Milton's Sonnets & the Ideal Community

Milton's Sonnets & the Ideal Community

Anna K. Nardo

UNIVERSITY OF NEBRASKA PRESS • LINCOLN & LONDON

174058

Publishers on the Plains

UNP

Library of Congress Cataloging in Publication Data

Nardo, Anna K.   1947–
  Milton's sonnets and the ideal community.

  Includes bibliographical references and index.
  1. Milton, John, 1608–1674. Sonnets. 2. Sonnets,
English—History and criticism. 3. Community
in literature. I. Title.
PR3567.N3   821′4   79–17221
ISBN 0–8032–3302–7

The publication of this book was assisted by a grant from
The Andrew W. Mellon Foundation.

For Neal Cronin

Contents

Acknowledgments

Like Satan, I too owe a "debt immense of endless gratitude," but unlike the fiend, I do not feel it as "so burdensome, still paying, still to owe." On the contrary, it is a joy to acknowledge my debt to two generous teachers and friends. Professor Robert B. Hinman first alerted me to the need for a book on Milton's sonnets, suggested several approaches to individual poems, and directed my original research and writing, even though he was released from any official obligation to my graduate work. Professor Irene Samuel, who has never had any official obligation to my work, devoted hours to reading subsequent versions of the manuscript and making cogent suggestions for revision. Her encouragement throughout the project helped me persevere. In their enthusiasm and learning, kindness and intellectual honesty, vision and rigor, Professors Hinman and Samuel have given me models of excellence in teaching and scholarship.

My debt of gratitude also extends to Professors Michael Lieb, Joseph Anthony Wittreich, Jr., Harry Rusche, J. Paul Hunter, John Fischer, and Lawrence Sasek, all of whom read the manuscript at various stages of development and suggested revisions which improved the book. Bainard and Christine Cowan helped prepare the manuscript for publication with careful typing and patient proofreading. Generous financial assistance—in the form of a four-year graduate fellowship from Emory University, summer research grants from the Louisiana State University Research Council and the American Council of Learned Societies, and funds for typing from Louisiana State University—allowed me to complete the project. And the editors of *Genre* and *Explorations in Renaissance Culture* graciously consented to the republication of portions of "The Submerged Sonnet as Lyric Moment in Miltonic Epic," *Genre* 9 (1976): 21–35; and "Renaissance Syncretism and Milton's Convivial Sonnets," *EIRC* 4(1978): 32–42.

Personal debts are less definable than professional ones, but Dr. Nita L. Nardo and Dr. Julian R. Gomez know how much I owe them. Finally, for my husband, Neal Cronin—who not only read, reread, and proofread this book, but endured cheerfully all the vicissitudes of its composition—I look forward to a lifetime to

afford him praise,
The easiest recompense, and pay him thanks,
How due!

Abbreviations

AnM	*Annuale Mediaevale*
Apology	*An Apology against a Pamphlet Called "A Modest Confutation of the Animadversions upon the Remonstrant's Defense against Smectymnuus"*
Areop	*Areopagitica*
BNYPL	*Bulletin of the New York Public Library*
C	*Comus*
CD	*De doctrina Christiana (The Christian Doctrine)*
CM	*The Works of John Milton*, 18 Vols., gen. ed. Frank Allen Patterson (New York: Columbia University Press, 1931–40)
DDD	*The Doctrine and Discipline of Divorce*
Def 2	*Johannis Miltoni, Angli, pro populo Anglicano defensio secunda . . . (The Second Defense of the English People)*
Educ	*Of Education*
EIC	*Essays in Criticism: A Quarterly Journal of Literary Criticism*
Eikon	*Eikonoklastes*
EIRC	*Explorations in Renaissance Culture*
ELH	*Journal of English Literary History*
ELN	*English Language Notes*
ELR	*English Literary Renaissance*
ES	*English Studies: A Journal of English Language and Literature*
Hirelings	*Considerations Touching the Likeliest Means to Remove Hirelings out of the Church*
HLQ	*Huntington Library Quarterly: A Journal for the History and Interpretation of English and American Civilization*
JHI	*Journal of the History of Ideas*

LangQ	*Language Quarterly*
LC	*Library Chronicle*
MiltonQ	*Milton Quarterly*
MiltonS	*Milton Studies*
MLN	*Modern Language Notes*
MLQ	*Modern Language Quarterly*
MSE	*Massachusetts Studies in English*
Music	*At a Solemn Music*
N&Q	*Notes and Queries*
OED	*Oxford English Dictionary*
PL	*Paradise Lost*
PMLA	*Publications of the Modern Language Association of America*
Pollard and Redgrave	*A Short-Title Catalogue . . . 1475–1640*, comp. A. W. Pollard and G. R. Redgrave
PR	*Paradise Regained*
Prol	*Prolusiones oratoriae (Academic Exercises)*
RCG	*The Reason of Church Government Urged against Prelaty*
RES	*Review of English Studies: A Quarterly Journal of English Literature and the English Language*
SA	*Samson Agonistes*
SP	*Studies in Philology*
SR	*Sewanee Review*
SRen	*Studies in the Renaissance*
TKM	*The Tenure of Kings and Magistrates*
TLS	[London] *Times Literary Supplement*
TSLL	*Texas Studies in Literature and Language: A Journal of the Humanities*
UTQ	*University of Toronto Quarterly: A Canadian Journal of the Humanities*
UWR	*University of Windsor Review*
Variorum	*A Variorum Commentary on the Poems of John Milton*, gen. ed. Merritt Y. Hughes (New York: Columbia University Press, 1970–)
Wing	*A Short-Title Catalogue . . . , 1641–1700*, comp. Donald Wing
YM	*The Complete Prose Works of John Milton*, gen. ed. Don M. Wolfe (New Haven, Conn.: Yale University Press, 1953–)

Milton's Sonnets & the Ideal Community

Introduction

As a Cambridge undergraduate asked to write merely some rhyming jokes for a "Vacation Exercise," John Milton interrupted the jocularity to promise to his "native Language . . . service in some graver subject," hoping that someday she might, he says,

> clothe my fancy in fit sound:
> Such where the deep transported mind may soar
> Above the wheeling poles, and at Heav'n's door
> Look in, and see each blissful Deity
> How he before the thunderous throne doth lie,
> Listening to what unshorn *Apollo* sings.[1]

At twenty-three no "bud or blossom" of fruitful deeds had appeared; still, he confidently prophesied about the outward results of his "inward ripenes,"

> Yet be it less or more, or soon or slow,
> It shall be still in strictest measure eev'n,
> To that same lot, however mean, or high,
> Toward which Time leads me, and the will of Heav'n.[2]

Although at thirty-four he had temporarily postponed the pursuit of his poetic ambitions in order to serve the state in controversial prose, he dared to "covnant with any knowing reader, that for some few yeers yet I may go on trust with him toward the payment of what I am now indebted, as being a work not to be rays'd from the heat of youth." Indeed, he hoped this work might be "something so written to aftertimes, as they should not willingly let it die."[3] Twenty-five years later—after marital unhappiness, family deaths, illness, and blindness; after political revolution, civil war, the frustration of his hopes for a godly community, and the threat of execution as one of the regicides—Milton, now approaching his sixties, paid the promised debt of a lifetime: he published *Paradise Lost*. Within the next seven years, he published *Paradise Regained* and *Samson Agonistes*, revised and reprinted his minor poetry and major epic, then died.

Amidst personal and national turmoil, he eventually realized the unified vision which had shaped his life as if it were a work of art. Indeed, he believed a poet's life must be a "true Poem, that is, a composition, and patterne of the best and honourablest things" (*Apology*, YM 1:890). Although this passage in *An Apology for Smectymnuus* emphasizes the poet's virtuous actions which are a "patterne" (an example) of the heroic deeds he sings, the words *composition and patterne* may also suggest Milton's concern with the shape of a poet's life. It should become a harmonious "composition [orderly arrangement] and patterne [design]" in which God's providence and man's efforts combine to create a work of art. Milton ordered his own poetic career according to traditional ideals of decorum. Following Virgil and Spenser, he believed that a great poet must master the pastoral before attempting the epic. And he composed Ovidian elegies, sonnets in Italian and English, and odes before experimenting with pastoral elements in companion poems, masques, and laments in Latin and English. All this generic experimentation prepared him to pursue "things unattempted yet in Prose or Rhyme" (*PL* 1:16) in the monumental epics and tragedy of his last years.

This passion for shapeliness and harmony of form, which guided his poetic career, influenced every task Milton undertook. Despite the varied occasions and the heat of unpredictable controversy which spawned his pamphlets, he later described them as a unified program of reform, advocating the "three varieties of liberty without which civilized life is scarcely possible, namely ecclesiastical liberty, domestic or personal liberty, and civil liberty" (*Def 2*, YM 4[1]:624). Following his lead, modern critics have found unity and patterns throughout his canon. Michael Lloyd has described the thirteen English poems of *Justa Edovardo King Naufraugo* as a collaborative effort in which *Lycidas*, coming at the end of the section, echoes and organizes the themes of the previous poems. Louis L. Martz has called attention to Milton's dating the poems in his 1645 edition and arranging them first by genre, then by chronology. This pattern, Martz believes, "creates the growing awareness of a guiding, central purpose that in turn gives the volume an impressive and peculiar sense of wholeness." And Arthur E. Barker has argued for reading *Paradise Lost, Paradise Regained,* and *Samson Agonistes* as a trilogy about man's first and subsequent falls, and his potential for regeneration.[4]

Long praised as masterpieces of the single-sonnet style, Milton's sonnets have only recently been described as an intentional unit. In his edition of the sonnets, E. A. J. Honigmann considers them a coherent work of art (if not a sequence) unified by themes, images, and subgroupings. William McCarthy has suggested that the twenty-five poems may be read as a sequence in which the career of an "implied author," who is not necessarily Milton himself, forms a double pattern of continuity: "a human career in its three conventional phases of youth, maturity, and old age" and "a Christian career which unfolds against the background of traditional cosmology"—heaven, Eden, the fallen world, and hell. Mary Ann Radzinowicz has argued more convincingly that the sequence is composed of five subgroups, "which in stages present . . . the political discoveries of the periods to which they belong," thereby recording "a process or struggle which . . . issues in the poet's offering his experience to his nation as exemplary."[5] But half the sonnets do not mention, much less focus on, the human or Christian career of an "implied author" or an exemplary poet. In Sonnets 2, 9, 10, 13, 14, 15, 16, 17, 18, 20, 21, and "On the new forcers of Conscience," Milton scarcely refers to himself, devoting the sonnets entirely to counseling civic leadership, chastising civic corruption, lamenting heroic martyrdom, inviting friends to fellowship, and praising beauty, talent, and virtue. Despite my disagreement about precisely what unifies the sequence, I will build on the foundation of these pioneering studies as I try to define the ordering principle of Milton's sonnet sequence and thus to increase our understanding of the passion for order and harmony that unified his life as well as his works.

1.
"Wov'n close, both matter, form and stile": The Sequence and the Ideal

Few men have sustained the unity of purpose that informed John Milton's life. One by one he deliberately mastered almost every poetic kind available in the Renaissance, and one by one he consciously reshaped each into an instrument fit to express his own poetic vision. His elegy, masque, epic, and tragedy all develop from well-known literary traditions, but each is unique, virtually transforming its genre. It would seem odd if Milton had ignored the most popular poetic kind in the Renaissance, the sonnet sequence. He did not. Predictably, however, he evolved a sequence from established models that was startlingly original in style and subject.

The unifying element found most often in sonnet sequences since Dante and Petrarch has been the "proud fair" or *donna angelicata* to whom the poems are addressed. The beloved can become a coy mistress, a tyrant, a Circe, or the ideal of beauty, chaste love, and religious devotion during the sequence's development and thus provide a focal point for innumerable variations on the theme of love. Although Milton does praise his beloved, he also invites a friend to dinner, retaliates against detractors, advises generals, worries about his career, and condemns a bloody massacre. Amidst this multiplicity, however, there is a unifying element in his sonnets. Instead of centering them on the courtship of a "proud fair" or devotion to a *donna angelicata*, he dedicates them to the ideal of a godly community.

Perhaps this assertion will seem less gratuitous if we consider J. W. Lever's description of the Renaissance sonnet sequence:

> It was preoccupied with an over-riding, all-important engagement of the self with an other; hence with the exploration of a polarity. That "other" might stand in the position of mistress, friend, or even

godhead; in any case a relationship was created which drew into its magnetic field the poet's whole personality; his sense of his environment; his response to nature, time and mutability; his political, religious or philosophical beliefs.[1]

Each of Milton's sonnets is an engagement of self with "other"—an "other" that might be a bird, an imaginary Royalist soldier, or a murmuring, impatient inner self.[2] The sonnets which detail these individual engagements are "wov'n close, both matter, form and stile" so as to present the larger communal ideal which Milton envisioned for England. It is true that most sonnet sequences focus on an individual. But it is also true that few of these sequences can be read in one sitting. Their length is frequently excessive, their pattern of theme and variation is often monotonous, and their sweetness soon cloys. Because each of Milton's sonnets presents a different facet of his ideal, the sequence provides the variety of tone and subject matter necessary to overcome a serious limitation of this extended lyric form. The ideal of a community permeates the sequence, but each sonnet maintains the lyric intensity of a unique one-to-one engagement.

Much has been written about the people in Milton's life—enough to make it unnecessary to refute again the once popular stereotype of the dour, unsociable Puritan. Even if Edward Phillips had not told us that Milton enjoyed an occasional "gawdy-day," we could have surmised as much from the sonnets, which present a sociable man who appreciated wine, music, company at table, and feminine graces. The most significant "other" to him, however, was not one person, but an ideal so compelling that it inspired his desire to write a poem for "the honour and instruction of [his] country" (*RCG, YM* 1:810), absorbed his literary talent for the twenty years during which he wrote most of his sonnets, and cost him (he believed) his sight. The ideal of the New Jerusalem he hoped to help build was neither a cold abstraction nor a fanatic's utopia, as his sonnets prove. A living, inclusive community, it could embrace a member of the King's Music and the lord protector, an Italian beauty and a New Model Army general. The abstract ideal takes on life because of each sonnet's lyric intensity and the variety of the sequence.

The claim that Milton, so often praised as a master of individual sonnets, wrote a sequence raises a host of questions about arrangement and chronology, about the omission of political sonnets from the 1673 edition and the inclusion of the "Canzone" and *sonetto caudato* ("On the new forcers") in the sequence. The complex problems of chronology, omission, and inclusion must await the discussion of the individual sonnets.[3] But one obvious reason to consider the sonnets as a unit is that in both the 1645 and 1673 volumes of minor poetry Milton himself grouped them together under the heading "Sonnets."

That leaves the question of arrangement. Surely, the skeptical might ask, would not a poet of such architectonic skill as Milton have arranged his sonnets so that their unity would be immediately apparent? Lever has, in fact, asked the same question about a puzzling collection of sonnets by another poet of proven architectonic skill and answered it thus: "It is arguable, indeed, that Shakespeare, writing perhaps over a period of years, never intended to produce a formal sequence, or at any rate did not settle upon a satisfactory order."[4] The same may apply to Milton's sonnets. Yet few deny that Shakespeare's sonnets form a sequence, although many may argue over the precise nature of their unity. Perhaps one solution to this puzzle lies in an understanding of the demands of the form itself. A sonnet sequence is necessarily a mélange. Whereas each highly structured lyric crystallizes a moment of intense experience so that a great sonnet might be called an ordered cri de coeur, a sequence, on the other hand, records an emotional life over an extended period of time (and we all live notoriously unruly emotional lives). Although sequences may hint at a temporal progression or sketch a shadowy plot, we do not demand the shapeliness of the *Divine Comedy* from the *Vita Nuova*, or the dramatic unity of *Othello* from Shakespeare's sonnets. Milton's sonnets lack the symmetry of *Paradise Lost*, because a sonnet sequence presents not one integral work of art, but a collection of captured nows in the duration of the poet's engagement with that which matters most in his life.

Nonetheless, to centuries of readers, Dante's and even Shakespeare's collections have seemed more like sequences than Milton's. The reason may lie in the very nature of what each poet idealizes. Beatrice possesses such beauty and virtue that she is sufficient to sustain all the longings which will ultimately lead Dante to the beatific vision of divine love. And Shakespeare's friend embodies a transcendent ideal which can conquer time—although, when ideal friend confronts all-too-real "dark lady," the resulting conflict leads the poet to an earthly vision of the complexities of human love. Milton's sonnets, however, lack such apparent focus precisely because the ideal which inspired them is not only complex, but inherently heterogeneous. No one person could embody the godly community Milton envisioned. Composed of individuals, each different but all one, this ideal is best expressed in *Areopagitica*, Milton's paean to the freedom to be unique. In describing the search for Truth, which he compares to Isis's quest to find and reunite the mangled limbs of Osiris, he insists that each man's separateness must be respected, for God's temple cannot be built of identical blocks: "Nay rather the perfection consists in this, that out of many moderat varieties and brotherly dissimilitudes that are not vastly disproportionall arises the goodly and the gracefull symmetry that commends the whole pile and structure" (*YM* 2:555). In religion, politics, and aesthetics Milton explored the relationship between unity and diversity. His providential God allows individual free will, his ideal commonwealth preserves freedom of speech and worship, and his epic includes a stunning variety of literary kinds: hymns, orations, love songs, allegories, soliloquies, and philosophical debates, among others. Similarly, his sonnet sequence maintains the uniqueness and intensity of his engagement with each individual while sustaining the unifying ideal of a godly community.

Milton begins and ends his sonnets with poems about the traditional focus of the Renaissance sonnet sequence, whether she be the love he longs for in "O Nightingale," the "donna leggiadra" who first touched his adamantine heart, or the "late espoused Saint" who has left him alone and blind, with only the "trust to have / Full sight of her in Heaven." Between the youthful sonnets of hoped-for love and the mature sonnet of the hope of heaven, he wrote seventeen which illuminate some facet of his ideal community on earth. He defends the home from the devastation of war (Sonnet 8) and marriage from those who misunderstand the meaning of the bond (11, 12). He praises, advises, and enjoys his friends, both male and female (9, 10, 13, 14, 20, 21). He counsels generals and statesmen (15, 16, 17) and condemns those who would destroy true religion by forcing consciences or persecuting dissenters ("On the new forcers of Conscience," 18). Finally, he examines his own role as poet and public servant, who must struggle against the pressures of time (7), the frustrations of blindness (19), and the temptation to total self-reliance (22) in order to reach beyond the self in service to the ideal godly community he wishes to see become a reality.

Although startlingly original, Milton's sequence evolved from established models, and his choice of an ordering principle is a logical development from preceding sequences not only in Italy, but also in France and Elizabethan England. The first sonnets he is known to have possessed are by della Casa and were discovered bound together in one volume with sonnets by Varchi and Dante's *Convivio*. These three remnants of Milton's library can tell us much about how he used received tradition. As F. T. Prince has shown, Milton learned a style from della Casa very different from either contemporary Italian Marinism or typical Elizabethan mellifluence. From Varchi, he probably learned the social and occasional function of the sonnet. A sixteenth-century Italian humanist, historian, and frequenter of great houses, Varchi often received sonnet letters and tributes. Obliged by social custom to reply with another sonnet, Varchi composed many such acknowledgments, some of which follow the same rhyme pattern (some even using the same rhyming syllables) as the sonnet which initiated the correspondence.[5] In Italy the sonnet had long been a social institution. At literary or social gatherings, such as those Milton attended during his European tour, gentlemen, as well as professional poets, recited or sang sonnets addressed to friends, patrons, statesmen, warriors, princes, and men of letters on a variety of subjects from the nature of love to the corruption of local government.

From Dante's *Convivio* Milton learned how a collection of lyrics can expand into a nearly encyclopedic "banquet" of knowledge intended for public benefit. Although Dante did not fulfill his plan to provide commentaries for fourteen of his canzoni in this volume, the four he completed justify writing about the self, vindicate his native language, explain the four levels of allegory, discuss heavenly cosmology, examine the nature of friendship, define nobility, and argue for the necessity of universal monarchy. Nearly all the major concerns of his life as poet and public servant are examined in the prose commentaries that accompany the four lyrics. So too, Milton used a sequence of lyrics to explore the problems he faced as poet, as concerned private citizen, and as government official: problems such as the frustrations of his poetic vocation (7, 19), the relation of a man of letters to an embattled society (8, 22), the use and abuse of language (12, 13), the separation of church and state (17, "New forcers"), and the nature of a good governor (15, 16, 17). Of course, he did not write canzoni, nor are the sonnets an essay in the tradition of lyric plus commentary. Still, these collections of lyrics do show both poets mulling over a variety of ideas crucial to their private and public lives before attempting their masterpieces.[6]

Although the centuries between Dante and Milton produced countless sequences of love sonnets, some important poets found the sonnet sequence a fit vehicle for exploring social and political ideals and realities. Short groups of political sonnets, such as Petrarch's stinging attacks on the papal court and Giovanni Guidiccioni's patriotic laments for the divided and chaotic state of Italy, were praised and imitated, and Joachim Du Bellay wrote two sequences which confront the problems of communities. *Les Regrets* and *Les Antiquités de Rome* were composed during his stay in Rome as secretary to his uncle, a cardinal. Observing at first hand the decadence, hypocrisy, and intrigue of the papal court and keenly feeling his homesickness for France, he turned *Les Regrets* into an examination of his complex and bitter relation to a wholly corrupt society. *Les Antiquités*—to be translated by Milton's favorite, Spenser—mourns the fallen grandeur of the once magnificent civilization that preceded the present-day corruption. Thus Du Bellay reshaped the sonnet sequence into an instrument capable of sounding the poet's personal engagement with the political, moral, social, and cosmic issues that confront an entire civilization.

In England, the sonnet naturally centered on the court society, as imitating Petrarch became a fashionable pastime. From the beginning, however, Wyatt and Surrey improvised with Petrarchan form and content—Wyatt veiling allusions to court intrigue under the guise of referring to his lady, and Surrey bitterly satirizing Henry VIII's gluttony and lust in a fiction of an Assyrian king.[7] The checkered careers of these two poets (now in, now out of favor) indicate how the court society indirectly determined the early fate of the English sonnet. Tudor monarchs, trying desperately to solidify their power, unify the nation, and work out a religious settlement, were not likely to allow even a part-time sonneteer much freedom to speculate openly on religious or political issues. Such imposed limitations, the desire of poets to establish England's place in the Renaissance flowering of European literature, and the unassailable eminence of Petrarch made it nearly inevitable that the burgeoning sonnet sequences in the last years of the century concern romantic love.

Nonetheless, minor poets who preceded Milton did experiment with different patterns of continuity for their sequences.[8] Sir John Davies satirized Petrarchan excesses in nine "gulling sonnets." Giordano Bruno published in England a series of Italian sonnets and commentaries called *Degl'eroici furori*, which condemn Petrarchan passion while they use its imagery to expound a mystical religion of divine contemplation. George Chapman composed "A Coronet for His Mistress, Philosophie." John Donne wrote holy sonnets far superior to other religious cycles published by Barnabe Barnes, Henry Constable, and Henry Lok. And John Taylor, the Water Poet, published an elaborately illustrated volume of execrable sonnets, each spoken by a different king or queen of England. Even such a brief summary indicates that, during the late sixteenth and early seventeenth centuries, English sonneteers were broadening their attitude toward the content of the sequence.

In fact, in the court poetry of Elizabeth's reign the Petrarchan pattern itself took on an entirely new significance. A virgin queen whose wit, accomplishments, and vanity were well known; whose brilliant appearance was frequently displayed in portrait and progress; who summoned masters of art, music, and literature to her court; who surrounded herself with courtiers, disapproved of their marrying, and played courtship games with many of the eligible monarchs of Europe—Elizabeth was naturally idealized in count-

less poems, including sonnets.[9] Sometimes, she was characterized
as a lovely chaste lady, Belphoebe or Diana. Sometimes, she was
praised as the just ruler, Gloriana or Astraea returning from
heaven to usher in a new Age of Gold. Not infrequently, she became
a royal Laura in sonnets which praised her beauty in the traditional Petrarchan conceits—a beauty that also commanded the
obedience due to a sovereign. In one of Fulke Greville's sonnets, the
red and white roses that appear so often in the sonnet-lady's
countenance become the roses of Lancaster and York united in the
Tudor rose, Elizabeth. Constable addresses both the public queen
and the private beauty in a sonnet which marvels that

> so many minds remain
> Obedient subjects at thy beauty's call!
> So many hearts bound in thy hairs as thrall!
> So many eyes die with one look's disdain!

And Raleigh's prefatory sonnet to *The Faerie Queene* portrays
Petrarch in tears as the "Graces" desert Laura's tomb to attend the
Faerie Queen. Surely these "Graces" represent not only "faire
Love, and fairer Vertue," but also the civilizing arts and ac-
complishments fostered in the Elizabethan court, the same
"Graces" Sir Calidore envisions decking an avatar of Elizabeth on
Mount Acidale.[10]

Although panegyric sonnets had certainly been written before,
the development of the English sonnet sequence had taken a new
turn. Now all the aesthetic, religious, and political ideals of English
Renaissance civilization could be presented in individual sonnets
and sequences using an extremely popular established form.[11] Innumerable Platonizing sonneteers had seen the feminine charms of
their ladies as shadowing transcendent philosophical or theological
ideals; it was an easy step to dedicate sonnets to a virgin queen who
embodied the ideals of a civilization. Needless to say, Elizabeth
deliberately encouraged this idealization. Faced with religious
unrest, fractious nobles, European wars, and such unflattering attacks on her sex as John Knox's *First Blast of the Trumpet Against
the Monstrous Regiment of Women*, she knew how to use a literature (including sonnets) that exalted unselfish and devoted service

to a lady—exactly the service required to maintain a stable, unified nation.

Elizabeth succeeded almost miraculously in sustaining the loyalty of her people and the stability of England, even during the difficult years that ended her reign. Her death, however, and the accession of James opened an ever-widening breach between the culture of the court and the newly established culture of large sections of the population outside the court circle. The gap had great consequences for literature in general and for the sonnet sequence in particular—consequences that prepared for the Miltonic sequence. But how the form evolved from collections of panegyrics addressed to an ideal female monarch into a sequence dedicated to the ideal of a godly community is a question that requires attention to the historical context in which Milton wrote his sonnets.

Because of James's conflict with his Parliament, the court lost its former eminence as the center of English civilization where the ambitious and talented sought honorable careers in public service. James's coterie of favorites was hateful to a gentry whose political, moral, and religious ideals were leading them to question both royal prerogatives and the administrative centralization of the Elizabethan church and state. Indeed, all over Europe in the seventeenth century there was what H. R. Trevor-Roper has called a "general crisis." New societies demanding decentralization and laicization were coming into conflict with older Renaissance states ruled from the top by Christian princes with costly, ever-expanding bureaucracies of governmental and religious administrators. Fed by the religious fervor of the Reformation and Counter Reformation, this European "general crisis" resulted in both a proliferation of new theories of community and a series of revolutions seeking to modify or even replace the centralized Renaissance state with these new communities.[12]

Puritanism, especially Calvinism, was a driving force in redefining these communities in two ways. First, by insisting on the justification by faith, not works, Puritans turned the focus of religious experience inward, sometimes exalting the will of each believer above church dogma. Although, to Calvin, man's will was far from free, one ultimate result of this internalization was belief in Christian liberty. Freed from Mosaic law by the new dispensation of Grace, some Puritans wanted to interpret the Scriptures according to their consciences led by the Holy Spirit. And the desire for religious freedom led to the desire for political freedom. Second, by denying the mediational power of priests, saints, and even some sacraments, and by emphasizing man's aloneness before God, Puritans set in motion a leveling process that undermined the feudal and hierarchical conception of the state. Instead of a microcosm of God's harmoniously ordered macrocosm, the Puritan state became a voluntary covenant between human will and divine commandments. The new covenantal form of community sought to replace the parish with a gathered church of free believers, the sacrament of marriage with a civil agreement between yokefellows, and the theory of the divine right of kings with a social contract.[13]

Although the interiorization of religion and the creation of covenant communities actually resulted in the modern secular state, Puritans intended to build a holy community, to imitate the *Regnum Christi*, or Kingdom of God, on earth. Having begun his reign at the Incarnation, Christ would not perfect his Kingdom until the Second Coming. Still, Puritans worked feverishly in the interim to transform their earthly community into a communion of saints. Emphases differed, but most Puritans identified the Kingdom by four referents: the spiritual Kingdom of virtue and love, which each Christian possessed within his soul by the assurance of Grace; the communion of believers composing a church, whether a visible fellowship or an invisible unity transcending time and space; the society transformed by the saints into a holy commonwealth, which would be continually reformed until the final perfection; and the Kingdom of Glory, when Christ would rule with the saints on earth until all things were made new.[14] This fourfold perspective on the Kingdom moves outward and upward from man's soul at the center, inspired by Grace and eager to serve; through concentric circles of community, each perfected by the force of man's redeemed will; to the divine circumference, where God and man will unite.

In practice, achieving the earthly Kingdom of God did not prove to be an easy ascent from center to circumference. Particularly in England, where civil war and regicide abolished the courtly ideal for eighteen years, each step upward precipitated an avalanche of conflicts. Emphasis on the spiritual, inward Kingdom fragmented the community of belief—producing protean forms of religious expression, from the rational advocacy of Christian liberty to the irrational prophesies of self-proclaimed messiahs. Individual churches, each of which believed itself to be sheep and the others goats, shared so little fellowship that the ecclesiastical Kingdom seemed unattainable. After the bishops and king were removed, factions could not agree on precisely how society should be reformed to create the political Kingdom. And, especially in the 1650s, millenarians, or Fifth Monarchy Men, frightened the conservative reformers by preaching and acting as if the eschatological Kingdom of Glory was at hand. Nevertheless, between 1642 and 1660, Parliamentarians and New Model Army generals, Presbyterians and Independents, Levellers, Diggers, Quakers, Familists, Seekers, and Anabaptists (to name only a few) set themselves the task of building a new community.

During these years England was a kaleidoscope of political and religious experimentation, from democratic army debates to one-man rule, from aristocratic Catholics to conventicles of tinker-and-tailor Ranters. Few Englishmen could avoid asking such questions as these: What constitutes a community—the inhabitants of a place or a communion of the elect? How does the individual function within the community—with freedom of conscience or subordinate to a national religious discipline? How does the City of Man relate to the City of God—as Babylon or as a step on the way to the New Jerusalem? The impulse to build a new community opened debate on issues that went far beyond the original questions of who controlled ship-money or how ministers dressed. Soon the English presses were flooded with broadsides, sermons, guide books, sectarian tracts, radical manifestoes, and learned treatises which attacked the monopolization of knowledge within the privileged professions, criticized the existing educational structure, discussed the relations between the sexes, theorized about private property and the franchise, and calculated the time of Christ's Second Coming to usher in the final community of the saints. What had begun as a movement to protect Parliament's prerogatives and purify the church resulted in an all-encompassing scrutiny of every aspect of English society.[15]

Although he felt that he had the use of only his left hand in controversial prose, Milton joined the fray, confronting these diverse issues both as a private citizen in his pamphlets and a public servant in Latin defenses and other commissioned treatises. Delaying the promised masterwork, he devoted his literary efforts between 1642 and 1660 primarily to making the godly community a reality. Never a Ranter, Leveller, or Digger himself, nor a Presbyterian either after the goal of removing the bishops was accomplished, nor a member of any definable sect—Milton was nonetheless immersed in the radical milieu and its exciting experimentation with new forms of communal organization.[16] England, he envisioned in the early years of the Long Parliament, was "the mansion house of liberty" where some men sat with poised pens "by their studious lamps, musing, searching, revolving new notions and idea's wherewith to present, as with their homage and their fealty the approaching Reformation: others as fast reading, trying all things, assenting to the force of reason and convincement" (*Areop*, YM 2:554).

In these hopeful years he sometimes seemed to believe that the ascent from the center, the spiritual Kingdom, through the perfected church and the holy commonwealth to the circumference, the Kingdom of Glory, would be easy and swift. In a fervent prayer in *Animadversions* (1641), he takes the present success of reformation as a sign that Christ's "Kingdome is now at hand" with Christ himself "standing at the dore." He begs, "Come forth out of thy Royall Chambers, O Prince of all the Kings of the earth, put on the visible roabes of thy imperiall Majesty, take up that unlimited Scepter which thy Almighty Father hath bequeath'd thee; for now the voice of thy Bride calls thee, and all creatures sigh to bee renew'd" (*YM* 1:707). But in the controversies over divorce, licensing, toleration, and tithes, he became so disillusioned with the Presbyterians and the Long Parliament that, at times, an abyss seemed to separate redeemed man from the reformed church and state, not to mention the Kingdom of Glory. Although never abandoning his hopes for a godly community—not even on the eve of the Restoration when he published *The Ready and Easy Way to Establish a Free Commonwealth* (1660)—he shifted his focus to the internal, spiritual Kingdom. The first step toward the ideal community was to perfect the inner man, and since Christian liberty was necessary for self-perfection, the primary duty of the holy commonwealth was to guarantee and protect liberty of thought and expression. The precise disposition of political power (whether republic, oligarchy, or one-man rule—all of which Milton supported at various times) concerned him far less than the preservation of freedom of conscience.

By the time he came to write *The Christian Doctrine*, he had clearly defined the relationship between the individual, the earthly community, and the Kingdom of Heaven. Because the Kingdom of Grace began with Christ's first coming, each man may achieve "incomplete glorification" in this world: he may be "justified and adopted by God the Father and . . . filled with a certain awareness both of present grace and dignity and of future glory, so that [he has] already begun to be blessed" (*YM* 6:502). From this "union and communion" with the Father and Son arises communion with all others who have been adopted and made members of Christ's body, and this "communion of saints" becomes a mystical body, "the invisible church," which "need not be subject to spatial considerations: it includes people from many remote countries, and from all ages since the creation of the world" (*YM* 6:500). After explaining the origin of the godly community, Milton discusses, in chapters on Christian liberty, church discipline, and man's duties to his neighbors, how the individual must live in the earthly community until the time of his "complete glorification" in the heavenly community, which will begin with "the coming of the Lord to judgment, when he, with his holy angels, shall judge the world" (*YM* 6:614). But Milton adds a cautionary note, "Christ will be slow to come" (*YM* 6:618).

Meanwhile, in the heat of controversy over issues as various as the right to marital harmony and the right to regicide, Milton worked to establish a godly community in the fallen world. Despite the wide-ranging subjects of his prose works, when he looked back in *A Second Defense* on his past accomplishments, he saw a coherence to his writing:

> Since, then, I observed that there are, in all, three varieties of liberty without which civilized life is scarcely possible, namely ecclesiastical liberty, domestic or personal liberty, and civil liberty, and since I had already written about the first, while I saw that the magistrates were

vigorously attending to the third, I took as my province the remaining one, the second or domestic kind. This too seemed to be concerned with three problems: the nature of marriage itself, the education of the children, and finally the existence of freedom to express oneself. [*YM* 4(1):624]

Whether or not he began his pamphleteering with this plan in mind, the statement shows that he defined community broadly and saw all its variety as composing a harmonious whole. In order to present his total ideal to the nation, he had to write about love, sex, marriage, divorce, children, the role of women in society, the power of language, war, economics, governing bodies, international politics, tithes, and church government. But he did not limit his examination of these issues to his prose; they are the subjects of his sonnets as well.

During these confused attempts to remake society from top to bottom without king or court, while Milton's left hand was constantly at his nation's service, his right hand was not completely idle. Between 1642 and 1660 he wrote all but the earliest of his sonnets, each of which presents his intense engagement with a real person, event, or issue important during this period of reformation. As a sonneteer, he fell heir to a single-sonnet tradition rich in humorous, occasional, satiric, heroic, friendly, and elegiac sonnets, and to a sequence tradition which had broadened its content to include the ideals of a civilization. Thus literary tradition and social upheaval converged to inspire his recruiting the form, which had previously flourished in the court, into the service of godly *civitas*.

But Milton fell heir to much more than a tradition of poetic kinds and an England that had need of him. His Cambridge prolusions, his early poetry, and his record of readings during the extended period of private study at Horton reveal that he was steeped in the culture of antiquity and Renaissance humanism. His Commonplace Book indicates that, long before he sallied out and saw his adversaries in the noisy pamphlet brawls of the 1640s and 50s, he had carefully studied the questions he would address in his prose and sonnets.[17] Thus we face the tired old question: Was Milton a humanist or a Puritan? In considering the sonnets, however, the question takes on meaning if it is slightly altered: Was his ideal community the product of broad Renaissance culture or the immediate wave of Puritan zeal to create a holy commonwealth in England? In a manner highly significant for the structure of each sonnet, it was both. The sonnet addressed to Sir Henry Vane, for example, praises this dedicated servant of the Parliament for his diplomatic skills, administrative abilities, and willingness to separate civil and spiritual power, a matter of heated contemporary debate among builders of the holy community. In the course of the sonnet, however, Milton compares Vane to a venerable Roman senator in the days of Hannibal. Here the immediate problems of creating the New Jerusalem—the Dutch negotiations and the church settlement—are vividly set forth, but the present struggles are also shown in relation to the efforts of the classical world to preserve civilization. Similarly, each sonnet details a unique engagement with a person, event, or partisan issue of the day, but each also asks its reader to consider this one moment in the light of man's ongoing fight against barbarity.

This overview of the evolution of the Miltonic sequence has already suggested the structure of the ideal community which the sonnets present. At the center is an individual—free and virtuous, with a calm and humble faith. Surrounding this "upright heart and pure" are the groups of significant "others" that form the society Milton envisioned: a beloved woman, the home, friends male and female, the nation, and Protestant Europe. Embracing all, of course, is a totally provident and beneficent God. Such a vast community is not static; it depends on a dynamic interchange of love and service among men and between man and God. The individual can best serve society and God by using his free will to perfect the center. Only then can he reach out in love and service to the surrounding "others." For example, the Italian sonnets and "O Nightingale" present a young Milton longing to serve both the Muse and Love, and hoping that his virtuous heart will be a worthy gift for his lady. Later sonnets of praise and friendship honor those who have also achieved inward strength and can, therefore, serve the community—whether, like Lady Margaret Ley, by preserving a noble father's good name and virtue or, like Cromwell, by defeating rebellious Scots. Not all the sonnets, however, praise the successful process of self-perfection and service to the community. Sometimes the center is frustrated and anxious; thus sonnets like

"How soon hath Time" and "When I consider" dramatize the struggle to restore a calm, humble faith that God will allow the individual to serve in His own way and time. Sometimes barbarous detractors surround the individual, railing at his attempts to serve the community; thus sonnets like "A Book was writ of late" and "I did but prompt the age" humorously but severely chastise the enemies of civlization. Sometimes the entire nation is attacked from without by hostile rumors or open rebellion, and threatened from within by spiritual tyranny or corruption; thus sonnets to Fairfax and Cromwell recall the warriors from peripheral battlefields to the more difficult warfare at home, the struggle to establish civic virtue at the heart of government.

If the center can perfect itself for love and service, both individual and nation can advance toward the final community that was never far from Milton's mind. In *Lycidas* he calls it "the blest Kingdoms meek of joy and love" where all are entertained by glorious, singing saints "in solemn troops, and sweet Societies" (ll. 177, 179). In the sonnets he describes it as the heaven that will grant him the full sight and completed embrace of his wife, or the marriage feast to which the Bridegroom will assuredly take the wise virgin of Sonnet 9, or the angelic host who both speed throughout the universe and simply wait on the Lord.

Despite all the impediments which the sonnets detail—ignorance, brutality, tyranny, corruption, the pressures of time, and blindness—the ideal community they present is a progress, from each individual center through the earthly community to the divine circumference. Although most of the sonnets capture only one moment, the complete progress can be clearly seen in at least one sonnet. The elegy to Catharine Thomason describes a woman whose inner "Faith and Love" have ripened her soul "to dwell with God." Emanating from this virtuous center, her "Works and Alms and . . . good Endeavour" performed earthly service and then followed her to the heavenly community where now she drinks from the same "pure immortal streams" which bathe the locks of Lycidas.

While the sequence as a whole presents this progress from individual center to eternal and infinite circumference, each sonnet also forms a focal center which expands into larger perspectives.

beginning in an immediate and intense lyric engagement of poet and "other," the sonnet ultimately asks the reader to see this person, event, or issue through a wide-angle lens.[18] For example, "When I consider" begins in small, cramped quarters—the divided soul of a fretful man who feels benighted and frustrated in his desire to serve his community and God. By the end, however, a vast panorama has unfolded in which a calmly assured servant stands and waits before (and upon) a mighty king whose legions of angels range the cosmos. Often this expansion of perspective within one sonnet is accomplished by classical or biblical allusions. The immediate situation of "Captain or Colonel, or Knight in Arms" presents a defenseless poet trying to placate a soldier who threatens his home. In mock humility and wry amusement, the poet bribes the warrior with promises of eternal fame. But soon the imaginary episode has become one skirmish in the eternal war between the preservers of civilization and its destroyers. For all his tone of self-depreciation, Milton portrays himself as the heir to Pindar and Euripides—poets whose civilizing word has the power to transcend time and space, "what ever clime the Suns bright circle warms." In the end the reader is convinced that the "Muses Bowre" has worth and even strength far superior to the conquering armies of Alexander the Great, and certainly to the spear of a petty Royalist officer.

These examples of widening perspective demonstrate the two complementary ways in which single sonnets in Milton's sequence depict an individual center's quest for service to the divine circumference: a temporal way and a transcendent way. Although sonnets like "Captain or Colonel, or Knight in Arms" dramatize only one moment in the historical struggle for civilization, their allusive resonance reminds the reader that present efforts are part of an ongoing process which includes heroic achievements of the past and ultimately leads to the Kingdom of God. But, because Milton's God is a god of presence as well as a god of history, in each moment, each soul, and each effort to imitate the Kingdom of God on earth, his transcendence can become immanent. Thus some of the sonnets, like "When I consider," offer a transcendent ideal in which the individual tries to penetrate to the radiant calm at the center of his soul where God and his Kingdom are wholly and already present.[19]

This ideal of a community found in the sonnets shares views central to works like *Comus* and *Lycidas*, which preceded Milton's efforts to help make the godly community a reality, and to the major poems, which arose from the ashes of those defeated efforts. At least three of these works present man's pre- and postlapsarian relations to a community in ways that will illuminate some of the questions confronted in the sonnet sequence.

A paradigm for the ideal movement from each individual center through the earthly community to the divine circumference may be found in the scenes of prelapsarian bliss in *Paradise Lost*. Recounting her first conscious moments, Eve remembers gazing with delight on her own image in a pool, then being led by a voice to Adam, whom she finds at first less delightful, but in whose image and for whom she was made. Like all her sons and daughters, Eve must overcome the temptation to self-love and isolation; she must move from self to a community by performing her earthly service as helpmeet to her husband, preserver of her garden home, and mother of the human race. Had she held the center firm through Satan's temptation, her (and Adam's) progress would have been unimpeded until, as Raphael predicts,

> Your bodies may at last turn all to spirit,
> Improv'd by tract of time, and wing'd ascend
> Ethereal, as wee.
>
> [5.497–99]

But because Eve pridefully sought immediate exaltation of the self to godhead rather than patient service to Adam, her children, her home, and God, the easy and promised progress from center to circumference was broken.

In his informative visit, Raphael makes it clear to Adam and Eve that spiritually and physically, morally and cosmically, "the scale of Nature" in their unfallen world is "set / From centre to circumference" (5.509–10). Where the center of the cosmos is and where the circumference, however, are puzzling. In the famous plant simile, the angel shows how all things move in a circular motion proceeding from and returning to God (5.469–90). In his description of heaven, we see how angelic hosannas and dances "in Orbs / Of circuit inexpressible . . . / Orb within Orb" (5.594–96) center upon God's throne. In the discussion of astronomy, Adam

marvels at the circling stars and planets which seem spatially to
center on the earth, more specifically on himself and Eve. Although
he dismisses Adam's vain speculations on geocentrism and helio-
centrism, Raphael emphasizes that the entire cosmos does indeed
center on the couple morally. If they withdraw from God's orbit by
denying him love and service (as Satan spatially withdrew his
followers from the angelic circle around God's throne), then the
animals will cease their obedient circling around man, husband
and wife will no longer enjoy their perfect circle of mutual love,
and "the Poles of Earth" wrenched "twice ten degrees and more /
From the Sun's Axle" will render "Oblique the Centric Globe"
(10.669–71). Where is the center, where the circumference of these
orbs within orbs?

Ironically, Satan himself clarifies the paradox that we have
already seen underlying the ideal community in Milton's sonnets.
Addressing the earth before beginning the temptation that will end
all this harmonious circling, Satan says,

> As God in Heav'n
> Is Centre, yet extends to all, so thou
> Centring receiv'st from all those Orbs.
> [9.107–9]

Ideally, in a prelapsarian world, both God and man's "upright
heart and pure" are at the center because, according to a well-
known Hermetic definition, God is a circle whose center is
everywhere and whose circumference is nowhere. But even in "this
dark world and wide" after the fall, when an impatient murmurer
restores faith to his center, he suddenly finds himself at the circumference of the universe before the throne of a king upon whom
thousands of angels center their flight.

The progress from isolation to communion, which was so easy
for unfallen Eve and has become so difficult for fallen man, also
faces the benighted Lady of *Comus*. In a provocative study, Gale
H. Carithers has shown how the masque "is animated by an ideal
of community":

> This ideal of community, explicitly stated nowhere but actuating
> speech and action everywhere, appears to be no less a conviction than
> that the true earthly fulfillment of man is free participation in loving,
> God-seeking society. Such loving concord, permitting orientation and
> aspiration towards "the Palace of Eternity," would seem to be the

cosmos to "disinherit *Chaos.*" And the two appear to be concurrently available, never far apart.[20]

Alone in a wood at nightfall, the Lady is threatened by chaos in the form of Comus's lustful designs. The "poor hapless Nightingale," as Thyrsis calls her, must be rescued from isolation, darkness, and danger and restored to polis and cosmos in the form of a feast attended by her family and the larger community Egerton represents as the earl of Bridgewater and lord lieutenant of Wales. What ultimately leads the Lady and her brothers to the "loving, God-seeking society" at the festival, says Carithers, is the masque itself, which moves "by song, dance, and story to establish the stylistic, aesthetic, intellectual, moral primacy of something contrasting with pastoral and broader than 'courtly,' the superiority of—call it—the civic, or the communal."[21]

Comus's lust and her isolation in the dark wood are not, however, the only dangers threatening the Lady. In order to defend herself from Comus's persuasions and threats, she must retreat to her inner consciousness: as she staunchly maintains, "Thou canst not touch the freedom of my mind" (l. 663). Although necessary, her defense freezes her in total isolation, "in stony fetters fixt and motionless" (l. 819), and Sabrina's "precious vial'd liquors" must release her from imprisonment and unite her to her family. Here Milton explores a dilemma he will confront in several sonnets: how to reconcile the necessary perfection of the self with the self-transcendence necessary to reach out in love and service to the family, the nation, and God.

Indeed, three years after the production of *Comus* he faced this problem again in *Lycidas.* In the opening lines, concern over the unfinished task of self-perfection and the resulting poetic unripeness makes him hesitant to perform the necessary service, to mourn the death of a fellow member of the university community. But the "bitter constraint, and sad occasion dear" of the unseasonable death of one who "knew / Himself to sing" forces the young poet out of isolating self-concern. In the poem, contributed to his classmates' collection of formal elegies, Milton calls the whole university, in the guise of conventional pastoral characters, to mourn the passing of one member of its community. He also calls all nature (winds, waves, rivers, vales, and flowers) to join the procession of mourners because, despite the brutal fact of death, nature should be in harmony with the human community. Peter, "the Pilot of the *Galilean* Lake," also appears among the mourners, lamenting the death of one good shepherd and condemning the greedy who survive.

Here, in what has often been seen as an extraneous digression on the corrupt clergy, Milton reminds the university community that it has a responsibility to others beyond its cloistered walls; it must feed the "hungry Sheep." The corrupt clergy were once members of the university, but they have renounced all responsibility to the flock they pledged to care for in becoming clergymen. Now they are only "such as for their bellies' sake, / Creep and intrude and climb into the fold" and care only "to scramble at the shearers' feast," a feast of lucrative church livings and pluralities. Yet, beyond the corruption of a failed community in the fallen world, Milton envisions the perfect heavenly community. Edward King is finally apotheosized to a realm where "entertain him all the Saints above, / In solemn troops, and sweet Societies," where he becomes one of the community of the blessed at the foot of God's throne.

Although critics have long debated the significance of Milton's resurrection of the pastoral elegy's quaint machinery for his contribution to his classmates' modest tributary volume, the choice of genre also demonstrates that, despite death and corruption, King is not completely cut off from the earthly community. By choosing this traditional form and loading it with mythological allusions, Milton can unite himself and King to Theocritus, Bion, Moschus, and the ancient heritage of Western literature. By accepting the conventions, he can participate in the community of poets who have mourned for their fellows since the first Sicilian pastorals, poets like Virgil, Petrarch, Boccaccio, Castiglione, Marot, Ronsard, and Spenser. The young Milton, poetically unripe, forced to write before his "season due," feels himself only an insignificant junior member of this noble community, but he dares to hope for a similar tribute:

> So may some gentle Muse
> With lucky words favor my destin'd Urn,
> And as he passes turn,
> And bid fair peace be to my sable shroud.
>   [Ll. 19–22]

Through his choice of the pastoral elegy, the poet also attempts to link his reader (in 1637 or the eternal present of the poetic experience) to this extended community of mourners. An elegy is a "melodious tear," an ordered expression of pain, and each experience of the poem symbolically reenacts grief for loss. *Lycidas* then stages this reenactment which binds us all to the communities of the dead and the poets who mourn.

Even in so early a poem Milton presents the temporal and transcendent quest for the ideal community that will unify his sonnets. In the opening lines communal necessity forces the isolated poet to mourn, to exorcise self-concern over poetic unripeness, and to assert the existence of a caring human community. In portraying the communities of friends, scholars, and the church, he shows how each isolated man is part of wider circles of communion, including the natural world and the blessed children of God. Finally, the conventional pastoral elegy connects this present death to an ancient tradition, to the brutal truth that death has indeed undone so many, and to a community of future mourners for the dead and readers of *Lycidas*.

Because the ideal community presented in Milton's sonnet sequence is consistent with his entire canon and because each sonnet presents both an immediate engagement of self with other and a historical or transcendent perspective on that engagement, three concurrent methodologies are required. First, comparisons of the sonnets to Milton's other poems will clarify the major concerns of the sequence. Since the work of Edward S. Le Comte, no one can doubt the remarkable consistency of ideas, themes, and images in Milton's poetry.[22] Second, an examination of contextual details about the real person, event, or issue addressed in each sonnet will illuminate the immediate engagement. Milton has been fortunate in his editors, and such scholars as John S. Smart, E. A. J. Honigmann, and William Riley Parker, along with many others, have amassed a wealth of detail (which I will appropriate) about the occasions of the sonnets. Third, an exploration of the allusions, both direct and oblique, that widen the perspectives of the sonnets will clarify each poem's contribution to the sequence's complete ideal. Thanks to many studies proving the richness and thematic unity of figurative language in Milton's major works, few critics

now condemn his allusiveness as mere filigree.[23] A fourteen-line
miniature provides even less room for nonfunctional ornament
than an epic, and in Milton's sonnets no such embroidery intrudes.
Because the sonnets often address specific readers he knew to be a
"fit audience," they reverberate with allusions that evince his ideal
of a godly community.

2.
Service in the Train of Love:
Love Sonnets

Eight of Milton's sonnets, including the first and last, which frame the sequence, are love sonnets of the type that proliferated throughout Europe during the Renaissance. Readers have often had trouble imagining the Milton of the strong-willed, righteous stereotype as a romantic lover. Nonetheless the love between man and woman was a lifelong concern of his, examined in youthful elegies, the divorce pamphlets of his middle years, and the epic and tragedy of his full poetic maturity. But to Milton love must accompany cultivation of the "upright heart and pure," a cornerstone of his morality and theology. Thus his love sonnets present a dynamic tension between self-concern and reaching out toward the beloved. Although he employs some conventions of Dante, Petrarch, and the poets of *amour courtois*, the love described in these eight sonnets is neither self-absorbed passion nor self-abnegation before the beloved. Milton modifies the traditions of love poetry to suit the balanced love he reaches toward.

His first sonnet, "O Nightingale," written in his early twenties, wins praise from Honigmann as a sensuous and delightful lover's "complaint" based on the medieval tradition that in spring the song of the nightingale, if heard before the cuckoo, presages love.[1] Other critics, however, have glanced over it as a pleasant youthful exercise. But "O Nightingale" is more than either the sensuous "complaint" of a courtly lover pining in the French troubadour tradition or mere juvenilia. It announces the sequence's major theme of self-transcendence and touches on many of the concerns Milton explores not only in the sonnets, but in his later poetry and prose as well.

The speaker longs for fulfilled service to both love and the muse; but each year, for no apparent reason, he has been thwarted, just as an older and wiser Milton will find himself frustrated in his desire

27

to use "that one Talent which is death to hide" although his "Soul [is] more bent / To serve therewith [his] Maker." In his first youthful sonnet Milton approaches the poised tension he achieves in his famous Sonnet 19, between frustration at the demand for "day-labour, light deny'd," and "patience to prevent / That murmur." Here, although the nightingale "from yeer to yeer [has] sung too late" for "no reason," the poet still waits in the train of Love and the Muse. But the young lover is also concerned with "Time the suttle theef of youth," as the twenty-three-year-old aspiring poet will be when he laments in Sonnet 7 that his "late spring no bud or blossom shew'th." He implores the nightingale, "Now *timely* sing, ere the rude Bird of Hate / Foretell my hopeles doom," a doom of unfulfilled love and unaccomplished poetic service, in much the same spirit as he will later be tempted to envy "more *timely*-happy spirits" who have already begun to serve the muse (emphases mine). The young, frustrated lover must wait for another spring; the young poet must wait for that poetic fulfillment "toward which Time leads [him], and the will of Heav'n"; and the blind bard must wait like the seraphim who, paradoxically, serve merely by standing before God's throne.

Alone, the young lover must wait in the coming darkness, in expectant silence "when all the Woods are still," or amidst the raucous din of "the rude Bird of Hate," for the song that will lead him to love. Throughout his career Milton will show a continued concern with those who must wait alone, in darkness and silence or amidst barbarous noise, for a voice or sign. As an epic poet Milton must wait for Urania's "Voice divine" to visit his slumbers nightly when he has

> fall'n on evil days,
> . . . and evil tongues;
> In darkness, and with dangers compast round,
> And solitude.
>
> [*PL* 7.25–28]

So too the Son in *Paradise Regained* must go alone into "the bordering Desert wild, / And with dark shades and rocks environ'd round" in order to learn "how best the mighty work he might begin / Of Savior to mankind" (l.186–87, 193–94). Each of these figures—the young lover, the blind poet, the Son—starts in isolation longing to transcend the self so that he may serve the muse and love, or "justify the ways of God to men" (*PL* 1.26), or "enter, and begin to save mankind" (*PR* 4.635). Each feels a duty to a larger community, an obligation that requires service to others as well as perfection of the self. Thus Milton's first sonnet, by dramatizing both the youthful lover's frustrated isolation and his longing for fulfilled service, introduces that dynamic tension between self-concern and a desire for self-transcendence which will become one of the unifying themes of his sonnets and continually reappear in his major works.

"The rude [uncivilized, unmusical] Bird of Hate"[2] may thwart the lover's reaching out to love, but the nightingale's "soft lay" can prevent the poet's isolation by driving off "the shallow Cuccoo's bill." So too the later Milton, as poet and pamphleteer, will find himself beset by railing detractors, "a barbarous noise . . . Of Owles and Cuckoes, Asses, Apes and Doggs" (Sonnet 11), by what he characterizes in *Paradise Lost* as

> the barbarous dissonance
> Of *Bacchus* and his Revellers, the Race
> Of that wild Rout that tore the *Thracian* Bard
> In *Rhodope*.
> [7.32–35]

So too he will continue to hope that song and poetry may drive off or silence such barbarians. In *Paradise Lost* he implores Urania's divinely poetic voice to "drive far off" the Bacchantes, and in Sonnet 11 he recalls how Latona, the mother of Apollo, turned into frogs the hinds who dared to rail at the future god of poetry and song. Thus as civilizing agents, Orphic song and even the "soft lay" of a nightingale can drive away dissonance and encourage man's reachng beyond the self.

Milton's probable source for the sonnet, Sir Thomas Clanvowe's *The Cuckoo and the Nightingale*, includes a love debate in which the nightingale asserts the civilizing power of love:

> For Love his servaunts ever-more amendeth,
> And from al evel taches hem defendeth,
> And maketh hem to brenne right as fyr
> In trouthë and in worshipful desyr.[3]

The debate ends as the narrator awakes from his dream vision and throws a rock to drive away the "lewde cukkow" (as Milton hopes to shun "the rude Bird of Hate") who slanders love by calling it rage in the young and dotage in the old. Since the seventeenth century attributed this poem to Chaucer and printed it with his works, in imitating it Milton may have seen himself as an heir to "him that left half told / The story of *Cambuscan* bold" (*Il Penseroso*, ll. 109–10)—an heir who also hoped to serve the muse by continuing Chaucer's and Spenser's work in perfecting English poetry.

Not only does the nightingale's song have poetry's power to banish isolation and rudeness and to lead its hearer to the sweet society of love, its "liquid notes . . . close the eye of Day," and while it sings, "the jolly hours lead on propitious *May*" as in a dance. Here Milton describes the bird's song as part of that cosmic musical harmony, thought to govern time and the seasons, which became such an important poetic commonplace for medieval and Renaissance poets. Thus the young poet's desire to hear the nightingale and serve the muse also becomes a desire to join the choir of universal concord in self-transcendent celebration. Sometime near the composition of his first sonnet Milton delivered his second Cambridge prolusion, "On the Harmony of the Spheres," in which, albeit playfully, he defends the belief, "We may well believe that it is in order to tune their own notes in accord with that harmony of heaven to which they listen so intently, that the lark takes her flight up into the clouds at daybreak and the nightingale passes the lonely hours of night in song" (*YM* 1:237).[4] The song of the nightingale (or even the aspiring poet) may thus be a lowly, though not insignificant, part of the divinely harmonious consort of the universe.

Although its song joins the celebration of divine harmony, the nightingale by its nature warbles "at eeve": it sings in the dark. According to myth, its song arises from the terrible suffering of Philomela. After her brother-in-law Tereus raped her and cut out her tongue, she was mercifully changed into the nightingale. Now she sings despite the dark of night and the darkness of her own tragedy: her metamorphosis has also transmuted her pain into a beautiful song of hope and love. Similarly, the young lover, who identifies the nightingale with his own hopes for fulfillment in love and successful poetic service, sings his sonnet despite frustration and isolation. (So later the blind poet will exhort himself to sing in the dark, "as the wakeful Bird / Sings darkling" [*PL* 3.38–39].) And the song itself, although no love has come, is a form of self-transcendence. "O Nightingale" does more than lament the woes of the forlorn lover; the poem turns outward, away from self-pity toward hope for another spring, another chance at fulfilled service to love and the muse. Out of the darkness comes the nightingale's promise of love, and out of isolation and frustration comes the young lover's song of hope.

As a singer in the dark, the nightingale reaches beyond isolation and makes of suffering a song which, by leading its hearers to love, can civilize; cancel the "rude," "barbarous" forces that surround the poet; and attune to God's cosmic harmony those who listen. Although in "O Nightingale" the young poet is frustrated in seeking an object for his love, in the six poems that immediately follow, the Italian sonnets, Milton takes his first successful step toward the ideal community: he falls in love.[5]

Young Milton, though serious and earnest, dedicated to study and absorbed in preparation for his poetic calling, was not immune to female charm, as his Latin elegies demonstrate. During his rustication from Cambridge, he tells his friend Diodati in Elegy 1 that he spends much of his time girl-watching and has decided that beautiful English maidens surpass all others. Even in his tireless study of "the sage and serious poet Spenser" he would have found not only the lesson of temperance, which he refers to later in *Areopagitica*, but also an insistence on the need to reach beyond isolated maleness and femaleness to union. Throughout *The Faerie Queene* Britomart and Artegall, Timias and Belphoebe, Amoret and Scudamour, Marinell and Florimell quest after one another, for each is incomplete without the other.

The Spenserian emphasis is obvious in Milton's concept of love. He abjures the *amour courtois* which Denis de Rougement describes in *Love in the Western World*: "The passion of love is at bottom narcissism, the lover's self-magnification, far more than it is a relation with the beloved. . . . Passion requires that the *self* shall become greater than all things, as solitary and powerful as God."[6]

According to de Rougement, the hopeless and adulterous passion of courtly love leads only to death. But for Milton the object of love is never the self, exquisitely and fatally branded by love; it is the other. He regularly portrays selfish passion as a perversion of the mutual love he exalts. For example, Dalila, in an attempt to justify her betrayal, says to Samson,

> I knew that liberty
> Would draw thee forth to perilous enterprises,
> While I at home sat full of cares and fears
> Wailing thy absence in my widow'd bed;
> Here I should still enjoy thee day and night
> Mine and Love's prisoner.
>
> [*SA*, ll. 803–8]

Her love is as much a prison to Samson as his blindness.

Even in the most traditional love poetry he ever wrote, his Italian sonnets, Milton avoids both courtly love and the debased Petrarchan tradition. He exalts a love that is neither the narcissism of passion nor the abasement before the beloved so often expressed in "Serenate, which the starv'd Lover sings / To his proud fair, best quitted with disdain" (*PL* 4.769–70). Both extremes are equally mistaken and both lead to death; indeed, the two extremes are nearly one, as Adam demonstrates in his fall. At once narcissistic in his passion and self-abasing in his argument, Adam prefers Eve— and with her, Sin and Death—to his own right reason—and with it, God.

For the most part, English critics have slighted the attitude toward love presented in Milton's Italian sonnets, considering them mere literary exercises in a foreign language and a poetic tradition equally foreign to the Miltonic sensibility. F. T. Prince calls them "less love-poems than slightly amorous compliments," and argues that "Milton could scarcely lose self-consciousness in a passion so largely literary in nature." The Italian critic, Sergio Baldi, examines Milton's use of the language and classifies the "Canzone" and five sonnets as Petrarchan in the sixteenth-century Italian tradition.[7] Undoubtedly the poems employ the conventional imagery that Petrarch's imitators had used for nearly three centuries, but Milton, striving for a balance between self-concern and self-transcendence, appropriates such commonplaces to his own artistic purposes.

He begins Sonnet 2 with a geographical reference which hints at his beloved's name, Emilia. According to John S. Smart, "The use of allusions, sometimes recondite and far-fetched, to convey the name of the person celebrated by the poet is common among Italian writers of sonnets, who love to play upon words and to follow up any associations they may suggest."[8] Since "il nobil varco" refers to the most "famous ford" in the world, the Rubicon, perhaps it is not too "far-fetched" to see Milton's writing this first explicit love sonnet as his crossing of a Rubicon, similar to, though certainly less momentous than, Julius Caesar's. In fact, when he announces to Diodati in Sonnet 4 that he is in love, he expects his friend to be as amazed as he is that one who used to resist love so stubbornly and jest at its snares has been trapped.[9] In reaching out to love, the young poet is crossing the barrier of self that separates him from others. The decision to love is dangerous; once involved with another, one can hardly turn back. In his final sonnet he is still trying to escape from the imprisonment of isolation and blindness into union with his beloved.

Sonnet 5 is Milton's most conventionally Petrarchan poem. The lady's eyes, which are the sun to her lover, cause a warm vapor, a sigh, to arise in his breast. The poet is distressed because it is imprisoned there, and when it finally does escape into the air, it becomes frozen or congealed (like the captive Lady of *Comus* who, fixed in virtuous resistance, can be reunited to the community only with Sabrina's help). Here, as in the nightingale sonnet, the would-be lover's desire to express his love is thwarted, but much as the poet of Sonnet 1 waits hopefully to serve love and the muse, the young lover of Sonnet 5 awakes after a night of lament to a hopeful dawn crowned with roses. Although superficially Petrarchan in imagery, the sonnet presents the central issue of all the love sonnets (and an important concern in all Milton's works), the desire to transcend the self in love and service.

Earlier, too, in the first Italian sonnet, Milton employs such Petrarchan commonplaces as the arrows and bow of love, but Emilia is hardly the usual "proud fair" ridiculed in *Paradise Lost*,

who wounds and then ignores the "starv'd Lover." Her gentle spirit
rather

> dolcemente mostrasi di fuora
> De' suoi atti soavi giamai parco,
> E i don', che son d'amor saette ed arco.

("sweetly reveals itself—bounteous in pleasant looks, and the gifts
that are the arrows and bow of Love.")

The lady does not stand aloof. Similarly in Sonnet 3, the beloved
Emilia is the youthful shepherdess who nurtures in the poet the
strange and beautiful plant of a foreign tongue. Although the
reader is not told directly that Emilia returns the poet's love, both
these sonnets imply a greater degree of mutuality than is conventional in Petrarchan sonnets. Also in Sonnet 4 Milton explicitly
denies that the "treccie d'oro" ("tresses of gold") and "guancia ver-
miglia" ("rosy cheek") of the Petrarchan mistress beguile him.
Moved beyond "quel ritroso io ch'amor spreggiar soléa / E de'
suoi lacci spesso mi ridéa" ("my stubborn self, that was wont to
despise Love and often laughed at his snares"), he is led out of his
isolation by the lady's lofty and modest manners, the calm radiance of her gaze, her knowledge of several languages, and her
lovely singing. And in all his later sonnets about women, Milton
praises their virtues and accomplishments, not the physical beauty
celebrated by most Petrarchan lovers.[10]

Emilia's singing even has Orphic power to draw the hearer
beyond his stubborn self ("quel ritroso io"):

> Quando tu vaga parli, o lieta canti
> Che mover possa duro alpestre legno,
> Guardi ciascun a gli occhi, ed a gli orecchi
> L'entrata.
>
> [Sonnet 2]

("When thou speakest in beauty, or singest in joy, so that the trees of
the mountains might be moved, let him who is unworthy of thee
guard well the entrance of his eyes and ears.")

In Sonnet 4 her singing, which might lure the moon from mid-
hemisphere, is implicitly compared to the Siren song heard by
Ulysses: "E degli occhi suoi avventa sì gran fuoco / Che l'incerar

gli orecchi mi fia poco" ("And from her eyes there darts such fire that to close my ears would avail me but little"). Although as powerful as the Sirens', her singing does not lead to destruction. Rather its effect, as Sonnet 6 shows, is to urge the lover to perfect his heart into a worthy gift for his beloved.

Prince argues that Milton used Italian in these sonnets, as he used Latin in his elegies, because he "instinctively preferred the protection of an alien tongue and a literary convention when it was a matter of seeing himself as a young lover."[11] But Milton makes of his decision to write in Italian an important symbol of self-transcendence. In Sonnet 3 he compares his use of a foreign tongue to a beautiful and strange plant timidly spreading its leaves in an unfamiliar climate far away from its more genial native spring. Despite its alien surroundings, the plant hesitantly unfolds its leaves, as the poet opens himself to the beloved, reaching beyond his native language and metaphorically exchanging the fair Thames for the fair Arno. When the laughing youths and maidens of the "Canzone" question his daring to write in Italian, he quotes his beloved's words, "Questa è lingua di cui si vanta Amore" ("This is the language in which Love takes pride")—the language that allows communication with his lady in her native tongue, not his own.

The youths of the "Canzone" continue to rebuke the poet, reminding him of his poetic calling, a matter of intense concern to young Milton:

> Così mi van burlando. Altri rivi
> Altri lidi t'aspettan, ed altre onde
> Nelle cui verdi sponde
> Spuntati ad hor ad hor a la tua chioma
> L'immortal guiderdon d'eterne frondi:
> Perche alle spalle tue soverchia soma?

("And thus they jest with me—'Other streams, other banks await thee, and other waves, on whose green margin there sometimes grows, to crown thy head, the immortal guerdon of unfading leaves. Why place upon thy shoulders a superfluous load?'")

But the objections of his friends are irrelevant; Milton never conceived of his calling so narrowly.[12] From his earliest sonnet to

Paradise Regained, he consistently saw himself as serving in the train of both the muse and love, a love that starts in virtuous attraction to women and grows to include "Patience and Heroic Martyrdom."

Sonnet 6 is the brilliant culmination of Milton's attempts in the Italian sonnets to achieve the delicate balance between self-consciousness and self-transcendence. This young, gentle, and simple lover longs in the opening quatrain to fly from himself ("fuggir me stesso") and make, in devotion to his lady, a humble gift of his heart. Here he has indeed crossed the Rubicon separating lover and beloved, the ford from which there is no return. But immediately, in the following quatrain and tercet, he lists the proved virtues of his "upright heart and pure." His heart is faithful, dauntless, loyal, and in its thoughts fair, wise, and good. In danger, "s'arma di se, e d'intero diamante" ("it arms itself with itself, as with complete adamant"). The repeated reflexives emphasize the unyielding independence of his heart, which ignores chance and envy, common hopes and fears, while it pursues genius and lofty worth in service of the muse. After this elaborate catalogue of self-praise, a masterful touch of irony undercuts the effect of boasting: "Sol troverete in tal parte men duro / Ove Amor mise l'insanabil ago" ("Only there will you find it less hard, where Love placed its incurable sting"). He admits that, far from being hardhearted, he not only desires to reach out, to fly from himself, to give his heart away, but has allowed the lady to reach in and touch his inviolability.

Even though the last line of the sonnet suggests the trite image of Cupid's arrow, Milton is again adapting Pertrarchism to his own poetic ends. The conventional image allows him to achieve a real irony, which critics have too seldom seen in his works. Here young Milton deflates his own pride, resisting the temptation to narcissism that Eve faced at the pool where delight in her own image almost prevented union with her beloved. Although egotism may threaten to usurp this sonnet, the poet reestablishes a balance between self-concern and self-transcendence by acknowledging the power of love.

Milton ends his sonnets as he began them, with a poem of reaching beyond darkness and isolation toward love. No longer a "donna leggiadra," the woman he loves is now a childbearing wife, the Puritan ideal of woman. And, no longer a lonely young man, the poet is now a blind widower. The movement from self toward beloved dramatized in the final sonnet of the sequence resembles Adam's dream vision of his wife-to-be, whom, he tells Raphael, *"methought I saw, /* Though sleeping" (*PL* 8.462–63; emphasis mine). Like the speaker of the sonnet, Adam finds his wife only to lose her:

> Shee disappear'd, and left me dark, I wak'd
> To find her, or for ever to deplore
> Her loss.
>
> [*PL* 8.478–80]

But whereas unfallen Adam recovers his wife immediately, the fallen speaker must await the millennium for the embrace that will bring him out of dark loneliness.

In fact, Sonnet 23 portrays Milton as doubly isolated—imprisoned by the "night" of physical blindness and cut off from the communion of marriage by his wife's death. Unlike Hercules, *"Joves* great Son," who had the "force" to rescue Alcestis from the grave, Milton must remain passive as his lost wife stoops to him. Nonetheless, he does reach out to her with his mind: *"Methought* I saw my late espoused Saint" (emphasis mine); and the entire poem takes on the force of a dream vision. Here the poet's imagination has power to break all barriers to communion: death no longer separates man and wife, blind men may see angels, and matter and spirit may embrace. Yet despite imaginative self-transcendence, the actual attempt to embrace the beloved fails, much as the poet's desire to reach out to love in the nightingale sonnet is thwarted. In both sonnets, at twenty and fifty, Milton has finally to wait alone in darkness, whether to serve love or to achieve the heavenly vision of his beloved.

That Sonnet 23 is a miniature drama, depicting interrupted movement from the isolation of a benighted "I" to union with the "late espoused Saint," is one of the few aspects of the sonnet upon which critics agree. Debate has been lively, however, over the precise direction of the movement and the identities of the dramatis personae. Is the drama temporal and should the sonnet then be examined typologically? Is it spiritual, requiring an analysis of the Neo-Platonic stages of the vision? Is the "Saint" Mary Powell, Katherine Woodcock, or an ideal *donna angelicata?*[13] And is "I" the blind widower, John Milton, or Everyman? In order to see how this sonnet maintains the balance between self-concern and self-transcendent love which we have noted in Milton's other love sonnets and how it functions as part of the sequence as a whole, we must venture answers for these questions raised by previous critics.

The three similes ("like *Alcestis*," "as whom washt from . . . child-bed taint," "such, as yet . . . in Heaven") which structure the sonnet (and, therefore, the dream vision as well) present a temporal movement from classial times, when Herculean "force" rescued Admetus's wife from the underworld; through the Hebrew era, when ritual "Purification in the old Law" was thought sufficient to save childbearing women from death; to Christianity, the new dispensation based on the "trust" in Christ that saves all men from the grave. This temporal movement is also typological in at least three ways: first, Renaissance poetry often figured Hercules as a type of Christ (see the *Nativity Ode*, ll. 227–28); second, the "old Law" ritual sacrifice of doves and lambs required after childbirth (Lev. 12:6–7) prefigures the sacrifice of the crucified Christ, the Lamb of God; and third, the white vestments and radiant purity of the vision represent a power beyond the types of Herculean "force" or "old Law" ritual—the cleansing power in the blood of the Lamb that will turn the taints of all the chosen to whiteness (Rev. 7:14).[14] Although in reality the dreamer is passive and must be "enclin'd" to, in his vision he moves temporally and typologically toward the final heavenly community, where the Lamb will re-clothe the faithful in white robes and shepherd them "unto living fountains of waters: and . . . wipe away all tears from their eyes" (Rev. 7:17).

The dramatic movement presented in these three similes is spatial and spiritual as well as temporal and typological. In the comparison to Alcestis, a wife, who sacrificed herself so that her husband might live, is brought from the underworld back to earth. In the comparison to the purified Jewish woman, a wife, who has successfully preformed her appointed service of bearing children, has entered into a new state of womanhood on earth. Certainly for

Milton, childbirth was a woman's glory, not her shame.[15] The "child-bed taint" referred to in the sonnet is not the impurity of woman qua woman; it is original sin, which is not only transmitted to all men by the "child-bed," but will be washed away by woman's labor in the "child-bed" because "blest *Mary,* second *Eve*" (*PL* 5.387) will become a God-bearer on earth. In the comparison to the full sight of the "Saint" in glory, a wife, who has become a new Bride of the Lamb (Rev. 19:6–9) and hence literally a "late [recently] espoused [to Christ] Saint," has passed from earth to heaven.[16] Thus the seemingly passive dreamer in Sonnet 23 moves vertically as well as horizontally toward the marriage feast of the Lamb as he envisions the service of three wives on three levels: one who was willing to descend to the underworld for her husband, one who served mankind on earth by bearing children, and one who, although now the Bride of Christ in heaven, stoops to raise her earthbound husband to glory.

But the movement toward the final community fails. Why does the sonnet end in an interruption of the vision? Critics favoring Neo-Platonic readings find the narrator's plight in the last line hopeless because they stress the abyss separating matter and spirit in one of three ways: by making the "I" an Everyman who faces "the generally human problem of the Ideal in our world"; by asserting that the "I" has not yet reached "the ideal of purifying Christian zeal" that the wife has attained; and by accusing the "I" of intellectual blindness caused by an "affectional egocentricity" that makes him refer to the Bride of the Lamb as "*my* late espoused Saint" and "*Mine*" (emphases mine).[17] On the other hand, biographical critics, whether they favor Mary or Katherine, point to the poignancy of John Milton's (not the persona's) physical blindness and loneliness after the death of his wife. At least four important questions seem to be at stake in these debates. Does the responsibility for the failure of the vision rest with the dreamer? Who is the dreamer? Who is the "Saint"? Upon our answers to these questions depends our answer to a fourth: what attitude should the reader take to the dreamer?

In other famous passages in which Milton has dramatized himself, he does not portray failure. The autobiographical section of *The Reason of Church Government* justifies the entrance of a scholarly poet into the fray of pamphlet warfare, and the *Apology for Smectymnuus* defends the author against libels of unchastitiy. In *Lycidas* the young poet's hopes for fame are not defeated, merely redirected. Not even Sonnet 22, in which the wounded veteran of the pamphlet wars comes perilously close to boastful self-reliance, allows the speaker to fall into the sin of pride (see Chapter 7). Whenever Milton refers to his own physical blindness, he does not ultimately consider it a symbol of spiritual blindness, as Colaccio suggests he does in Sonnet 23. Quite the contrary, his blindness becomes both a painful human loss ("Ever-during dark / Surrounds me, from the cheerful ways of men / Cut off" [*PL* 3.45–47]) and a symbol of prophetic vision ("Celestial Light / Shine inward . . . that I may see and tell / Of things invisible to mortal sight," [ll. 51–55]). Nor does the persona of Sonnet 19 fail to control his anger and frustration over loss of "light." Hence Neo-Platonic readings of Sonnet 23 which emphasize the speaker's failure to attain exalted vision seem improbable in view of Milton's characteristic manner of self-dramatization. And finally, few readers respond to the last line of the sonnet by concluding that the overly possessive husband got the "night" of spiritual blindness he deserved.

The question of the identities of the dramatis personae remains. Does the sonnet dramatize Everyman seeking an ideal *donna angelicata* or John Milton dreaming of either Mary Powell or Katherine Woodcock? Perhaps all parties in the controversies would agree that the sonnet begins in a particular occasion, lamenting a personal loss ("Methought I . . . my . . . me . . . Mine . . . I . . . my . . . me . . . I . . . my") which might refer to either wife: Mary, who died as a result of childbirth, or Katherine, who survived the period of purification referred to in Leviticus. Most would also agree that the sonnet alludes to the cause of death in a graphic simile ("as whom washt from spot of child-bed taint"). Incidentally, if the "Saint" is Katherine, there may even be a pun on her name (*katharos* = "pure").[18] Thus the drama begins like Milton's other sonnets in an immediate engagement of self with other; but that immediate engagement, also as in many of his sonnets, must be seen through a wide-angle lens. Comparing Sonnet 23 to John Donne's sonnet on his deceased wife, E. M. W. Tillyard observes that, while Donne's poem is wholly self-centered and particular, Milton's both centers on his wife as a real woman and places her in a social context with its references to Alcestis and Hebrew women.[19] Perhaps then the richest reading would consider the speaker to be first, John Milton, and second, one among many husbands (like Admetus) who have lost and (at least for a moment) recovered wives; so too, the "Saint" is first, John Milton's wife, and second, one among many wives who have died in childbirth and become the Bride of Christ. Without the particularity the sonnet loses its intense poignancy, without the social context its universality.

As we have seen, the full context includes all time from the classical era to the millennium and all space between the grave and heaven. But an abyss separating matter from spirit does not cause the failure of the vision. There is no such abyss. The "Saint" who inclines to "embrace" physically her husband could not be a mere disembodied angelic ideal any more than could Raphael, who dines in Eden: in Milton's cosmos "one Almighty is, from whom / All things proceed, and up to him return . . . one first matter all" (*PL* 5.469–72). Since matter and spirit are inseparable, it may not be crucial to an understanding of Sonnet 23 to know which wife the poet envisions, but it is important to realize that he sees a real woman, not an unidentified ideal. In fact, she could not serve as Milton's ideal unless she were real. As easily as Raphael eats the material food offered by Adam and transforms it into his own spiritual essence, the childbearing woman becomes the saintly ideal. Milton's wife is, in a literal sense, more a *donna angelicata* than either Beatrice or Laura, for she is characterized as both a flesh-and-blood woman (*donna*) and an angel.

In fact, the spiritual movement toward the final community does not fail at all. In his imaginative vision Milton has seen his wife (albeit veiled) clothed in white and radiating "love, sweetness, goodness" at the marriage feast of the Lamb. It is rather the expanse of time separating the 1650s from the Second Coming that halts the temporal movement of the sonnet. Such Neo-Platonic visions which Milton describes here as "my fancied sight" were regularly available to him, although earthbound and blind—even visitations from his heavenly muse who, he says, "[visits] my slumbers Nightly" (PL 7.29). The completed "embrace," however, must wait. Matter can become spirit, and Milton can "trust" that he will join his wife in heaven, but not until Raphael's prediction that "*time* may come when men / With Angels may participate" (*PL* 5.493–94; emphasis mine) comes true. Eve fell by accepting Satan's false offer of instant godhead and ignoring Raphael's gentle admonition to wait: "Your bodies may at last turn all to spirit, / Improv'd *by tract of time* . . . If ye be found obedient" (ll. 497–98, 501; emphasis mine). Milton, however, painfully learned the lesson of expectant waiting in both patience and readiness, making it one of the central themes of his sonnets (and his major poetry as well).

Alone in a life he characterizes as "night," the speaker of Sonnet 23 must wait until he also becomes the Lamb's "espoused Saint." So too the Son in *Paradise Regained* must wait to begin his kingship on earth, the lady of Sonnet 9 must imitate the wise virgins of the parable who await the coming of the Bridegroom, and the twenty-three-year-old poet must wait for the "will of Heav'n." And the darkness of Sonnet 23 is more bleak than the night in which the young lover awaits the nightingale or the epic poet awaits the voice of his muse or blind Samson awaits a call to service. The same man who once saw himself surrounded by the vast community of anxious and listening Europe in *A Second Defense* now sees himself alone and lonely in the dark. Even so, he is sure that his desire to reach beyond blindness, isolation, and the earthly prison of life in order to unite with his beloved will be fulfilled "in Heaven without restraint." As the frustrated young lover hopes for another spring (Sonnet 1) or, after a night of lament, awakes to a dawn crowned with roses (Sonnet 5), the blind widower can say, "Yet once more I trust to have / Full sight of her."[20] Milton's final sonnet of the sequence approaches the remarkable balance between hope and despair presented at the end of *Paradise Lost*. While neither the epic nor the fourteen-line miniature denies the tragedy of loss, both assert self-transcendent hope and love reaching toward an ultimate community, the central theme of Milton's sonnets as of his life's work.

3.
"The better part":
Sonnets Addressed to Female Friends

Sonnets 8–14 were probably written between November, 1642, when a Royalist move against London, the occasion of Sonnet 8, was expected, and December, 1646, when Catharine Thomason, to whom Sonnet 14 is addressed, died.[1] During these years England was in the midst of warfare—either the actual Civil War or warring factions who were trying to establish a new basis for community. Amidst the physical warfare, pamphlet wars, and political battles of this period, it may at first seem incongruous that Milton wrote three sonnets addressed to women (9, 10, 14), one sonnet in defense of his home (8), and two sonnets justifying his divorce treatises (11, 12). Although earlier he had fought in the pamphlet wars over church government, in these years his published prose focused exclusively on one of the three elements in the broad ideal of a community he set forth retrospectively in A Second Defense: that is, "domestic or personal liberty," which involves, he said, "three problems: the nature of marriage itself, the education of the children, and finally the existence of freedom to express oneself" YM (4[1]:624).[2] He called for domestic freedom in order to present his total ideal at a time when the English community was being completely rebuilt and when, despite the chaos of war, the battle for liberty might still be won. To this end, in both prose and sonnets of this period, he examined the role of women in the home and the larger society, the function of marriage in fostering domestic and civic harmony, and the power of the word both to educate and to civilize despite the threats of physical warfare and the barbarism of ignorance. Three sonnets from these years addressed women who (not unlike Alcestis, the Hebrew women, and the "Saint" of Sonnet 23) served the godly community on domestic, civic, and transcendent levels.
Although many readers have agreed with Dr. Johnson that

Milton had a "Turkish contempt of females," *Paradise Lost* and
the divorce tracts suggest the opposite: that he assigned woman a
significant, if secondary, role in the quest for the ideal community.
Unfallen Eve is exalted as the preserver of both the human race
("Mother of Mankind" [*PL* 5.388]) and her future family's home.
She lovingly prepares Raphael's meal (5.331–49), names the
flowers (11.273–85), and shares with Adam their pleasant gar-
dening duties (4.610–32). Even after her sin, she is promised that
the curse of painful labor will ultimately result in the glorious
service of her daugher Mary in bearing the "Seed of Eve" who will
redeem all sin. Milton explicitly contrasts her to the "Bevy of fair
Women," whom Michael shows Adam in the vision of future
history. These women have become what unfallen Eve never was,
mere sexual objects,

> empty of all good wherein consists
> Woman's domestic honor and chief praise;
> Bred only and completed to the taste
> Of lustful appetence, to sing, to dance,
> To dress, and troll the Tongue, and roll the Eye.
> [*PL* 11.616–20]

Dalila is like these harlots who do not serve the community.
Although she claims to have become a national heroine by en-
slaving Samson, her patriotism is only treachery because she
betrayed what should have been her primary bond—the sacred
trust that holds home and family, husband and wife together.
Obviously, for Milton, as for many Puritans, woman had a call to
significant biological and domestic service to the community.[3]

Women were not, however, to be merely breeders and
housewives; Milton understood feelingly God's words at the
creation of Eve, "It is not good that the man should be alone" (Gen.
2:18). In fact, Adam is even willing to argue with his Maker (*PL*
8.379–436) to attain what Milton calls in *The Doctrine and
Discipline of Divorce* "an intimate and speaking help" and "the
apt and cheerfull conversation of man with woman, to comfort
and refresh him against the evill of solitary life" (*YM* 2:251, 235).
The divorce tracts are devoted to proving that the primary function of marriage is to provide this "conversation," not to produce

offspring.[4] Thus, for Milton, woman is above all a companion to whom he can reach out to escape self-imprisonment—to whom he does reach out, as we have seen, in his love sonnets and, as we shall see, in his sonnets of praise for virtuous women.

The occasion of Sonnet 9 is unknown, as is the identity of the "Lady" addressed. Although likely candidates, such as one of Catharine Thomason's daughters, Alice Egerton (the "Lady" of *Comus*), Mary Powell, and a Miss Davis (whom Edward Phillips said Milton considered marrying after Mary's desertion), have been suggested, the only facts supplied by the sonnet itself are that she is young ("in the prime of earliest youth"), that recently some people have peevishly reproved her virtues ("at thy growing vertues fret their spleen"), that Milton encourages her pursuit of virtue despite her critics, and that she is familiar with the Bible. The sonnet contains direct references to the "broad way" to destruction mentioned in Matt. 7:13-14, the story of Christ's visit to Mary and Martha related in Luke 10:38-42, the Book of Ruth, and the parable of the wise and foolish virgins found in Matt. 25:1-13; it also contains verbal echoes of John 3:19-21 ("deeds of light") and Rom. 5:3-5 ("Hope that reaps not shame"). Since the immediate engagement of self with other is clouded, the only access to this sonnet is through the wide-angle lens provided by its allusive richness. Through these references Milton praises the young girl's service to the community.

The "Lady" finds herself in a situation which Milton came to know well and which he would later recreate as the plight of many of his major characters: she is alone in her virtue and assailed by detractors. Like the lonely young lover who hears only the "rude Bird of Hate," the misunderstood pamphleteer surrounded by a "barbarous noise," Abdiel jeered at by Satan's army, the Son and Samson patiently enduring the taunts of Satan and Harapha—the virtuous lady waits among fretful critics for a reward that will bring her out of isolation to a communal celebration with "the Bridegroom with his feastfull friends." In the meantime, however, she merits Milton's praise for the lonely work of perfecting the center by imitating traditional models of Christian womanhood.

She has chosen "the better part with *Mary*, and with *Ruth*." According to Luke, a sudden visit from Christ produced very different responses from the two sisters of the household: Martha busied herself with the domestic necessities of serving while Mary listened to Christ's teachings. When Martha complained that her sister was not helping to serve, Christ replied, "Martha, Martha, thou art careful and troubled about many things: But one thing is needful: and Mary hath chosen that good part, which shall not be taken away from her" (Luke 10:41–42). The "better part" is to learn, not to pursue housewifery; virtue and learning contribute to "apt and cheerfull conversation" far more than does domestic expertise. If Milton intends the allusion to be understood literally, we may conjecture that the young lady's detractors would have preferred that she imitate Martha's busy housekeeping rather than Mary's desire to learn. If, in addition, the allusion resonates to include Mary, the mother of Christ, the lady is being compared to a woman whose heart, according to *Paradise Regained*, had been "a storehouse long of things / And sayings laid up" (2.103–4) and who had learned "to wait with patience" and readiness for the fulfillment of prophecies concerning her Son, the same Bridegroom awaited by the wise virgins to whom the lady is compared at the end of the sonnet.

In equating her with Ruth, Milton again portrays her as serving in other than domestic and biological ways. Choosing to follow her mother-in-law Naomi after her husband's death, Ruth knowingly forsook her womanly role of mother, preferring virtues of loyalty and love to biological fulfillment. Naomi entreated Ruth and Oraph to remain in Moab: "Go, return each to her mother's house. . . . The Lord grant you that ye may find rest, each of you in the house of her husband" (Ruth 1:8–9). When the widowed daughters-in-law persisted in their desire to follow her, Naomi asked, "Are there yet any more sons in my womb, that they may be your husbands?" (1:11). Whereas Oraph agreed to remain, Ruth chose Naomi's people and even her God. Paradoxically, because Ruth chose "the better part" of faith, she did achieve maternal fulfillment. Not only did she win the love of Boaz, but she became great-grandmother to David, from whose house Christ descended. Like Mary, the mother of Jesus, she became one of Eve's daughters through whom the promised Seed was to come.

Yet the lady's service includes not merely the passive virtues exemplified in Mary's attentive listening at Jesus' feet and Ruth's loyalty in following Naomi. Hers is not "a fugitive and cloister'd vertue, unexercis'd & unbreath'd, that never sallies out and sees her adversary" (*Areop, YM* 2:515). Running after "that immortall garland," she "with those few [is] eminently seen, / That labour up the Hill of heav'nly Truth." The young lady is no pedestaled beauty praised by an adoring Petrarchan lover; she is praised for climbing to eminence on her own. Like the wise virgins of the parable, she has actively pursued virtue by filling her lamp, not with oil that produces light, but with "deeds of light." As Ruth actively went to the fields to glean after the reapers hoping to win Boaz's favor, the lady's "deeds" also include "Hope that *reaps* not shame" (emphasis mine).

This verbal echo of the Ruth story at line 11, separated by changes in imagery and syntax from the original allusion in line 5, should alert the reader that the sonnet's allusive density connotes some less obvious ways in which the lady's pursuit of virtue resembles the deeds of Mary, Ruth, and the wise virgins, all of whose service was both active and passive. Ruth went to the field, but passively waited for Naomi's kinsman, Boaz, to notice her. Later she deliberately anointed and dressed herself to seek a husband. She came to the threshing floor at midnight (the Bridegroom will reward the wise virgins at "the mid hour of night"), waited until Boaz returned from a feast (the Bridegroom will include the wise virgins among his "feastfull friends"), lay down at his feet (Mary sat at Jesus' feet), waited for him to awake (the wise virgins waited in readiness for the Bridegroom), and then boldly requested, "Spread . . . thy skirt over thine handmaid; for thou art a near kinsman" (Ruth 3:9). Boaz commended both her bold actions and her known chastity; thus she is like the lady of Sonnet 9 in that their "Hope . . . reaps not shame."[5]

In this complex texture of mutually reflecting allusions, the young lady of the sonnet is likened to virtuous women who were each surrounded by disapproving, alien, or opposing groups: Martha reproved Mary, Ruth was a Moabite in Bethlehem, and the foolish virgins demanded oil from the wise. But all were ultimately rewarded with acceptance by a bridegroom: Mary was praised by Jesus, Ruth became Boaz's wife, and the wise virgins entered the

marriage feast. In the meantime, however, these models of
Christian womanhood learned to wait in readiness for their
reward: Mary listened attentively to Jesus; Ruth anointed and
clothed herself, then waited for Boaz's approval; and the wise
virgins attended the Bridegroom with full lamps. Paradoxically,
even their passive waiting became active service. By responding to
her detractors with "pity and ruth" rather than "anger," the lady
shows that she too has attained the radiant calm at the center of an
"upright heart and pure" which allows her to serve as she merely
stands and waits. Even in such a minor sonnet, Milton examines
the paradox of creative waiting that structures *Paradise Regained*,
Samson Agonistes, and two of his most famous sonnets (7, 19).

Perfection of the center, however, leads inevitably to the circumference, as this sonnet demonstrates in picturing the temporal
and spatial progress of a young pilgrim who labors "up the Hill of
heav'nly Truth." The poem moves from the lady's virtue in the
"prime of earliest youth" to the "mid hour of night" when she will
be rewarded as the Bride of the Lamb, and from earth's deceptive
"broad way and . . . green," which she has "shun'd," to the
heavenly "bliss," into which she is assured "entrance." At the
circumference the reward for her lonely self-perfection will be
participation in a glorious community, as Ruth's reward was full
acceptance into Bethlehem society. After Boaz publicly declares his
intention to marry her, "the people that were in the gate, and the
elders" welcome her as an important member of their community:
"The Lord make the woman . . . like Rachel and like Leah, which
two did build the house of Israel" (Ruth 4:11).

The lady's future community is previewed as "the Bridegroom
with his feastfull friends," but this allusion refers to an entire
complex of Old and New Testament symbolism of which the
parable of the wise and foolish virgins is only one element. The
feast to which the lady is assured entrance is the final feast of glory,
the marriage feast of the Lamb, which is described in Revelation,
alluded to throughout the Gospels, and prefigured in the Song of
Songs. Here she will be rewarded for being both "the true war-
faring Christian" of *Areopagitica* (*YM* 2:515) and for awaiting in
readiness the Second Coming. The "Virgin wise and pure" will
enter into a heavenly marriage where her virginity will become

true womanly fulfillment. Whereas now she must hold herself aloof
from those who "at [her] growing vertues fret their spleen," in the
ultimate feast all the virtuous will unite in the joyful community.
Perhaps Milton even intends her to see the contrast between the
heavenly feast being offered her and the mundane feast over which
Martha busied herself so needlessly. In choosing "the better part"
of listening to Jesus' teachings, both the lady and Mary seek "divine
Philosophy" which the younger brother in *Comus* calls "a perpetual feast of nectar'd sweets, / Where no crude surfeit reigns"
(ll. 478–79). But their reward in heaven will be a full feast of song,
nectar, and dance such as Lycidas enjoys (*Lycidas*, ll. 172–81).
Sonnet 9, *Lycidas*, and *Comus* all demonstrate the importance of
the feast to Milton's concept of the ideal community; the feast also
becomes a crucial image in other sonnets where it represents the
consummate harmonious community of the godly. Further
discussion of this image must, however, be postponed until Sonnet
20, an actual invitation to a feast, is considered.

Whereas Sonnet 9 praises a young lady's private virtues, which
Milton can only predict will eventuate in service to and acceptance
by a more congenial community than that of her present critics,
Sonnet 10 commends an adult woman's "noble vertues," which
"all" who know her acknowledge and which allow her to manifest
to the world the integrity of her father, a noted public servant.
Whereas we can only speculate about the identity of the young lady
of Sonnet 9 and the occasion of the poem, we know that Lady
Margaret Ley was the daughter of James Ley, the earl of
Marlborough, who had served James I and Charles I as lord high
treasurer and lord president of the Council. We also know from
Edward Phillips's *Life* that, during Mary Powell's residence with
her family (1642–46), Milton frequently visited Lady Margaret
and her husband, who were his neighbors, finding her "a Woman
of great Wit and Ingenuity [who] had a particular Honour for him,
and took much delight in his Company."[6]

We may also assume that, despite the Royalist sympathies of the
Ley family, Milton found Lady Margaret's household a place
where, during these early years of the Civil War, he could find
support for his own political views. Her husband, John Hobson,
served in the Parliamentary army and her father, Milton believed,

had practiced civic virtues he greatly admired: scrupulous honesty
and support of parliamentary government.[7] In describing the earl
as "unstain'd with gold or fee," Milton alludes obliquely to his
pronouncing sentence as chief justice of the Court of the King's
Bench in 1621 during Lord Bacon's trial for bribery. In asserting
that "the sad breaking of that Parlament / Broke him," Milton
perhaps repeats a family tradition related to him by Margaret that
the news of Charles's dissolution of Parliament on March 10, 1629,
hastened the earl's death, which occurred four days later.

Although the sonnet arises from the intercourse of a genial
company of friends who honor the contributions to civilized
community made by public servants of the past, Lady Margaret,
her father, and Milton himself are seen against a background
tainted by political corruption, abrogation of the rights of
Parliament, and warfare possibly "fatal to liberty." Of course, the
financial scandal alluded to occurred in 1621, the breaking of
Parliament in 1629, and the "dishonest victory" in 338 B.C. (the
battle of Chaeronea in which Athens and Thebes lost their independence); but these events all had parallels in the chaos of
1642–46. During these years when Milton frequented Margaret's
house and probably wrote the sonnet, ballads and jokes abounded
denouncing a corrupt Parliament who borrowed money "on the
public faith,"[8] nor had anyone yet forgotten the equally "sad
breaking" of the Short Parliament in 1640, and Royalist victories
that might be "fatal to liberty" were still to be feared until the New
Model Army proved itself in the Parliamentary victory at Naseby
in 1645. Thus Sonnet 10 portrays civilized communities of the past
and present as menaced by destructive forces which long ago killed
an aged orator and champion of freedom (Isocrates, who died of
grief over Athens's loss of liberty), which recently "Broke" a
devoted public servant, and which still threaten the peace, honesty,
and freedom of the English community.

The octave focuses on the contrast between the surrounding
world's corruption and violence ("breaking," "Broke," "Kill'd")
and the earl's inward virtue ("more in himself content"), which
sustained him in both public and private life. Not until the sestet
does praise of the father become praise of the "Daughter," barely
introduced in the first line. But the sestet establishes, in firm op-

position to the octave's catalogue of malignant forces, Margaret's power to preserve her deceased father's good name and virtues by keeping them alive in her praise of him and in her own actions as well. Both father and daughter have served the community first by perfecting the center and then by putting their "noble vertues" to work even in the midst of a hostile and dishonest world.

Biographical evidence suggests, however, that Margaret's service began even before her father's death. Smart notes that of the earl's numerous family only she and one sister remained in his house during his old age and were provided for in his will.[9] This fact, coupled with the sonnet's allusions to details of her father's life which only she could have revealed, indicates that she fulfilled, in at least one way, Milton's ideal of womanly service to the community: she served the home and family by preserving her father's life and good name. But her service transcended the domestic sphere. Her verbal praise has made Milton, "though later born, then to have known" the earl, see him "living yet." Not only has she provided a picture of his virtue in herself and given her troubled age a model of just and honest community service by her words, but she has also given her father the immortality of fame, an important Renaissance goal as the author of *Lycidas* well knew. Indeed, if Honigmann's speculations are correct, the fame she sought for her father was of a more lasting kind than oral praise to a friend.

Because the sonnet devotes more attention to the earl than to his daughter and emphasizes the daughter's description of the father, Honigmann believes that Milton may have written Sonnet 10 as a commendatory verse to accompany a biography by Margaret for one of James Ley's posthumously published manuscripts. Although the actual publication was probably delayed by exigencies of war, as was Lawes's *Choice Psalms* (1648) for which Milton wrote Sonnet 13, Milton may have written the verse ahead of time as he did with the sonnet to Lawes (1645). The line, "So well your words his noble vertues praise," would then refer directly to the biography which Margaret intended to prepare as a preface to one of her father's legal treatises.[10] If so, Margaret was a preserver not only of her father's life and good name, but also of his life's work, and not only through her spoken praise, but also by means of the written word, which Milton was to call later "an immortality" (*Areop, YM* 2:493). In any case, whether her praise of her father was oral or written, her service to the community extended beyond the domestic sphere.

In addressing to Margaret a sonnet with a reference to Isocrates' death after the battle of Chaeronea, Milton shows respect for her learning and intelligence. She was no "sullen masse whose very company represents the visible and exactest figure of lonlines it selfe," as *Tetrachordon* (*YM* 2:670) describes the woman incapable of being a companion as well as a housewife. Because she was a "Woman of great Wit and Ingenuity" who could entertain a man of such vast knowledge as Milton (and perhaps write a life of her noble father), she also fulfilled the second half of Milton's ideal of womanly service. It seems likely that, during the period of his wife's desertion, she provided a measure of that "apt and cheerfull conversation of man with woman" he valued so highly.

As we have seen, Sonnet 10 sets Margaret's threefold service to the community (concern for her family, her neighbor, and the wider community to whom she praises her father) against a background of corruption, tyranny, and war. The contrast makes her virtues and actions shine all the brighter. In fact, a pun on her name in the final words of the sonnet furthers this intentional contrast. That Milton enjoyed such linguistic guessing games as were popular among Italian sonneteers has long been acknowledged. Four examples suggest that the sonnets are full of them: in Sonnet 2 he conceals Emilia's name in a geographical reference, in Sonnet 11 the allusion to Christ's counsel against "casting Pearl to Hoggs" includes a pun on an opponent's name (Bacon), in Sonnet 13 an unstated pun on Lawes's name arises from the allusion to Dante and Casella, and in "The new forcers" the sting in the sonnet's tail depends on the reader's knowledge that *Priest* derives from the Greek root *Presbyter.*[11] In the last words of Sonnet 10, Milton puns on the name *Margaret* ("margherita"), meaning "pearl," just as Torquato Tasso and Claudio Tolomei had done before him. In fact, Milton's use of the pun draws on a long-standing tradition, both literary and religious, of comparing women to pearls.[12]

Because she models her father's high standards, and by her praise has preserved his good name so that future generations may see him "living yet," Milton describes Margaret in the sestet as a living emblem of her father's virtue shining in a tainted world. To emphasize her symbolic function and highlight the contrast to her darker surroundings, Milton culminates the sonnet with the submerged pun, which we may reasonably expect a woman of such "Wit and Ingenuity" to have appreciated, honoring her in the image of a pure and radiant pearl.

As well as radiance, the final pun emphasizes the worth of the virtue which the daughter embodies. Perhaps Milton, like many other poets who had used the pun, intends to compliment Margaret as the pearl of great price mentioned in Matt. 13:45–46. "Again," says Jesus, "the kingdom of heaven is like unto a merchantman, seeking goodly pearls: Who, when he had found one pearl of great price, went and sold all that he had, and bought it." Since the sonnet's opening quatrain praises James Ley for preferring the purity of inner virtue at the price of shunning lucrative bribes, and the sestet portrays Margaret as the symbol of that virtue, the pun in the final line suggests that, in name and deed, she typifies the precious pearl of virtue for which one must forego worldly riches. Indeed, according to the family tradition Milton repeats in Sonnet 10, James Ley lost all he had, his life, in the cause of civic virtue.

Whether one considers its radiance or worth, the pearl image makes concrete the relation between Margaret's and her father's virtue. She is herself "Honour'd" for possessing virtue through which she honors her father by shining like a pearl before a later age as an emblem of his purity. Similarly, she typifies the virtue whose worth justifies her father's worldly sacrifices. Although the pun on Margaret's name may seem recondite, it helps Milton accomplish the difficult task of complimenting both daughter and father in fourteen lines with grace and economy.[13]

In some ways Sonnet 14, "On ye religious memorie of Mrs Catharine Thomason my christian freind deceas'd Decem. 1646," is the complement to Sonnet 9, addressed to the unknown lady. Where the young girl of Sonnet 9 must "labour up the Hill of heav'nly Truth" by performing "deeds of light," the "Works and

Alms and . . . good Endeavour" of Catharine Thomason are
already on their way "up to joy and bliss for ever." And where the
unknown virgin actively awaits the Bridegroom's coming to take
her "to bliss," Catharine has attained her reward and now rests,
drinking the waters of life (Rev. 22:1,17) at the marriage feast of
the Lamb. In another sense, however, Sonnet 14 is the complement
to Sonnet 10 because, as we shall see, Milton alludes to Catharine's
earthly service which, like Margaret's, has extended beyond the
domestic sphere.

Although the sonnet itself depends on abstractions ("Faith . . .
Love . . . Death . . . Life . . . Works") and numerous biblical
allusions to present its eulogy, we know a great many details about
its subject. She was the wife of George Thomason, the famous
collector of over 22,000 Civil War and Interregnum pamphlets;
she was also the niece and ward of Henry Fetherstone, a bookseller
and prominent official in the Stationer's Company (warden in
1635, 1639; master in 1641) to whom her husband was once
apprenticed. Although the mother of nine children, she was widely
read, perhaps even learned. That Milton knew the family well is
likely for three reasons: several of his pamphlets appear in the
Thomason collection with the words *"Ex Dono Authoris"*; in 1647
he sent a letter by Thomason to his friend Carlo Dati in Florence;
and he refers to Catharine in the manuscript title of the sonnet as
"my christian freind."[14] His friendship with the family probably
began very early. In *A Second Defense* he says that, during his
years of retired study at Hammersmith and Horton (1632–38), he
occasionally visited London "to purchase books" (*YM* 4[1]:614).
Perhaps he met Thomason then; at any rate, during his trip to Italy
the book dealer wrote him a letter, now in the Barberini collection
in the Vatican Library. Hanford, who discovered the letter,
believes that the friendship with Thomason, in fact, secured Milton
an easy entrance into the Vatican because Holste, the librarian,
eagerly sought book-buying information from him.[15] His long-
standing intimacy with the family naturally prompted Milton to
compose a sonnet in praise of Catharine when she died.

The poem, however, seems to lack the personal details that
enliven his other sonnets. While R. L. Ramsay attributes its ab-
stractness to Milton's use of allegorical themes from morality plays

as a source, Honigmann classifies it as an epitaph, a genre that often uses personifications. Universally the poem has been condemned as commonplace and lacking in a sense of felt loss over the death of a real person.[16] But perhaps the poem is neither so simple nor so abstract as its critics have assumed.

In Sonnet 14, Milton confronts a tough problem he had already wrestled with in *Lycidas*, but solves it in a way that points toward *Paradise Lost*. In both *Lycidas* and Sonnet 14 death is a great separator, severing the soul from the body, removing the dead from the living, and terminating the earthly service that the deceased once performed so well. But in this sonnet Milton describes what may appear to be a violent separation as a process of growth. In the first two lines we learn that the two headings which Milton believed comprehended all of Christian doctrine (*CD*, *YM* 6:128), faith and love, never parted from Catharine, either in life or death. Her soul is likened to a plant, such as the one described by Raphael (*PL* 5.479–90), which grows and ripens until flowers produce "Spirits odorous," fruits produce man's "vital spirits," and man produces right reason, the essence of the soul, which will one day "dwell with God." In fact, the entire sonnet is devoted to Catharine's easy ascent from matter to spirit. To emphasize that death is a process of growth, not a separation, Milton has deviated from the Italian norm he so often followed, by constructing a sonnet with no volta (turn of thought) at all. Although the first six lines focus on the "earthly load" and "the grave," soon the rising movement toward heaven and the forward narrative progression take over: "Staid not behind . . . pointed . . . Follow'd thee up . . . led them on . . . up they flew . . . spake . . . thenceforth bid . . . drink." Thus the poem describes a continuous assumption into heaven which resembles Raphael's organic image of spiritual degrees more than the sudden apotheosis of *Lycidas*.[17]

In presenting a temporal and spatial movement toward heaven, the sonnet also explains the theology whereby earthly service can be transformed into heavenly song. From the earthly point of view, which dominates the sonnet's first quatrain, it seems that "this earthly load . . . doth sever" us from true "Life." The second quatrain and the sestet, however, are devoted to proving that, though our bodies rest in the grave, our works do not. Catharine is not justified "before the Judge" by "Faith" alone because "by works a man is justified, and not by faith only" (James 2:24). Since both are necessary, both "Faith" and "Love" (which manifests itself in "Works") ascend with her (Prov. 31:10–31, Acts 10:4, Rev. 14:13). Faith points the way for her works because only faith makes man capable of love. We can see this hierarchy clearly in a negative example from *Paradise Lost*. Eve, failing to have faith that in God's time she will become a goddess, falls; then, without the faith that had sustained their mutual love, Adam and Eve become mired in lust and petty bickering. Catharine, in contrast, provides a positive example: since "Faith" "parted from [her] never," it eventuated in "Love" which produced "Works and Alms and . . . good Endeavour." Works are called her "hand-maids" because they are both the deeds of her hands and the way in which abstractions like faith and love were made manifest in her life. Thus through the ripening power of "Faith" and "Love," the "Works and Alms" of her earthly service find themselves, in the last two lines of the sonnet, singing her praises before the throne of God and ensuring her a place of eternal rest and fulfillment in the community of the blessed. Although Milton's mortalism does not intrude itself into this sonnet for his "christian freind," he does show that death cannot separate all earthly things from the soul. Here matter has become spirit, and service has become song, adding still more "glorious Theams"[18] to the hymns at the marriage feast.

Theologically, at least, this sonnet is neither simple nor commonplace. Not only does it present the complex interrelations among matter, spirit, faith, love, and works, but it also confronts the mystery of Providence. In the final scene Catharine is judged and rewarded because of works which arose from faith. Earlier, however, "Faith" had pointed the way to heaven with "her golden rod," the golden reed / rod of Rev. 11:1, 21:15. In these cryptic prophecies, John is shown the city of Jerusalem, the faithful who have become the Bride of the Lamb (21:9–10); then he and an angel measure the city / Bride with a "golden reed" or "a reed like unto a rod." Commentators and Milton himself in *The Reason of Church Government* (YM 1:752) identified this reed / rod with "discipline," which measures the community of the faithful, judging them perfect in every respect. Hence in the sonnet, "Faith" both holds the measuring rod of judgment and makes Catharine's soul worthy to be measured by enabling her to perform good works. The circle of divine providence has been completed in Catharine's life as Raphael describes it in Eden: "One Almighty is, from whom / All things proceed, and up to him return." The sonnet's structure as well as this biblical allusion create the sense of a completed circle: in the opening lines "Faith" is characterized as the ripener with the goal of heaven already established, in mid-sonnet (l. 7) "Faith" points toward the goal, and in the final lines Catharine is judged worthy "to dwell with God," the fate planned for her in line two and prepared for her by the measuring rod of discipline. Indeed, the coordinate construction and run-on lines of the one-sentence sestet hasten the sonnet and Catharine simultaneously to the completion of "rest."

Although it devotes much of its complexity to presenting the relations among aspects of Christian doctrine, Sonnet 14 was intended to praise a specific woman's service, emphasizing that her earthly works are acceptable in heaven. Why, in praising a woman he probably knew very well, does Milton focus on her "Works"? Another look at what we know of Catharine's life and her husband's collection may suggest an answer. Her lifelong connections to bookmen, both guardian-uncle and husband, allowed Catharine the opportunity to become not only learned, but a collector in her own right. George Thomason's will indicates that she owned an extensive library which he prized highly and willed separately from his other possessions to his children, "hoping," he says, "that they will make the better use of [it] for their precious and dear mother's sake."[19] It is likely that Catharine was George's helper in the difficult and sometimes dangerous work of amassing his collection. In his own narration of the collection's history, he claims to have sustained the "Burthen" of his collecting secretly over a period of twenty years "in which time hee Buryed three of them who tooke greate Paines both day & night w*th* him in that tedious Imploym*t*."[20] One of these may have been Catharine herself.

But did Milton know of her library, her help with the collection, or even the supposedly "secret" project itself? For several reasons it is likely that he knew of all three. As we have seen, he knew the family well for many years. Then too his own pamphlet gifts stopped with Catharine's death, which suggests that they may have even been intended for her rather than George. And the collection was not completely secret. Records show that the king, a few noblemen, and other booksellers knew that Thomason was collecting licensed pamphlets, although they may not have known the extent of his unlicensed holdings. Moreover, although his politics later clashed with Milton's, a man who tried to collect objectively everything written for twenty years must have shared with the author of *Areopagitica* a belief in the immense power of the written word and with the future author of *The History of Britain* a sense of history.[21] Milton would have approved and encouraged his work.

Certainly, he approved the "Works" of Thomason's wife. Like Lady Margaret, Catharine had performed valuable community service which extended beyond the domestic sphere, despite the burdens of raising nine children. The "Works and Alms and . . . good Endeavour" which Sonnet 14 praises probably refer to the collecting of her own library and to her help in her husband's labor of love, as well as to her pious gifts and care for her extensive family. She did indeed fulfill Milton's ideal of the wife who not only is a helpmeet to her husband, but can also provide "apt and cheerfull conversation." And her reward, to drink her "fill of pure immortal streams," is a fitting one for a preserver of the written word, which Milton defined as "the pretious life-blood of a master spirit, imbalm'd and treasur'd up on purpose to a life beyond life" (*Areop, YM* 2:493).

In the broad concept of a community which he examined in the prose of 1642–46, Milton showed that the role of women in society, the proper basis on which to build domestic harmony, education, and the free publication of ideas were not isolated issues, nor merely peripheral to the work of determining the structure of church and state. All these problems had to be confronted by the builders of the holy community. In the three sonnets of this period addressed to women, we have seen all these concerns blend to suggest how women can contribute to the nation's efforts. He praises women, all of whom have chosen "the better part" of perfecting the self and actively serving the community in areas beyond woman's usual domestic labor. The virtuous lady of Sonnet 9 is likened to Mary, who sought Jesus' teaching, not Martha, anxious over the dinner. Lady Margaret Ley imitates and praises her father's virtues so that her beleaguered country still has a model of just and honest community service. And the "Works" of Catharine Thomason, despite her death, have both won her immortality in heaven and left succeeding ages a priceless record in books. In contrast, three other sonnets of this period show Milton surrounded on all sides by a threatening war-world. From sonnets of praise for successful service, he turns to sonnets of ridicule and chastisement against the enemies of the godly community.

4.

"The Muses Bowre":
Sonnets Defending Domestic
Peace and Freedom

In Sonnets 8, 11, and 12, the often "fugitive and cloister'd" domestic world "sallies out and sees her adversary," the war-world of England in the 1640s. One sonnet laughs at an enemy soldier with gentle irony, another mocks the ignorant reading public with humorous satire, and a third rails at rude detractors with direct castigation. Despite their differences of tone, all three use the same weapon, the power of the word, for similar purposes, to preserve the home and the institution of marriage from physical violence and uncivilized ignorance.

Although we need not take Milton's deleted title for Sonnet 8 literally ("On his dore when ye Citty expected an assault"), defense of the home was a serious matter in the seventeenth century. One popular Puritan conduct book emphasizes that the Tenth Commandment places the house first in listing a neighbor's possessions one must not covet and adds this jeremiad: "The curse and vengeance of God is due unto those which are spoilers of houses. . . . It were a fowle faulte . . . to build houses for the harbour and helpe of mankinde at the first, and after to destroy and pull downe those which he hath built."[1] Less hysterical, but no less serious than the conduct books, the flourishing subgenre of country house poetry depicted the home as a microcosm of a well-ordered state and a nurturer of poetry and religion (Ben Jonson's "To Penshurst"), a peaceful refuge from the vices of urban life (Robert Herrick's "A Country Life: To His Brother"), and even a final outpost where the struggle against chaos continues within the bounds of the home itself (Andrew Marvell's "Upon Appleton House"). Early in the century, Puritans in particular had good reason for insisting that the home be preserved. While feudal, monastic, and courtly societies had employed other ties of allegiance and hierarchical systems to maintain order and discipline, the home was the center of Puritan communities. Beginning in the sixteenth century, when there were too few preachers to satisfy the country's growing hunger for the Word and the state suppressed laymen's conventicles, dissenters had increasingly been forced to turn their homes into informal and often secret churches. Soon the home became a school, church, and governing body all rolled into one, and authors of Puritan conduct books never tired of exalting the home as not only "the Schoole, wherein are taught and learned all the principles of authoritie and subjection," but "even a kind of paradise upon earth."[2]

Milton too believed that the home was potentially a paradise. Although Adam and Eve, once "Imparadis't in one another's arms," must leave their paradisiacal home to wander through a fallen world seeking "thir place of rest," they leave "hand in hand" with the promise that they can create temporary homes in the "paradise within" and the paradise of their mutual love to sustain them in the pilgrimage to their final home. Sonnets 8, 20, and 21 temper these specifically Puritan attitudes with a broad humanist culture, representing the home as the nurturer of friendship, learning, poetry, and music. As a young man, Milton enjoyed a cultured home life; his father, an accomplished composer, fostered his genius by hiring private tutors and later making the family home a haven where he could spend five postgraduate years in retired study. Indeed, he highly valued and intended to preserve "the Muses Bowre."

Although the events of 1642 that necessitated preparations to defend his home were real enough, the engagement between poet and soldier described in Sonnet 8 is probably a fiction. Early in the war, London was threatened by a Royalist attack which, if carried out, might have ended the Parliamentarians' hopes. Londoners, frightened by reports of the pillaging Royalist cavalry, worked anxiously in early November, preparing earthworks and mustering the 24,000 men who, on November 13, blocked the advance of the king's forces without a battle. During the excitement or shortly thereafter, Milton wrote Sonnet 8, a vignette in which a poet-speaker offers a bribe of fame to an enemy soldier in return for sparing the poet's house.[3]

However seriously the poem defends the importance of the home to a community, the fancied situation is comic. Milton asks his reader to imagine that a brief note in sonnet form tacked on a poet's door may prevent devastation by a Royalist cavalry notoriously eager for booty. He characterizes the poet-speaker as submissive, even fearful, despite his claims to poetic power. His doors are "defenceless," although Milton was proud of his swordsmanship.[4] He invokes "Captain or Colonel, or Knight in Arms" as one might beg, "Anyone, whoever you are, spare my home!" He even stoops to bribery, hardly the act we would expect from the poet who praised the integrity of Lady Margaret's father. Finally, he flatters the comparatively low ranking officer who, if he spares the house, may be classed with Alexander the Great. This is going too far; even the imaginary soldier should realize by now that he is being mocked.[5]

The poet has contrived his submissive tone all along to please the victorious officer he addresses and thereby to set him up for a comedown. A fall from the heights of pride is necessary to prepare him for a serious lesson about the true nature of power. Throughout the sonnet, in fact, the poet's apparent submissiveness conceals pointed barbs. He meekly asks for mercy, "if deed of honour did thee ever please." Of course, he means that sparing his house is as worthy a deed as others the soldier may have previously performed. But may he not also be wondering if "deed of honour" has *"ever"* pleased the Cavalier he addresses? Pillage was not the only dishonorable act for which the Cavaliers were notorious.

He also offers the soldier the benefit of his knowledge of "charms," meaning songs (*carmina*) with magical powers. But Milton considered poetry far more than magical formulas. Quasi-divine, it arises from "devout prayer to that eternall Spirit who can enrich with all utterance and knowledge, and sends out his Seraphim with the hallow'd fire of his Altar to touch and purify the lips of whom he pleases" (*RCG*, *YM* 1:820–21). Of all the references in his poetry to *charm(s)*, only in unfallen Eve's love sonnet does Milton use the term to mean purely song (*PL* 4.639–56); everywhere else it carries overtones of deception (*PL* 2.460–62) or, at least, bedazzlement (*PL* 9.999) and is associated with or spoken by such charmers as fallen Eve, Comus, and Satan. And though the narrator of *Paradise Lost* praises heavenly music as "charming" (5.625–27) and says that "Song charms the Sense"

(2.555-57), he labels poetry that does nothing more than charm, "partial." There are, after all, ravishing poets in hell, but heavenly poets delight their hearers with truth, not with

> vain wisdom all, and false Philosophie:
> [which] with a pleasing sorcery could charm
> Pain for a while.
>
> [*PL* 2.565-67]

In Sonnet 8, then, the poet-speaker condescends to the officer, emphasizing a less exalted conception of poetry in order to make his bribe enticing to a Cavalier, whom he expects to be interested primarily in poetry's magical power to guarantee personal fame.

The third barb is subtle indeed. In order to forestall any fears the soldier may have that a superior officer will accuse him of being weak or softhearted for sparing a "Muses Bowre," the poet offers precedents of other ruthless warriors who were secure enough in their bravery to risk performing "gentle acts." In these double entendres and condescending offers, the poet simultaneously bows to military might and playfully punctures its inflated sense of superiority.

The serious lesson, for which these barbs prepare the officer, arises from the contrast in the sestet between the power of poetry to preserve civilization, "to save th' *Athenian* Walls," and the power of war to reduce it to "ruine bare," to raze "Temple" (church) and "Towre" (state) "to the ground." In opposing the creative and sustaining power of the "Muses Bowre" to the destructive power of the "spear," the poet-speaker alludes to two historical incidents in which poetry actually saved homes: Alexander's devastation of all Thebes except a house once occupied by Pindar and the Spartans' decision not to destroy Athens after hearing a chorus of Euripides' *Electra*.[6] Although the once awesome power of Alexander, Thebes, Sparta, and Athens has vanished, Pindar and Euripides remain alive to speak to men of 1642 and today, preserving the values of their past communities. Because the written word, the arms wielded by the "Muses Bowre," can transcend time and space, "what ever clime the Suns bright circle warms," the books of Pindar and Euripides have not only won them fame, but also metamorphosed Greek civilization into "an elementall life . . . that ethereall and fift essence, the breath of reason it selfe . . . an immortality" (*Areop*, *YM* 2:493). By comparison, Sparta's or Macedonia's wars of conquest have dwindled to mere background for literature we still value.

By the end of the sonnet, the soldier has been cajoled, bribed, condescended to, ridiculed, and finally shown the limits of his destructive might when contrasted to poetry's regenerative power to recreate the past.[7] Thus, when the sestet opens, "Lift not thy spear . . . ," the imperative represents both a plea and a veiled threat, because even a piece of paper tacked on a door can become a weapon that will continue to inflict wounds for centuries. The initially comic situation (sonnet versus spear) has become a serious confrontation between the forces of civilization and destruction. In fact, Sonnet 8 dramatizes only one battle in a centuries-long war in which Milton allies himself with the finest poets of ancient Greek civilization against past and present conquering armies who devastated Thebes, threatened to raze Athens, and hoped to pillage London. Because the sonnet invokes the past and promises to memorialize the soldier's clemency in the future, it places the present event in its proper perspective. Although the war is serious, the 1642 battle for London is only a skirmish; so Milton can face the Royalist attack with jesting detachment, confident that the truism is true: "The pen is mightier than the sword."

By means of playful irony and allusive resonance, Sonnet 8 puts the war-world in its place and successfully defends the home as the seat of poetry and civilization. But it addresses a double audience: while the speaker flatters, ridicules, and teaches the officer in the fictional situation, Milton is staging the scene for the amusement of a friend. Parker suggests that the sonnet may have been sent to John Hobson, who, Phillips tells us, was Lady Margaret's "very accomplished" husband and an officer in the Parliamentary army.[8] Whoever received the sonnet (perhaps even Margaret herself), we may assume that she or he was a "fit audience," who would not only detect Milton's irony at the officer's expense and enjoy the joke, but appreciate the significance of his allusions. One particularly recondite allusion supports the sonnet's contrast between the power of the "spear" and the "Muses Bowre."

Because the sonnet compares the poet's might to the warrior's, exalts the power of poetry to preserve civilization, refers to the destruction of Thebes, and mentions the ruining and saving of "Walls," it may include an allusion to the myth of Amphion and Zethus. Of these twin sons of Zeus and Antiope, Amphion became adept at music and Zethus at war. After destroying Thebes to avenge their mother's imprisonment, the brothers promised to rebuild its walls. But Zethus's strength could not match Amphion's music, which caused stones to follow him and fit themselves into place. Thus if the sonnet recalls to its reader this variant of the Orpheus theme, it offers still further evidence that the poet surpasses the warrior as the preserver of civilization.

But a more obvious example of how the allusive texture of this sonnet may convey meaning to its "fit audience" is the reference to "sad *Electra's* Poet." If the recipient valued Euripides as highly as Milton did, he would have read *Electra* and might remember the opening lines which deterred the Spartans from razing Athens and selling its people into slavery.[9] In this chorus, the women of Argos invite Electra to leave her desert home and join them in celebrating the feast of Hera, goddess of womanhood. Unlike Catharine Thomason and Sonnet 9's unknown lady, who either await or enjoy the final marriage feast, Electra cannot participate in festivals of womanhood; she is "unmated," as her name implies.[10] By marrying her to a peasant, her stepfather Aegisthus has kept her from wedding a powerful prince who might help her avenge the murder of her father, Agamemnon. She remains a virgin because the humble peasant refuses to sully her royal purity. Euripides' Electra is a bitter woman, barren and ragged; unlike Margaret Ley, she preserves her father's memory only to goad her cravings for vengeance, not to perpetuate his virtues.

The entire play, as well as the characterization of "sad" Electra, presents the perversion of a domestic community, a perversion caused at least in part by senseless warfare. Like her daughter, Clytemnestra has been treated brutally and, in turn, has become brutal: she has defiled the home by murdering her unsuspecting husband in his bath. Of course, Agamemnon had previously agreed to sacrifice their daughter, Iphigenia, to ensure favorable winds for the Greek ships, and brought home spoils, including a mistress, from the hideous sack of Troy. No one in *Electra* is innocent of crimes against the home, family, and civilized life—not even the avenging Orestes who desecrates a holy feast by killing Aegisthus at a public sacrifice. The final allusion of the sonnet thus invokes a cycle of interrelated Greek legends which are significant to the values the sonnet and sequence advocate. Milton would have the friend(s) who read the sonnet, and perhaps the Royalist officer as well, remember why Electra is "sad": her tragedy includes the frustration of woman's proper role as preserver of the home and civilization, the tainting of the home and family by vengeance and murder, the defilement of holy feasts, and the destruction of an entire civilization caused by a wanton's betrayal. Those who do recall Electra's tragedy will know what evil can be unleashed if the war-world is allowed to violate the home and family.

Inasmuch as Sonnets 11 and 12 defend Milton's divorce tracts, which themselves plead for domestic freedom, they join Sonnet 8 in protecting his ideal of home, marriage, and family from ignorance and barbarity. His ideal included much more than the rules for wifely behavior presented in the myriad domestic conduct books of the day. To compare the common Puritan and the specifically Miltonic attitudes toward marriage may explain the anger that animates Sonnets 11 and 12 and his resort to his enemies' tactics of name-calling and mockery.

Puritan theorists exalted marriage and family life to a position hitherto unknown in Western civilization. Marriage not only propagates the race, spreads the church, creates a community of earthly saints to become the communion of heavenly saints, and, in itself, represents church and state in little, but it also mirrors the universal cosmic harmony. In *Matrimoniall Honour*, a conduct book of 1642, Daniel Rogers delivered a paean to marriage:

> Oh, thou sweet amiableness and concord, what may not be said of thee? Thou art the offspring of God, the fruite of Redemption, the breath of the spirit: Thou art the compound of contraries, the harmony of discords, the order of Creation, the soule of the world: without which, the vast body thereof would soone dissolve it selve by her owne burden, as wearisome to it selfe, and fall in sunder by peacemeale from each other.[11]

Nowhere is this cosmic view of marriage more evident than in *Paradise Lost* where "two great Sexes animate the World" (8.151). Indeed, John L. Halkett has described the epic as the history of a marriage, where Adam and Eve's prelapsarian union, the prime object of Satan's envy, is echoed, varied, or distorted in angelic sexuality and concord, the magnetism of the elements, Satan's incestuous mating with Sin, and the mésalliance between the sons of God and the daughters of Cain.[12] After the fall, Adam and Eve's restored union is the domestic parallel to the "paradise within," the grace and order always potentially available to postlapsarian man.

Unfortunately, man and wife do not always create a domestic paradise, and when they fail, Milton believed their bond may be dissolved. In his divorce treatises he asserts that anyone who truly values marriage will allow divorce for incompatibility so that the ideal domestic community may become a reality: "Who therfore seeks to part, is one who highly honours the maried life, and would not stain it: and the reasons which now move him to divorce, are equall to the best of those that could first warrant him to marry" (*DDD, YM* 2:253). If, he argues, marriage is the foundation of the state and the mirror of cosmic concord and if the freedom to divorce will help create good marriages, then that freedom is essential to political stability and cosmic harmony.

In his address to Parliament prefacing *The Doctrine and Discipline of Divorce*, he assures the builders of the holy community that domestic liberty relies on the same principles by which they hope to reform every facet of English life, from constituting a sovereign power to educating the youngest child:

> He who marries, intends as little to conspire his own ruine, as he that swears Allegiance: and as a whole people is in proportion to an ill Government, so is one man to an ill mariage. If they against any authority, Covnant, or Statute, may by the soveraign edict of charity, save not only their lives, but honest liberties from unworthy bondage, as well may he against any private Covnant, which hee never enter'd to his mischief, redeem himself from unsupportable disturbances to honest peace, and just contentment. . . . For no effect of tyranny can sit more heavy on the Common-wealth, then this houshold unhappines on the family. And farewell all hope of true Reformation in the state, while such an evill as this lies undiscern'd or unregarded in the house. On the redresse wherof depends, not only the spiritfull and orderly life of our grown men, but the willing, and carefull education of our children. [*YM* 2:229–30]

Not only is the freedom to divorce necessary for civic concord; Milton goes on to insist that by God's "divorcing command the world first rose out of Chaos, nor can be renew'd again out of confusion but by the separating of unmeet consorts" (*DDD, YM* 2:273). Thus the creation and sustaining of both cosmic and civic harmony depend on divorce.[13]

Nor will divorce result in anarchy. For Milton, the freedom to divorce is dictated "by the known *rules* of antient libertie" (emphasis mine), and he writes of not only the "doctrine," but also the "discipline" of divorce. Throughout the treatise, he emphasizes that discipline and liberty form an inextricable union that avoids the extremes of slavery and license. But the rude detractors he rebukes in Sonnets 11 and 12 misunderstood the necessity of being able to break in order truly to bind marriages. One critic, still venting his spleen in 1660, long after the outcry that greeted the original publication of the treatises in 1643–45, accused Milton of opposing marital harmony and ridiculed "that other learned Labor of yours, which you style *Tetrachordon*, that is to say, a Fiddle with four strings; but, as you render it, a Four-fold Cord, with which you undertake . . . not to bind, but (most ridiculously) to unty Matrimony."[14] The criticism reveals a complete misunderstanding of what Milton had fully explained in his four treatises: that domestic liberty depends on the harmonious inner discipline which, after Christ's coming, replaced external law, and that the freedom to divorce, by "separating . . . unmeet consorts," fosters harmony in married life.

The Greek title of one of his treatises emphasizes this message. As a title, *Tetrachordon* performs at least two functions. It suggests that four seemingly contradictory biblical passages actually agree in permitting divorce for incompatibility, just as the Greek scale composed of four unlike notes produces a musical harmony. It also recalls an essential argument of *The Doctrine and Discipline of Divorce*: that domestic harmony demands the option of divorce for incompatibility. The title is thus part of Milton's strategy of persuasion, as it links divorce analogically to the fourfold scheme of Pythagorean cosmology. The educated seventeenth-century reader, whom the treatise addresses, still believed that God governed the universe by tetrads. He assumed that the well-tempered state, soul, body, and universe all rest on the harmonious combination of four elements. He found it significant that there are four compass points, four seasons, four qualities, four humours, four cardinal virtues, four evangelists, four trees in Paradise, and four corners of the cross. The list is almost endless.[15] And all these harmonious quaternions were thought to participate in the musical world soul to which all things are tuned. In the syncretist spirit of Renaissance humanism, biblical exegesis also assumed this Pythagorean faith in universal harmony. Commentators sought to match Old Testament prophecies to New Testament fulfillment, types to antitypes, even Holy Scripture to pagan writers like Virgil—always citing the parallels they discovered as proof that God created and sustained the universe in musical harmony.[16]

When Milton calls his "Expositions upon the foure chiefe places in Scripture which treat of Mariage, or nullities in Mariage" a *Tetrachordon*, he is playing no merely fanciful word game. The title is not only an echo of his faith in the universal harmony, but also the logical extension of his belief in Christian liberty. Because Christ freed man from the imposed righteousness of the Old Testament, all things not specifically prohibited by the Gospels (and he believed divorce for incompatibility was not prohibited) are now left to the disciplined liberty of the individual. By trying in *Tetrachordon* to harmonize Christ's apparent prohibition with Moses' permissiveness, Milton hoped to demonstrate how all parts of God's word participate in the world harmony which makes true marriages and allows man the freedom to break false ones. Only by allowing divorce, he insists, can man achieve that harmony in the home and commonwealth which leads to the final harmony and community at the marriage feast of the Lamb.

But in the sonnets which defend his ideal of domestic harmony, Milton again finds himself in the situation of Abdiel facing Satan's troops and the lady of Sonnet 9 facing her critics: he stands alone in defending truth, surrounded by scorn. The immediate occasion of the sonnets heightened his sense of alienation to anger, since his present detractors had been his allies. After the publication of his divorce treatises, the Presbyterians, whom he had supported earlier in the Smectymnuan controversy, were loud and virulent in their immediate and continued denunciation of Milton "the divorcer." They condemned him as a dangerous schismatic, placing his ideal of marital reform in the same category with the notoriously licentious views of such sects as the Family of Love and the Anabaptists.[17] He retaliated in Sonnets 11 and 12 by characterizing them as animals and barbarians. They are the "Owles" of ignorance, the "Cuckoes" of ingratitude and vanity, the "Asses" of stupidity and obstinacy, the "Apes" of mockery, and the "Doggs" of quarrelsomeness.[18] Barbaric Scottish names "that would have made *Quintilian* stare and gasp" have grown sleek on their tongues, but they are ignorant of Greek, the language of the first great civilization so treasured by Renaissance humanists. In fact, they hate "Learning wors then Toad or Asp."

As the allusion to "the barbarous dissonance / Of *Bacchus* and his Revellers" in *Paradise Lost* shows, Milton came to see harmonious civilization as a precarious attainment constantly under barbaric attack. He felt that he himself as scholar and poet had a special calling to defend culture and was horrified at the Bacchantes whose "savage clamor drown'd / Both [the] Harp and Voice" of his prototype, Orpheus. Similarly, in Sonnets 11 and 12 he fears that the cacophony of his detractors' "barbarous noise" and the "Cries" of the ignorant "stall-reader" will drown his earnest pleas for liberty. He wanted a community in which man attunes his domestic and civil life to the cosmic harmony implied in the title of his divorce tract, *Tetrachordon*—a community that would be the political counterpart to Orpheus's world, "where Woods and Rocks had Ears / To rapture" (*PL* 7.35–37). But like Orpheus, he finds himself in these sonnets as the beleaguered defender of harmonious cosmos amidst the din of chaos.

Sonnets 11 and 12 insist on two prerequisites for an ordered community: the individual center must seek inner perfection in order to serve the community, and the community must guarantee the center's freedom to do so. As the poet says in Sonnet 11, whoever loves liberty "must first be wise and good"; and Sonnet 12 makes clear by negative example the necessity of attaining that wisdom. But because his age hates learning, which perfects the center, it excoriates his promptings to free the center. As a result, neither freedom nor self-perfection is possible, and chaos is unleashed. In the sonnets, noise, not harmony, prevails, rustics rail at gods, the words *Licence* and *libertie* are confused, barbaric language replaces elegance, and learning is despised "wors then

Toad or Asp." Such confusion has resulted from trying to bind the center with external tethers and neglecting the virtue and learning that would free the center.

As the advocate of freedom in Sonnet 11, Milton associates himself with powerful allies. The liberty he supports is "antient": he has precedents as far back as Moses for his opinion on divorce and the distinction between license and liberty was forcefully drawn by many Roman worthies.[19] Also, since *Tetrachordon* and *Colasterion* were both published on March 4, 1645,[20] he compares his own "twin-born progenie," which advocate true domestic harmony and which he defends from attackers, to Latona defending her infant twins from railers. As the deities of music, healing, poetry, and chaste womanhood, the twins Apollo and Diana represent virtues and accomplishments which, as we have already seen in several sonnets, Milton valued highly as civilizing agents. (At least one syncretist mythographer of the Renaissance went so far as to compare the twins to Christ and his Church.)[21] Although Milton may seem a lonely champion of his ideal in this sonnet, he has marshaled in his allusions a formidable array of supporters who have defended ideals like his in the past.

Still, the ideals that once civilized Israel, Greece, and Rome must face the present "age" of bawling animals. By prompting his countrymen "to quit their cloggs," Milton has asked them to cease being enslaved animals and assume their birthright as Christian men and women: *cloggs* are "pieces of Wood, or such like, fastned about the Necks, or to the Legs of Beasts, that they run not away" (*OED*, *sb.*, Worlidge, 1669). Freed from the restrictions of Old Testament law, men should depend on their right reason and erected wills for making the choices necessary to live in an ordered human community. But Sonnet 11 shows that Milton's opponents have preferred their "cloggs" and thus sunk to the level of animals. He chooses to characterize his former allies as beasts not merely because he feels angry or betrayed, but because animals have neither reason nor will. A slave to appetite, a beast must be controlled by "cloggs" since it lacks the reason and will to distinguish between "libertie" and "Licence," a requirement for citizenship in a civilized community.

Paradoxically, the result of preferring external constraint has been "Licence." The rustics in Ovid's story not only ignored Latona's pleas that all men have a natural human right to sun, air, and water, but took no pity on her as a newly delivered mother, muddied the pool from which she would drink, and reviled both her and her nursing infants.[22] The rudeness of the "Hinds" had rendered them bestial before Latona transformed them into frogs, making their external form coincide with their actions. Here Milton suggests that, because his detractors have chosen the external "cloggs" fit for animals instead of seeking the virtues available to men, they have degenerated to the license of beasts; their cruelty toward one who pleads only for natural rights (as does Milton as well) has made them unfit to live in a human community. Their railing is indeed "barbarous," like the noise of Comus's bestial crew, who prefer licentious revelry in the dark forest, and with it enslavement to their appetites, above the inner perfection and freedom which allows the Lady to rejoin her family and the *civitas* they represent. Milton does not scruple to call his enemies beasts; like the "Hinds" who became "Froggs," their rudeness has already excluded them from the human community.

Sonnet 11 insists that external restraint and license go together and both are opposed to internal freedom and wisdom and virtue, a doctrine Milton repeatedly taught. In *The Tenure of Kings and Magistrates*, he argues, "None can love freedom heartilie, but good men; the rest love not freedom, but licence; which never hath more scope or more indulgence then under Tyrants" (*YM* 3:190). Then in *A Second Defense* he insists that goodness is not merely the prerequisite for liberty, but its definition: "To be free is precisely the same as to be pious, wise, just, and temperate, careful of one's property, aloof from another's, and thus finally to be magnanimous and brave, so to be the opposite to these qualities is the same as to be a slave" (*YM* 4[1]:684). The whole chain of ethical reasoning is complex, but Milton, with characteristic force and precision, easily telescopes it in Sonnet 11 into two puns: one on *Hoggs* and a second on *Licence*.

After explaining his attempts to free the age from external constraints and after describing the unrestrained and bestial attack inflicted upon him as a result, he ruefully comments, "But this is got by casting Pearl to Hoggs; / . . . Licence they mean when they cry libertie." Honigmann has offered a convincing argument that the lines include a topical allusion as well as the reference to Matt. 7:6 ("Give not that which is holy unto the dogs, neither cast ye your pearls before swine, lest they trample them under their feet, and turn again and rend you"). Two prominent Parliamentarians, both named Bacon, opposed Milton's libertarian ideals: one examined him in 1644 after he had published *The Doctrine and Discipline of Divorce* without a license; another helped prepare an ordinance in 1646 that would severely punish all heretics.[23] The name pun on *Hoggs*, then, coalesces the two extremes that Milton's free and virtuous man would naturally avoid. *Hoggs*, the men, were advocates of "Licence," meaning official permission—either for control of the press, which Milton flouted in publishing his divorce treatises and attacked directly in *Areopagitica*, or for control of individual religious expression, which he deplored throughout his career. On the other hand, the *Hoggs* of Matt. 7:6 are beasts who live by "Licence," meaning excessive or undisciplined freedom. With no reason or will to provide inner discipline, they can neither value pearls nor control their passions. In asserting that these swine mean "Licence" when they cry "libertie," Milton turns the detractors' argument against the freedom to divorce back upon themselves. Although they have accused him of advocating licentiousness, he knows that their misunderstanding of the internal constraints that produce true freedom makes them, not him, a prey to swinish "Licence."

Milton's condemnation of his enemies as "senceless" and dissolute has prompted some critics to suggest that he is referring not to the Presbyterians, but to the Independent lunatic fringe, some of whom had actually used his divorce treatises to justify their own desertion and elopement.[24] Obviously, both extremes of "Licence" are under attack here, and the bestial images used for both the "barbarous" slanderers of his ideals and the swinish abusers of them emphasize the essential kinship between the two extremes. The double puns support the sonnet's final judgment: that the advocates of external constraint (the Presbyterians) and bestial license (the Independent fanatics) are alike in their efforts to disrupt the harmonious community based on freedom and virtue.

The sonnet ends in a bleak vision of chaos with its "wast of wealth, and loss of blood." Despite a civil war fought for freedom, both Presbyterians and fanatics have shot far from the mark of that

virtue and goodness which alone sets men free. The conclusion is
bitter because, after a thirteen-line demonstration that the leaders
empowered to restructure the community are completely mis-
guided, the last line reminds the reader of the physical war that
was to clear the way for the New Jerusalem. But warfare by its
nature cannot establish the basis of Milton's ideal community—
that true liberty "which must be sought, not without, but within,
and which is best achieved, not by the sword, but by a life rightly
undertaken and rightly conducted" (*Def 2*, *YM* 4(1):624). Sonnet
11 describes the war as "wast" and "loss" not only because it had
cost so much in wealth and human life, but because it could do
nothing to make the ideal community a reality so long as
Englishmen preferred "cloggs" and "Licence" to "libertie" and
being "wise and good."[25]

While Milton's second sonnet on his detractors jests rather than
rails, it deplores as vehemently as its predecessor the age's
preference for the bestial and barbarous over the wise and
civilized.[26] Sonnet 12 focuses on the abuse of language rather than
liberty; but its concerns are civic as well as aesthetic, since for
Milton, to be a free citizen one must be both "*wise* and good."
Puritans and humanists alike considered language crucial to the
attainment of wisdom. As one earthly manifestation of the divine
word, language makes God's revealed will available to all who can
read and hear, and as that which distinguishes men from beasts,
language helps them realize their full humanity. Even in his
earliest prolusions, Milton expressed a Renaissance humanist's
faith in the civilizing power of language. The Greek poets, he
remarks,

> have attained an ample meed of honour and of glory by gathering
> together in one place and forming into organised communities men
> who previously roamed like beasts at random through the forests and
> mountains, and by being the first to teach, by their divine inspiration,
> all the sciences which are known to-day, arraying them in the
> charming cloak of fable. [*Prol* 1: "Whether Day or Night is the More
> Excellent," (*YM* 1:224)][27]

And while in Italy, he wrote to Benedetto Buonmattei, who was
preparing a systematic treatise on Tuscan, a letter which predicts

dire consequences for the civilization that allows the abuse of language:

> Whoever in a state knows how to form the manners of men wisely, to rule them at home and at war with excellent precepts, him before others do I think especially worthy of all honor. Next to him, however, is the one who tries to fix by precepts and rules the order and pattern of writing and speaking received from a good age of the nation, and in a sense to enclose it within a wall; indeed, in order that no one may overstep it, it ought to be secured by a law all but Romulean. For if we wish to compare the usefulness of the two men, the one alone is able to effect an upright and holy society of Citizens; the other alone can make it truly noble, and splendid, and brilliant, which is the next thing to be wished. The one provides, I believe, a noble ferocity and intrepid strategy against an enemy invading the boundaries; the other, with a learned censorship of ears and a light-armed guard of good Authors, undertakes to overcome and drive out Barbarism, that filthy civil enemy of character which attacks the spirits of men. Nor is it to be thought unimportant what speech people have, whether pure or corrupted, or how correct their daily use of it, a matter which more than once involved the welfare of Athens. Nay more, though it is the opinion of Plato that grave actions and mutations in the Republic are portended by changed custom and style in dressing, I should rather believe that the downfall of that City, and its consequent meanness of affairs, might follow blemish and error in speech. For when speech is partly awkward and pedantic, partly inaccurate and badly pronounced, what does it say but that the souls of the people are slothful and gaping and already prepared for any servility? On the other hand, not once have we heard of an empire or state not flourishing at least moderately as long as it continued to have pride in its Language, and to cultivate it. [*YM* 1:329-30]

Milton draws a direct causal relationship between the use of strong and elegant language and the mental alacrity which citizens need to guarantee their freedom and survival. If a people have allowed their language to become debased, they are prepared to become slaves themselves. The man who, like Buonmattei, preserves language from "Barbarism" is a public servant whose worth is second only to the lawmaker's. Thus when Sonnet 12 ridicules the public's preference for "awkward . . . and badly pronounced" names, more than a pedantic quibble is at stake. Milton views his countrymen's abuse of language as an indication of the same unwillingness to "quit their cloggs" that he lamented in Sonnet 11.

And the horror of his response to their indolence is similar. Sonnet 11 depicts a lonely champion of liberty surrounded by bawling animals who shun the responsibilities of freedom; Sonnet 12 casts him in the role he had assigned to Buonmattei. As a defender of the thoughtful language that makes men free, he challenges a reading public that prefers to slide backwards into the barbarous and bestial rather than rise to full humanity through learning and liberty. In their acceptance of harsh-sounding names, which they make even more harsh by mispronouncing (*Galasp* for *Gillespie*), Milton sees evidence of the debasement of language. Not only does he consider the "rugged names" inelegant in themselves (what Quintilian called *"barbarismi"*); he also fears that his countrymen have developed "like mouths"—that their speech has become as rugged and barbarous as the familiar names of Scottish generals so often in the news. The phrase "like mouths" may also be an allusion that reveals his deeper fears about the abuse of language while it ridicules the folly of the masses. Cicero tells the story of dour Crassus, whose only recorded laugh was prompted by an ass's preference of thistles to lettuce because thistles were more "like" his mouth.[28] The allusion jestingly proves the ignorant public asinine, but simultaneously betrays Milton's serious concern that if language, which first raised man from the state of wild beasts in the forests, is debased, men will regress to the bestial state. In fact, he says, they have already declined so far as to hate "Learning wors then Toad or Asp": they prefer even loathsome animals to learning.[29]

Milton wrote his treatises on domestic liberty in the first place as part of the ongoing battle to raise man from bestial slavery and license to a fuller humanity. His weapons were the tools of civilization, reasoned argument and persuasive rhetoric. He felt that, as an author who sought to defend harmony in married life, he must perform his task in imitation of the Author of all things who created that harmony. The Renaissance artist believed himself a "maker," an analogue to God, the creator and sustainer of the cosmos. Since Milton wanted his treatise on the harmony of biblical teachings on divorce to mirror the harmony of marriage, Christian doctrine, and the cosmos, he wove it "close, both matter, form and stile" and entitled it *Tetrachordon*. The substance, organization, presentation, and title of his argument were to lead his audience to the order available to those who can attune themselves and their community to the cosmic harmony woven by God into all things. But the immediate result was the cacophony of Sonnet 11's zoo and the barbarous ejaculation of an ignorant stall-reader, "Bless us! what a word on / A title page is this!"

Because his civilized efforts in defense of the community were met with rudeness, noise, vulgarity, and stupidity, Milton in both sonnets resorts to punishing his enemies with their own weapons. In Sonnet 11, he chooses ugly rhymes ("cloggs . . . Doggs . . . Froggs . . . Hoggs") and vulgar diction ("bawle"). In Sonnet 12, he employs choppy phrasing ("The Subject new: it walk'd the Town a while, / Numbring good intellects; now seldom por'd on"), bizarrely broken lines ("while one might walk to Mile- / End Green"), and contorted syntax (transposition of "like ours") in addition to harsh rhymes ("*Tetrachordon* . . . por'd on . . . word on . . . Gordon"; "Galasp . . . gasp . . . Asp") and vulgar diction ("Bless us!"). But his unpoetic discord serves concord: the harmony in married life that he predicts in the divorce tracts will result only from the "separating of unmeet consorts." He insists that satirical harshness and laughter at the ridiculous are not inconsistent with a serious concern for harmony, any more than divorce is inconsistent with honor for the marriage bond. In the controversial prose which defends his community ideals, he stoops from the Miltonic sublime to caustic mockery with a vehemence and gusto that have shocked his more delicate readers. But *An Apology for Smectymnuus* justifies the use of satire and thus reveals the purpose of the jangling discord of Sonnets 11 and 12:

> Now that the confutant may also know as he desires, what force of teaching there is sometimes in laughter, I shall returne him in short, that laughter being one way of answering *A Foole according to his folly*, teaches two sorts of persons, first the Foole himselfe *not to be wise in his own conceit*. . . . Next, it teaches the hearers, in as much as scorne is one of those punishments which belong to men carnally wise, which is oft in Scripture declar'd. [*YM* 1:903][30]

In Sonnet 11 the animals who rail are answered with railing, and in Sonnet 12 the ignorant stall-readers who use barbarisms are answered with barbarous rhymes and diction. Indeed, the fool is answered "according to his folly" because in Milton's cosmos "evil on itself shall back recoil" (*Comus*, l. 593), restoring goodness, wisdom, and harmony.

Although in both sonnets he assumes the satirist's role as the one good man condemning omnipresent vice, his allusions reveal that he does not face either noisy detractors or the foolish masses completely alone. He marshals reinforcements in Sonnet 12 by recalling past defenders of language and learning, as he recalled the god of music and the "rules of antient libertie" in Sonnet 11. Quintilian, the Roman rhetorician, was daily fare for seventeenth-century schoolboys, who would have been repeatedly instructed to avoid the disharmony of "rugged names" in formal compositions, never to "stare and gasp" while delivering the required orations, and to shun such barbarisms as the addition of unnecessary or the omission of necessary syllables ("Galasp").[31] Not only, then, is this teacher of centuries of students on Milton's side, but the enemy is portrayed as lacking even the rudimentary language skills of a schoolboy.

A second ally is Sir John Cheke, Cambridge's first professor of Greek and Edward VI's tutor. As one of the early English humanists, Cheke gave his students a key to a richer understanding of Greek civilization. Reading the Greek authors, either for the first time or in texts freed from corruption, many Englishmen were inspired with the new ideals of civic virtue that had excited humanists throughout Europe. In addition to his teaching duties, Cheke had served on a committee proposing more liberal divorce laws and had highly praised Martin Bucer, the reformer whose statements on divorce Milton translated.[32] By invoking the soul of Cheke, Milton recalls the dawn of both Renaissance humanism and Reformation zeal in England—the two forces he hoped would make the ideal community a reality. Although Cheke had deplored his own age as ignorant, Milton perceives it differently; in *Tetrachordon* he praises it as "the purest and sincerest that ever shon yet on the reformation of this Iland" (*YM* 2:716).[33] The sonnet also suggests that Cheke's age believed in the ideal of the philosopher king: in his day, the young sovereign ("King *Edward*"), as well as professional scholars (*"Cambridge"*), valued the learning Milton believed so essential to civilization.

Nor has learning been completely abandoned in his own age. His book reached its "fit audience . . . though few" in the "good intellects" who seriously considered it; but now, he laments, it is "seldom por'd on." Although no longer surrounded by noisy detractors, Milton faces two worse enemies in Sonnet 12: apathy and ignorance. Some cannot comprehend his title page, much less the learned argument in the book proper; others simply do not care enough about their own domestic liberty to read his work. He would have welcomed a reasoned reply to his divorce treatises and was frustrated that unthinking horror and rejection were all he aroused.[34] The apathy and ignorance he condemns in the sonnet, like the debasement of language, give evidence that Englishmen, aside from the few "good intellects," have become "slothful and gaping and already prepared for any servility." If, as Sonnet 11 claims, to be "wise and good" is to be free, Sonnet 12 demonstrates why the age refused "to quit their cloggs."

The remarkable consistency of Milton's thought is revealed in the six sonnets (8–12, 14) which either address women, protect his home from attack, or defend his ideal of marriage from ignorance and scorn. In each of the six he examines one or more of the elements named in *A Second Defense* as the components of domestic liberty: the purpose of marriage in relation to the individual, state, and cosmos (and as a corollary, the role of woman in the home and larger community); the importance of education; and the power of the written word to further the search for truth, which demands as prerequisite a free press. The six sonnets not only examine these issues, but also demonstrate their interdependence. Three praise women who value education and share Milton's belief in the immortality books can guarantee. The other three defend his ideal of a domestic community while insisting that learning and language are the basis for civilized life. Together, they indicate that whatever facet of community life an individual poem analyzes, the ideal that animates the sequence is whole and consistent.

5.
"Where shall we sometimes meet":
Sonnets Addressed to Male Friends

A harmonious community was always Milton's goal. Beginning with an internal quest to be "wise and good" (Sonnet 11), the individual strives to serve the earthly community through "Works and Alms and . . . good Endeavour" (14), and his service leads eventually to the heavenly community of "the Bridegroom with his feastfull friends" (9). Unfortunately, this potential harmony is all too frequently prevented by the "barbarous noise" (11) of misunderstanding and ignorance or by warfare, political or physical, which may be "fatal to liberty" (10). But the champion of the community has powerful weapons with which to fight for his ideal. Learning, language, and especially poetry can help him silence the surrounding discord and attune his "fit audience" to civilized life transcending the chaos of war.

In three sonnets addressed to friends, Milton envisions the civilized life of social man. The arts which have produced "well measur'd Song" (13) and the judgment which has learned "to measure life" (20, 21) enhance friendship; and arts, judgment, and friendship all foster the harmony of a cultured life. Even these sonnets of praise or invitation, though, hint at surrounding threats to concord among friends and within the state. Milton used the sonnet as a weapon when his ideal of domestic liberty was attacked; here he uses it to reach out to friends despite the separations threatened by partisanship, "the hard Season," or anxious overwork. Sonnets 13, 20, and 21 also defend his ideal community, but not by a counterattack; rather, they invoke the virtues and pleasures that Milton felt must be preserved even in the midst of war.

Placed near one sonnet that defends language from barbarism (12) and another that eulogizes a woman whose "Works" included the preservation of books (14), Sonnet 13, "To my Friend Mr. Henry Lawes," praises a musician who also honored language.[1]

Much as the author of *Tetrachordon* deplores the public's ignorance and preference for the bestial, Lawes stands aloof from "the throng" with its "*Midas* Ears." And much as the ending of Sonnet 12 lifts the reader above the noisy pamphlet warfare of a dull age by invoking an earlier one of great learning and zealous reform, the ending of Sonnet 13 links both Lawes and Milton to the grand tradition of poets and musicians epitomized by Dante and Casella. As Sonnet 13 ends with Casella's singing in Purgatory, where penitent souls "labour up the Hill of heav'nly Truth," Sonnet 14 begins with a soul's liberation from its earthly burden, then follows its steady ascent to bliss. At the summit, its good works become the "glorious Theams" of heavenly song that assure it a place at the marriage feast of the Lamb. This continuity among three dissimilar sonnets placed so close together indicates how the ideal of a community threaded throughout the sequence appears in repeated themes and techniques—such as the civilizing power of language; the divine harmony potentially available to man in song, marriage, and friendship; the hardships of a fallen world that threaten this harmony; and the perspective that sees the immediate engagement of self with other in relation to past communities and the progress toward the final community.

In Sonnet 13 Milton relaxes for a moment from the frustrating battle to "effect an upright and holy society of Citizens," focusing instead on the community of cultured men and their efforts to make society "splendid, and brilliant, which is the next thing to be wished."[2] Henry Lawes had shared this goal with Milton from their first acquaintance. As a member of the King's Music from 1630 until the Civil War, he had composed music for court masques by such celebrated poets as Carew; he wrote musical settings for lyrics by Jonson, Davenant, Herrick, Lovelace, Suckling, Waller, and many other Cavalier poets; and he was a significant figure, if not the first, in the reform of English music. Following the innovations of Italian humanists who tried to recreate the music of classical antiquity, as they conceived it, Lawes and other English musicians rejected the older polyphonic style (for example, madrigals, many of which Milton's father had composed) because it obscured the lyrics. The reformers believed that music, like the other arts, must instruct as well as delight.

Without words or with incomprehensible lyrics, music is merely sensuous gratification, but if it enhances the meaning of its lyrics (as in the declamatory air), then song becomes a powerful means of engaging the hearer—both soul and sense.[3] When poet and musician complement each other's art, they wield a civilizing power to rival the fabled Orpheus. Together, they may help man measure his life according to the harmony of creation, perhaps making his society "upright and holy" as well as "splendid, and brilliant."

Lawes had served and honored not only "English Musick" and "Verse," but also a young aspiring poet, John Milton. In 1634, when the earl of Bridgewater commissioned him to produce a masque, Lawes was accustomed to mingling among the gay courtiers and poets of high society. But he chose as his collaborator Milton, an unknown poet, thirteen years his junior. Later, when Lawes published *Comus*, he complimented his unnamed friend in a dedicatory letter: "Although not openly acknowledged by the Author, yet [the masque] is a legitimate offspring, so lovely, and so much desired, that the often Copying of it hath tired my Pen to give my several friends satisfaction."[4] More complimentary even than his praise is the manner in which he published *Comus*. He edited carefully and probably consulted Milton about which version to use. And although printed masques were usually full of costume, set, and stage directions, Lawes published Milton's copy, thereby granting the poetry priority over the printed re-creation of the dramatic production.

Lawes's service to his collaborator extended beyond their work on *Comus*. When Milton was planning his trip to Italy, he had to procure permission from the Privy Council to visit Rome, a special privilege not often granted, because officials feared the militant Catholicism spawned by the Counter Reformation. Although authorities often inserted specific clauses in passports forbidding travel to Rome, Lawes secured permission for Milton through court influence, bypassing the tedious and often fruitless bureaucratic appeals.[5] Since Lawes had been such a kind friend and a colleague in Milton's goal to raise English arts to the heights reached elsewhere in Renaissance Europe, Sonnet 13 both addresses him familiarly as *"Harry"* and praises him formally as the nation's first musician.

Specifically, Milton envisions his musical accomplishment as a civilizing force. Instead of the chaos of previous polyphonic song, in which the musical line might accent words unimportant to the meaning or draw out a short syllable to an inordinate length, Lawes's songs are "well measur'd." They "span / Words with just note and accent" and avoid the error of "committing [misjoining] short and long" syllables and notes. In Milton's view, Lawes has brought order and true harmony to English music, while the opposition scan "with *Midas* Ears." Like the king who was awarded ass's ears for preferring Pan's pipe to Apollo's lyre, they hear like asses, beasts who prefer cacophony to harmony. Lawes, in contrast, eschews the barbarous woodland Pan and follows the god who ruled the muses and was the patron of the civilizing arts of medicine, music, and poetry. He has become "the Priest of *Phoebus* Quire," and like Apollo himself, has harmonized the arts of music and poetry. Much as the young lover of Sonnet 1 believed that the nightingale's song could deter "the rude Bird of Hate" and the angry pamphleteer of Sonnet 11 remembered that Apollo's mother could turn railing "Hinds" to "Froggs," Milton, in praising Lawes, again attributes to song the power to triumph over discordant and "barbarous noise."

The antithesis of both raucous detractors and the ignorant and inelegant "stall-reader," Lawes has served English music and taken his place in a tradition of artists and scholars who have carried on the task of civilizing their nations. His work will not be forgotten by "after-age" any more than Sir John Cheke's (12) or Pindar's or Euripides' (8) or, Milton hopes, his own. Indeed, in the work of perfecting English music and poetry, Milton aspires to and his compatriot is assured of "Fame" to rival Dante and Casella, who performed a like service for Italian. Earlier, in *The Reason of Church Government*, Milton had declared his hope "that what the greatest and choycest wits of *Athens, Rome,* or modern *Italy,* and those Hebrews of old did for their country, I in my proportion with this over and above of being a Christian, might doe for mine" (*YM* 1:812). By implicitly linking himself with Dante in Sonnet 13,

Milton reveals his desire to join the poetic community which has sung not only of a nation, but of man's universal striving toward God. Lawes, explicitly compared to Dante's musician friend Casella, also participates in these two tasks: he has helped reform English music, and the collection of his airs for which Milton wrote this sonnet contained *Choice Psalms* such as the "Hymn[s]" mentioned earlier in the sonnet.[6]

Sonnet 13 pays tribute primarily to Lawes's work in bringing a harmony between verse and music to English song, but it also memoralizes the concord of friendship, which can sustain friends despite warfare and separation. In the classical tradition revived in the Renaissance, friendship was often associated with the harmony of Pythagorean cosmology. And Cicero in *De amicitia* describes friendship as a natural part of the universal concord, which holds the elements together, compels animals to seek their kind, binds parents to children, and joins man to woman. So great is friendship's power, he asserts, that without it "no house or city could stand, nor would even the tillage of the fields abide." Montaigne, among other Renaissance followers of the friendship tradition, emphasized the ability of such relationships to transcend separation. "I know," he says, "that the arms of friendship are long enough to reach and join from one end of the world to the other . . . if one [man] does but stretch forth his finger, wherever he may be, all the sages on the habitable earth feel themselves assisted by it."[7]

In the allusion to Casella, whom Dante "woo'd to sing / Met in the milder shades of Purgatory," we see how Milton's tribute to *"Harry"* exemplifies the concord of friendship that can overcome separation. Among newly arrived spirits who are beginning their journey up the purgatorial mount, Dante sees one who

> trarresi avante
> per abbracciarmi, con sì grande affetto,
> che mosse me a fare il simigliante.[8]

("come[s] forward with so much affection to embrace me that it moved me to do the same.")

Immediately recognizing the poet whose canzoni he once set to music, Casella spontaneously rushes to meet Dante. Although they try three times to embrace, they cannot even touch because they belong to different worlds: Dante is flesh and blood, Casella a disembodied spirit. As the saddened shade gently draws away, Dante begs him to remain; and the musician, despite the separation of death, affirms his enduring love for the living poet:

> Così com'io t'amai
> nel mortal corpo, così t'amo sciolta:
> però m'arresto.
>
> [2.88–90]

("Even as I loved thee in my mortal flesh, so do I love thee freed; therefore I stay.")

Perhaps Milton hopes Lawes will see a similarity in at least two aspects of their relationship. Once collaborators, now they too belong to different worlds. An ardent Royalist, Lawes published *Choice Psalms* in 1648 with a courageous dedication to his former master, King Charles, at that moment a prisoner of the state. But Milton could ignore political expediency and allow his sonnet praising the avowed Royalist to be included in the volume. Their friendship and shared goal to perfect English music and verse transcended the separation imposed by partisan politics.

Although the tone in the octave is light, even jocular, with the final tercet's allusion to Dante and Casella it modulates to bittersweet, reminding the reader that mutual love must overcome a seemingly irreparable separation. Beyond the submerged reference to their opposing political views, Milton may expect Lawes, if not the reader of *Choice Psalms*, to catch a reference to another bar to their previous communion. In 1644, one year before the Cambridge manuscript dates the sonnet (February 9, 1645), Milton realized he was going blind.[9] The sonnet reaches out to a friend amidst the isolation of approaching blindness—a growing darkness that Milton may be comparing to the "milder shades of Purgatory." Similarly, in Sonnet 23, a living husband (like Dante) reaches out to his "late espoused Saint" (like Casella) despite the barriers of death and blindness. Sonnet 13 thus provides another example of Milton's attempts throughout the sequence to transcend the noise and darkness that threaten the communities of love, friendship, or the body politic.

In the allusion to Casella, Milton demonstrates one important

way to overcome darkness and separation. Although they meet in
the shadowy dawn in Purgatory, Dante asks his friend,

> Se nuovo legge non ti toglie
> memoria o uso all'amoroso canto
> che mi solea quetar tutte mie voglie,
> di ciò ti piaccia consolare alquanto
> l'anima mia, che, con la mia persona
> venendo qui, è affannata tanto!
> [2.106–11]

("If a new law does not take from thee memory or practice of the
songs of love which used to quiet all my longings, may it please thee
to refresh my soul with them for a while, which is so spent coming
here with my body.")[10]

Casella then sings his setting of one of Dante's allegorical love
songs to his Lady Philosophy, which enchants Virgil and the
spirits. Here, song bridges the gap between the dead and the living,
allowing friends and fellow artists to communicate mutual love
and honor without embracing. So too Milton's sonnet allows him
to praise a friend of the enemy's party who, as Casella had done for
Dante, once honored with music his own paean to "divine
Philosophy," *Comus.* In this resonant allusion Lawes, at least,
would see that both poets and both musicians sing under a shadow,
but their songs transcend the darkness and separation imposed by
either the "shades of Purgatory" or blindness or the English Civil
War.[11]

The musical communion between Dante and Casella is interrupted when Cato incites the pilgrims to hasten to their
penetential climb lest they delay their journey to God. Yet Dante
says of Casella's song, "La dolcezza ancor dentro mi sona" ("The
sweetness sounds within me still") (2.114). Although he and his
friend have to part, following separate ways to God, the harmony
of their friendship and shared song remains in his memory.
Similarly, Sonnet 13 memorializes the reciprocal honor Milton
and Lawes paid to one another in their verse and music, despite
their choice of contrary paths (Anglican and Puritan) to the
Kingdom of God.

Placed near sonnets about warfare and written in the midst of the Civil War, Sonnet 13 praises the concord and order available to civilized man in "well measur'd Song" and friendship. Despite political discord and the unwanted separation of friends, the sonnet seeks to preserve those values and relationships that make social life "splendid, and brilliant."

Although probably written ten years later, Sonnet 20 also praises the virtues and pleasures of cultured society in the midst of a hostile environment.[12] Because the wet fields and muddy roads of winter have prevented their usual outdoor meetings, Milton invites his young friend Edward Lawrence to share a cozy indoor dinner enlivened by song. The son of the learned president of Cromwell's council, Edward was Milton's junior by twenty-five years. Yet he was bright and precocious and had won the esteem of both William Davenant, the poet, and Henry Oldenburg, Milton's scientific friend who corresponded with Spinoza and later became the first secretary of the Royal Society.[13] All that is known of the earnest and personable Lawrence suggests that, despite his youth, he would have appreciated the temperate meal, refined entertainment, and companionship "by the fire" that Milton offers to dispel the winter gloom.

The "hard Season" that threatens to separate the friends may, however, include more than just inclement weather. As with so many lyrics of the Interregnum, more often written by Cavaliers, the winter becomes a symbol of political as well as physical storms whose raging may turn both a grasshopper and a king into a "Poore verdant foole! and now green Ice!"[14] Of course, neither Milton nor Lawrence was a Royalist fallen on hard times who sought consolation for his loss in friendship and wine; still, the seasonal metaphor applies. In the second year of Cromwell's Protectorate, Puritan England was beset by the hostility of Catholic Spain, a potentially bellicose trade rivalry with Holland, and exiled Royalists eager to avenge Charles's execution.[15] One year before the probable date of the sonnet, Milton himself had published his *Second Defense* in which he tried to justify the ways of his country to a predominantly hostile Europe. But it was a "hard Season" for him personally as well as politically; since 1652 he had lived in a perpetual winter of blindness. As he was to lament later in *Paradise Lost*,

> Thus with the Year
> Seasons return, but not to me returns
> Day, or the sweet approach of Ev'n or Morn,
> Or sight of vernal bloom, or Summer's Rose,
> Or flocks, or herds, or human face divine.
> [3.40–44]

Certainly, the rainy winter was the primary occasion of Sonnet 20's opening quatrain; but the season was, in truth, made trebly hard for Milton by political turmoil and blindness.

The day seems even more "sullen" because, in the first quatrain (four and five-eighths lines), the winter is described as "gaining" time on the friends. They may meet only "sometimes," and then merely to "wast" the day in an attempt to glean whatever may be "won" from the dreariness. Here the speaker measures time mechanically, tallying up the score of who has gained time and who lost it. Life appears to be a perpetual struggle to win one moment from an implacable winter, and this one moment may even be wasted. But in the midst of line 5 a less rigid view of time takes over the sonnet, allowing the lines to merge into one another (literally to "run / On") in imitation of the temporal flow:

> time will run
> On smoother, till *Favonius* re-inspire
> The frozen earth.

The second quatrain, in contrast to the mechanical measurement of gain or loss, measures time by the recurrent seasonal rhythm. The speaker expresses faith that time's smooth current will eventually bring back Favonius, the west wind of spring, to breathe fresh life into the seemingly dead earth. All he and his friend need do is keep time with the rhythm, relax all impatient fretting over "wast," and wait.

With this new perspective on time, the speaker can devote the third quatrain to describing how the friends may *live* (not *spend*) their time while awaiting the fulfillment of the rhythm in spring.[16] His description paints neither a "sullen day" nor a "wast" of time.

Once he no longer sees himself in a race, with winter always "gaining" on him, he can perceive the valuable indoor pleasures winter brings: a fire made all the warmer by the cold outside, food and drink made more cheery by the gloomy weather, and companionship made closer by limited mobility. In the invitation to share these pleasures, Milton incidentally alludes to the cultured leisure enjoyed in three great civilizations. Sonnet 20 is indisputably Horatian, and it would have reminded the intelligent youth of the Roman poet's love of grace, temperance, and conviviality among wise and virtuous companions. Horace's ideal of the civilized life heartened many poets (Milton as well as the more sober of the Cavaliers) during the times of political turmoil when such reasonable pleasures seemed to have all but disappeared.[17]

By offering Lawrence a meal "Of Attick tast," Milton recalls the leisure activities of a second civilization. Good taste among the ancient Greeks dictated a diet "light and choice," but their banquets, if Plato is to be believed, were also abundant feasts for the soul, where debates about serious and complex problems of philosophy were relished. In addition to Horatian conviviality and a Greek banquet, the friend will also enjoy a *"Tuskan* Ayre."

Milton first encountered this style of singing on his Italian trip where he visited Florentine academies, attended a musical entertainment at the Palazzo Barberini, and heard "Leonora Singing in Rome." The style so impressed him that, according to Phillips's *Life*, he shipped home "a Chest or two of choice Musick-books of the best Masters flourishing about that time in *Italy*,"[18] and, as we have seen, he praised his friend Henry Lawes for imitating the declamatory air first used by the Florentine *Camerata*. Milton never forgot the communities of learned and cultured men among whom he circulated in Italy, and much later as a Puritan apologist he still considered Italian society a model of civilized life. In *A Second Defense* he answers the slander that, as a youth, he travelled to "a refuge or asylum for criminals," by praising Italy as "the lodging-place of *humanitas* and of all the arts of civilization" (YM 4[1]:609). So in its promise of a *"Tuskan* Ayre," Sonnet 20 entices Lawrence with one of the delights of Renaissance Italian culture, the "Sphere-born harmonious Sisters, Voice and Verse" (*Music*, l. 2). Since in this style of singing the harmony of sound enhances the meaning of the lyrics, the airs to follow the feast may instruct as well as delight the company.

Because he has surrendered to the seasonal rhythm, Milton will be able to share with Lawrence the values and pleasures that have graced the leisure of cultured men in past and present civilizations. Paradoxically, by merely awaiting the spring, they may have "won" despite the rainy winter—"gaining" delight and instruction in song, virtue in practicing temperance, and wisdom in conversation. Indeed, this continuity of civilized life through time had been previewed in the opening line's allusion to the guest's heritage: "*Lawrence* of vertuous Father vertuous Son." But the sonnet intimates a Grace beyond graceful refinement.

Besides mechanical tallies and seasonal rhythm, Milton suggests a third conception of time. By alluding to the Sermon on the Mount, the second quatrain recalls that natural time, which promises to "re-inspire / The frozen earth," is itself animated by a greater force: divine providence. In the Sermon, Jesus exhorts his disciples to "take . . . no thought for the morrow" because, in his own time, God will feed the fowls, though they neither *sow* nor reap; array the *lilies*, though they neither toil nor *spin*; clothe the grass, though it will be cast into the oven; and even, he adds, "*clothe* you, O ye of little faith" (Matt. 6:26–34). When Milton remembers that spring will "*cloth* in fresh attire / The *Lillie* and Rose, that neither *sow'd* nor *spun*" (emphases mine), he not only abjures the opening quatrain's anxious computation of time, but sees beyond the seasons to "the kingdom of God" which Christ tells his disciples to seek first (6:33). When the day of that Kingdom is finally come, all of the righteous will be "arrayed in fine linen, clean and white" to join the marriage feast of the Lamb (Rev. 19:8). As the flowers wait through the winter to be reclothed in the spring and cultured men weather a "hard Season" of political unrest to reestablish their ideals of civilized life, Christians await the resurrection when they will likewise be reinspired and reclothed "in fresh attire" to join the final heavenly community.

As with so many of Milton's protagonists, particularly the lady of Sonnet 9 who waits in readiness for the Bridegroom to take her to the marriage feast, Milton and Lawrence must wait in the winter of a fallen world. But unlike the young lover of Sonnet 1 or the blind widower of Sonnet 23, they need not wait alone. Since

Christ's coming, the Kingdom of Heaven has already begun on earth, so that in the interim between the already and the not-yet, men may participate now in the Kingdom's festal joy. While they wait, Milton and his friends imitate the final community in a feast graced by virtue, mutual affection, and "immortal Notes." As both a Renaissance humanist and a Christian, Milton believed that the truly graceful mirrors the grace of God who rules the cosmos by the concord available to men in the self-perfection of temperance, the community of friendship, and the harmony of song. While the friends gracefully await the spring, they have already "won" a glimpse of Grace.

So too Adam feels himself already in heaven when, at a feast in Eden, he listens to his friend Raphael, "the sociable Spirit," speak words "with Grace Divine / Imbu'd."[19] The angel also finds in Adam "all comeliness and grace" (*PL* 8.210–23). Raphael enjoys the earthly food as much as Adam, and Adam enjoys the lofty conversation about cosmology, history, ethics, and astronomy as much as the angel. Thus their feast and conversation represent the graceful society of near equals and mirror the heavenly banquets which Raphael predicts Adam and Eve may one day share.

If we contrast the concord at this Edenic feast and its parallel in Sonnet 20 to Milton's discordant confrontations with the enemies of civilization, we can see how Sonnet 20 glimpses the transcendent, as well as the temporal movement toward the Kingdom of God. In Sonnets 8 and 12, Milton stands beside past defenders of civilization like Pindar, Euripides, and Sir John Cheke to carry on the historical battle for his community ideal. But Sonnet 20 works both historically (like Sonnets 8 and 12) and analogically (like Adam's and Raphael's feast). Although Horace's Rome, Plato's Greece, and modern Italy provide cultural ideals for Lawrence and Milton, their present communion as virtuous men already fulfills the hope of the prayer Jesus taught his disciples in the Sermon on the Mount: "Thy kingdom come. Thy will be done in earth, as it is in heaven" (Matt. 6:10). In the fellowship of virtuous friends, part of the Kingdom has already come.

A troublesome problem remains: the meaning of the sonnet's epigrammatic ending. Does "spare / To interpose them oft" mean "refrain from interposing these delights often" or "afford time to interpose them often"? Critical opinion is divided, and arguments based on linguistic precedent, Milton's supposed temperament, and his sources have provided no conclusive answer.[20] But in the light of the sonnet as a whole, only the second choice, "afford time," seems possible. As we have seen, the sonnet presents a tripartite movement. At first, the anxious speaker fears that time will allow the friends to meet only "sometimes." Then he accepts the smooth flow of time's seasonal rhythm. Finally, he realizes that to imitate the patient lilies of the field is to seek the Kingdom of God, and while he and his friend wait, they can share an earthly feast to mirror the divine one he is sure will come. The progress (similar to the movement in the sonnets on his twenty-third year and his blindness) is from fear to faith, anxiety to calm, and the isolation of "sometimes" meeting to the communion of "oft" enjoying "those delights." Since his companion's virtue is emphasized in the opening line, since the feast offers pleasures enjoyed by three great civilizations, and since it is a shadowy type of the true heavenly feast, surely Milton would want to "spare" time to interpose such graceful intervals among the worldly busyness a wayfaring-warfaring Christian must conduct on his temporal pilgrimage to Grace.

The temporal way is not the only way to the Kingdom of God, as the fretful worry of the opening quatrain shows. When Milton praises the man "who of those delights can judge," he is praising the wisdom of judging according to true worth, of measuring earthly life by a heavenly scale. This is, in fact, the meaning of the reference to the Sermon on the Mount. Christ illustrates his doctrine with birds and lilies because they do not sow, reap, gather, toil, or spin. They are not anxious Puritan workers concerned with "wast" and "gaining," who must seldom afford time for leisure; on the contrary, their whole life is a leisure of waiting for the free gifts of God. Certainly, it is "not unwise" to wait like the lilies of the field and while waiting to imitate the Kingdom to come. The last lines of the sonnet may even include a touch of understatement and irony: the man who can "judge" the true worth of this feasting is not merely "not unwise." He is far wiser than the anxious man whose tally sheet of his time forces him to "spare" (refrain) to interpose delights often among his sowing, reaping, gathering, toiling, and spinning.[21]

Sonnet 21 may have invited Cyriack Skinner to join Milton and

Lawrence at the same feast described in Sonnet 20. Both sonnets resemble Horatian convivial odes in offering "delights" (20) and "mirth" (21), promising the temperate enjoyment of wine, and complimenting the virtue of the guest's ancestry. The company would have been compatible since Cyriack was only six years older than Lawrence, also enjoyed the friendship of Oldenburg, and shared similar political sympathies. Cyriack was the grandson of Sir Edward Coke, the famous parliamentarian and chief justice of the King's Bench who angered James I by defending the supremacy of common law against claims of royal prerogative. Coke also defended common law in his influential "volumes," *Reports* and *Institutes of the Law of England*, to which Milton alludes in Sonnet 21. Most likely, both the son of Cromwell's learned minister, Lawrence, and the grandson of the noted parliamentarian, Cyriack, would have followed recent political developments with keen interest and debated them eagerly. Cyriack had as lively an intellect as Lawrence—if not livelier for having had Milton himself as a teacher.[22]

Whether or not the same festivity occasioned both sonnets, Sonnet 21 is also set in a "hard Season" of both domestic and international confusion. At home, the "Lawes" that Coke once "Pronounc't" as a judge and "taught" as an author are now twisted so that "Brittish *Themis*" is no longer impartial. Abroad, the volatile Charles X of Sweden keeps Europe at war; and, despite the 1655 treaty of friendship between England and France, the wary Puritan government cautiously watches the crafty Cardinal Mazarin. Also, as the winter weather described in Sonnet 20 threatens to separate the friends, Sonnet 21 counters a threat to separation: the guest's anxiety over international diplomacy and his diligent studies may prevent his accepting the invitation to mirth. Milton uses these two sonnets to sweep aside all obstacles to the communion among friends.

The persuasive strategy he adopts in Sonnet 21 to overcome Cyriack's reluctance echoes the previous sonnet's allusion to the Sermon on the Mount, almost as if the invitation to Lawrence lingered in his mind as he composed the one to Cyriack. In describing heaven as "mild" and God as freely dispensing gifts of cheer upon man without his own efforts, Sonnet 21 advocates the same attitude toward apprehensive striving found in Christ's

counsel to "consider the lilies of the field." When the invitation
reminds Cyriack how unwise anxious "care" is in reality, "though
wise in show," it may recall Christ's condemnation of the
Pharisees' hypocrisy in a passage from the Sermon on the Mount
which closely precedes the one alluded to in Sonnet 20: "Therefore
when thou doest thine alms, do not sound a trumpet before thee, as
the hypocrites do in the synagogues and in the streets, that they
may have glory of men" (Matt. 6:2). Also, by insisting that God
disapproves of the "care . . . That with superfluous burden loads
the day," the sonnet may reword Christ's judgment, "Sufficient
unto the day is the evil thereof" (6:34), which immediately follows
the passage alluded to in Sonnet 20. Thus the two sonnets are alike
in not only their Horatian tone, but their Christian ethics as well.

Both also advocate the proper measurement of life. As Sonnet 20
shows three ways to measure human time—by an anxious tally of
"wast" and "gaining," by seasonal rhythm, and by divine
providence—Sonnet 21 suggests three ways to measure human life.
The opening quatrain praises Coke's administration and teaching
of "Lawes," a form of political measurement necessary to maintain
the harmony of the state. The second quatrain refers to Euclid and
Archimedes, whose mathematics measures the world by lines,
planes, solids, and weights, describing the harmony of the cosmos.
And the sestet counsels Cyriack "to measure life" by God who "a
time ordains" for cheer as well as mathematics and statecraft.

Although advocating the third kind of measurement, the sonnet
does not deny the significance of law or mathematics. On the
contrary, it indicates how the active man measures life—as Coke,
the judge, or Charles X, the warrior, or Mazarin, the minister of
state; also how the contemplative man measures life—as Coke, the
teacher, or Archimedes and Euclid, the mathematicians. Milton
himself pursued both the active life, as Cromwell's Latin secretary,
and the contemplative life, as a scholar and a poet. Indeed, he
quotes Coke as a supporting authority in his prose, praises warriors
in Sonnets 15 and 16, commends Vane's predictions concerning
Dutch diplomacy in Sonnet 17, and advocates the study of
mathematics, which he himself probably taught Skinner, in his
treatise on education.[23] Yet Sonnet 21 shows how, finally, all these
ways are by themselves insufficient to the proper measurement of
life. Human laws, as the opening quatrain laments, may often be

wrenched from the "solid good" they were intended to preserve. Statecraft, as the reference to "the *Swede*" and "the *French*" implies, can become a dangerous second-guessing game that insures no "solid good." And Euclid and Archimedes, although unsurpassed in the science of measurement by numbers and in the geometry and physics of solids, often failed "to measure life" in order to reach "solid good." Later, Milton would assert the limitations of *scientia*, using similar geometric terms. In *Paradise Lost* Raphael answers Adam's questions about the heavens by jesting at astronomers who "gird the Sphere / With Centric and Eccentric scribbl'd o'er" (8.82–83). Perhaps, he adds, the earth "may of *solid good* contain / More plenty than the Sun that barren shines" (8.93–94; emphasis mine).[24]

Obviously, as Honigmann has observed, Milton is punning on *measure* and *solid* in Sonnet 21 to impress on Skinner the importance of interrupting his mathematical studies with some "mirth."[25] But in addition to these puns, the sonnet is full of recondite allusions, academic jokes between teacher and former pupil, which recall with amusement how, despite their brilliant discoveries in scientific measurement, Euclid and Archimedes sometimes failed at humane measurement. All the legends about these mathematicians available to Milton's age characterize both as intensely dedicated. In one of the few surviving stories about Euclid, King Ptolemy asked him "if there was not *a shorter road* to geometry than through the *Elements* [Euclid's famous text], and Euclid replied that there was no royal road to geometry" (emphasis mine).[26] If Cyriack, whose interest in geometry Milton thought strong enough to keep him at his books instead of the party, remembered this story, he would have found a double geometrical joke in the advice to "know / Toward solid good what leads the *nearest way*" (emphasis mine). Milton echoes both the standard Euclidian definition of the straight line as the shortest distance between two points and the anecdote about Euclid's scholarly earnestness.[27] The *Elements* may indeed be the "nearest way" to solid geometry, but not necessarily to "solid good." By advising his former pupil to "let *Euclid* rest," Milton literally counsels Cyriack to relax his studies for a while and allusively recalls a negative example of the busy scholar who allowed no one, not even a king, to rest from hard study.

More legends of Archimedes than Euclid were current in the seventeenth century, and all characterize him as a stereotypical absent-minded professor. Sir Thomas Browne exercised his fanciful wit at the mathematician's expense, and Robert Burton used him to laugh at the melancholy of scholars.[28] While an educated seventeenth-century audience could enjoy the jokes of Sonnet 21, a twentieth-century one may need to review the well-known stories first. Although a mechanical genius, Archimedes considered his practical inventions such as war machines or the water screw less valuable than his theoretical speculations. These musings often led him to propose fantastic projects like measuring the number of grains of sand that could be contained in a sphere the size of the universe. He disdained his useful inventions for lifting weights, but in the *Life of Marcellus* Plutarch records his claim "that if there were another globe of earth, he was able to remove this of ours, and passe it over to the other."[29] Sometimes he became so absorbed in his mathematics that he had to be carried forcibly to the baths. Once there, he drew circles and parallelograms in the ashes of the fire to heat the bath water and, after his bath, continued his calculations on his body, drawing in the oil used to anoint him. The baths, in fact, are the setting for the most famous legend of all. According to Vitruvius in *De architectura*, he solved the problem of how to determine if the king's crown were pure gold or alloyed with silver by noticing for the first time how much bath water his body displaced. Elated with his discovery and heedless of his nudity, he ran through the streets shouting *"Eureka!"* ("I found it!")[30]

Plutarch's account of Archimedes' death proves that such extreme preoccupation may be dangerous as well as embarrassing. Thanks to the mathematician's ingenious war machines, Syracuse withstood a long siege by the Roman army; but when the city was finally conquered, he was completely oblivious:

> Being in his studie when the city was taken, busily seeking out by himselfe the demonstration of some Geometricall proposition which he had drawne in figure, and so earnestly occupied therein, as he neither saw nor heard any noise of enemies that ran up and downe the citie, and much lesse knew it was taken: he wondered when he saw a souldier by him, that bad him to go with him to *Marcellus* [the

Roman commander]. Notwithstanding, he spake to the souldier, and bad him tarie untill he had done his conclusion, and brought it to demonstration: but the soldier being angry with his answer, drew out his sword and killed him. [Plutarch, *Lives*, p. 316]

In some versions of the legend, Archimedes is on the beach drawing figures in the sand, and he fails to notice the soldier until a shadow falls upon his circles.

In light of these legends, Milton's advice to "let . . . *Archimedes* pause" means more than "put down your books." It mocks the scholar's preoccupation and headlong haste, to remind Cyriack of the potential ridiculousness of overzealous study. But other parts of Sonnet 21 may also glance at these stories to reinforce its lesson about proper measurement and enhance the jocular tone that enlivens its invitation to mirth. In condemning the "care . . . / That with superfluous burden loads the day," Milton may have laced his more serious allusion to the Sermon on the Mount with a smile at Archimedes' inventions for lifting, perhaps even his boast about lifting the earth. And the offer of "mirth, that after no repenting drawes" may include a riot of puns which require a knowledge of both mathematics and the legends about these mathematicians.

The primary meaning of *drawes* is, of course, "brings"; thus Milton's and Cyriack's feast will bring no repenting after it. But in Barrow's 1660 edition of Euclid, *drawes* also meant "to add (*to, together*); to subtract (*out of*); to multiply (*into, in*)," as in "draw 3 into 4, there will be produced 12" (*OED, v.* 22); thus the friends' feast will not add or multiply repenting afterwards. This available meaning may highlight the contrast between humane measurement of life and mathematical measurement.

A third definition of *drawes* (in the seventeenth century, as today) is "to displace (so much depth of water); to sink to a specified depth in floating" (*OED, v.* 13); thus their feast will not draw repenting the way a ship draws water. This available meaning may recall Archimedes' discovery of water displacement while bathing, after which he did not "pause" to note his nakedness—an indiscretion that probably caused "repenting." The rhyme of "drawes . . . pause" connects the two verbs in a way that could alert a student of geometry, as Cyriack was, to the jest.

Fourth, *drawes* also means "to trace (a line or figure) by drawing a pencil, pen, or the like across a surface" (*OED, v.* 59); thus their feast will depict no scene of repenting afterwards. This possible meaning may allude to the fate of Archimedes, too preoccupied with drawing his geometrical figures to "pause" for the soldier who consequently killed him. These last two puns, by recalling his excessive concern for his studies, may not only enhance Milton's argument that occasional recreation is necessary, but also contrast the mathematician's intemperance to the temperance of the proposed feast. While Archimedes should have repented running naked through the streets and his shade surely did repent his scholarly preoccupation with drawing, Milton promises that Cyriack will not repent the mirth to be shared.

But Milton's light-hearted punning does not end here. A fifth meaning of *drawes* is "to cause (liquid) to flow from a vessel through an opening, to obtain (drink) from a cask, etc. by a tap or the like" (*OED, v.* 40); thus their feast may draw wine from the tap, but in such temperate measure that no repenting will flow after the wine.

These puns may seem too ingenious to be possible, and we cannot know which, if any, Milton intended. But the evidence favors accepting at least some of them: he probably taught his guest geometry, all the legends about Euclid and Archimedes are found in books he had read, and his other sonnets are full of puns. So are his major works; one example may suggest what a daring punster he was. At the nadir of *Paradise Lost*, when Adam and Eve, once blissful lovers, have become bickering enemies, Milton ventures a bold pun indeed:

> Thus they in mutual accusation spent
> The *fruitless* hours, but neither self-condemning,
> And of thir vain contést appear'd no end.
>   [9.1187–89; emphasis mine]

Also, Sonnet 21 has already prepared the reader to accept puns, particularly ones involving liquids. As Dixon Fiske has noted, the lines "resolve with me to drench / In mirth" suggest an offer of wine since *resolve* means both "to determine or decide upon (a course of action)" (*OED, v.* 14) and "to . . . reduce to a liquid or fluid state" (*OED, v.* 1). Milton wants Cyriack both to *decide* to "drench" his "deep thoughts" and to *dissolve* his "deep thoughts" in "mirth."[31] Obviously, at least part of the "mirth" he offers is vinous, and Honigmann has found a final pun in *cheerful hour* (full of liquid "good cheer").[32] "Solid good," it seems, does not preclude liquid refreshment.

All of this mirth is part of Milton's strategy of persuasion to overcome Cyriack's earnest reluctance. As Sonnet 20 tempts Lawrence by describing the meal and entertainment, Sonnet 21 gives Cyriack a sample of the sparkling wit to gladden their "gawdy-day." All we know of Cyriack indicates that he would have found such spirited conversation appealing. Later, in 1659–60, he participated in, and often chaired, the meetings of the Rota, a club of bright political speculators of republican sympathies who met nightly in a Westminster coffee house to discuss solutions to the governmental confusion. Aubrey's description of their meetings suggests the kind of discussions that Cyriack, himself "an ingeniose young gentleman," probably relished: "The discourses . . . were the most ingeniose, and smart, that ever I heard, or expect to heare, and bandied with great eagernesse." Nor do critics doubt any longer that Milton, with his "very sharp, biting and satyrical wit," heartily enjoyed the kinds of linguistic and academic humor found in Sonnet 21's puns and oblique allusions.[33]

Yet the laughter teaches an important lesson: man should measure life by the ordinances of a "mild" God who clothes the lilies of the field and sends him a "cheerful hour." He must work, but not all the time. And in the long run, as Milton would show in *Paradise Regained*, neither human laws, nor statecraft, nor scholarship alone will attune him to the "well measur'd Song" by which divine providence governs the cosmos. Only submission to the "will of Heav'n" will produce that internal harmony. So, when the occasion arises to join the concord among a community of friends, he should rejoice in this feast as both a blessing in itself and a foretaste of the Kingdom to come, the heavenly feast among the community of the blessed.

6.
"The Civill Sword":
Sonnets about Public Policy

In the majority of his sonnets, Milton speaks as a private citizen, illustrating his ideal of the civilized life. He seeks a beloved woman to end his loneliness, praises women who have served their homes and communities, defends domestic liberty, values concord and gaiety among friends, and reflects on his vocation. But in several sonnets, national and international politics intrude upon the ideal private and social life. Physical warfare may raze a poet's home (8) and has caused the death of a venerable statesman (10). Political partisanship and foreign policy threaten to separate friends (13, 20, 21). Corruption has stained the courts (10, 21). More dangerous still, the denial of true liberty has broken an aged, virtuous judge (10) and unleashed a scornful, ignorant mob (11, 12). Since public policy invariably affects private and social life, and the Christian is commanded to love and serve his neighbors, Milton insisted that each individual participate in a larger community than the home or friendships. Armed with both the left hand of prose and the right hand of poetry, he tried to influence public policy so that a godly community might be achieved. To this end, in Sonnets 15, 16, 17, 18, and "On the new forcers of Conscience," he confronts difficult questions about the use of the "Civill Sword," the physical and legal might of the state. May it be used against the soul? Which enemies of the commonwealth most need castigation? When is it best sheathed? And when is it useless?

The just power of the state became a crucial issue to all builders of the holy community—perhaps to Milton most of all. To him both the Reformation and Revolution began with the goal of freeing the individual soul from the external constraints of hierarchical, sacramental Catholicism and the citizen from the tyranny of a state that supported a similar system of church

government. Once the soul had been freed from external constraints, it could choose to perfect itself with God's guidance and
the light of reason and serve its fellows in voluntary harmony, not
forced hierarchy. Throughout his career, Milton described the
ideal community and its opposite using two geometrical images:
the circle or sphere and the triangle or pyramid. As early as *The
Reason of Church Government* (1642) he explained the differences
between these two symbols. Discussing prelacy's inability to
eliminate schism, he says,

> Prelaty ascending by a graduall monarchy from Bishop to Arch-
> bishop, from thence to Primat, and from thence, for there can be no
> reason yeilded neither in nature, nor in religion, wherefore, if it have
> lawfully mounted thus high, it should not be a Lordly ascendent in
> the horoscope of the Church, from Primate to Patriarch, and so to
> Pope. I say Prelaty thus ascending in a continuall pyramid upon
> pretence to perfect the Churches unity, if notwithstanding it be found
> most needfull, yea the utmost helpe to dearn up the rents of schisme
> by calling a councell, what does it but teach us that Prelaty is of no
> force to effect this work which she boasts to be her maister-peice; and
> that her pyramid aspires and sharpens to ambition, not to perfection,
> or unity. This we know, that as often as any great schisme disparts the
> Church, and Synods be proclam'd, the Presbyters have as great right
> there, and as free vote of old, as the Bishops, which the Canon law
> conceals not. So that Prelaty if she will seek to close up divisions in
> the Church, must be forc't to dissolve, and unmake her own
> pyramidal figure, which she affirmes to be of such uniting power,
> when as indeed it is the most dividing, and schismaticall forme that
> Geometricians know of, and must be faine to inglobe, or incube her
> selfe among the Presbyters, which she hating to do, sends her haughty
> Prelates from all parts with their forked Miters, the badge of schisme
> or the stampe of his cloven foot whom they serve I think, who ac-
> cording to their hierarchies acuminating still higher and higher in a
> cone of Prelaty, in stead of healing up the gashes of the Church, as it
> happens in such pointed bodies meeting, fall to gore one another with
> their sharpe spires for upper place, and precedence, till the councell it
> selfe prove the greatest schisme of all. [*YM* 1:789–90]

Milton contrasts the unity and perfection in a circular council to
the fragmentation and pride in a pyramidal hierarchy.

The concept of a rigid, formal hierarchy had dominated

European thought for centuries. Often called now the Great Chain of Being, it was for many early seventeenth-century thinkers the old order which once seemed to bind all men to one another and all nature to God. That there was order and unity in the cosmos Milton never doubted, but that the order was fixed and the unity imposed, he consistently denied. Many contemporaries feared that, if any part of the structure were removed, anarchy would result. Donne's famous lament, "'Tis all in peeces, all cohaerence gone," is only one of countless literary expressions of this view. But to Milton, the force and rigidity of the structure were the true causes of disorder and schism. Free the individual from the pyramidal hierarchy, he believed, and all men may choose to join the circle in a voluntary community. Only through choice are true harmony and unity possible.

Both symbols of a community reappear in *Paradise Lost*. The unfallen angels, who eat, sleep, sing, dance, and worship in harmonious circles around God's radiance, exemplify Milton's ideal of the well-ordered, unified, and freely chosen community. Their patterns are not rigid: they are "eccentric, intervolv'd, yet regular / Then most, when most irregular they seem" (*PL* 5.623–24). Nor are the angels forced to circle around the throne, as Satan's decision to "leave / Unworshipt, unobey'd the Throne supreme" (5.669–70) proves. The opposite of Milton's ideal is the pyramidal hierarchy of the fallen angels in Pandaemonium, where only "the great Seraphic Lords and Cherubim / In close recess and secret conclave" (1.794–95) may attend the tyrant, who sits "high on a Throne of Royal State" (2.1) while manipulating a sham democracy.

Combining the inclusiveness and equality of the circle with biblical imagery, Milton repeatedly describes his ideal community as a sheepfold or a pastor surrounded by his flock. The metaphor becomes almost obsessive, appearing early and late in his career: from *The Reason of Church Government* (1642) to *The Means to Remove Hirelings* (1658), from *Lycidas* (1637) to *Paradise Lost* (1667).[1] Like the circular council into which he advises prelacy "to inglobe" herself, this figure is inclusive; it is constructed to nurture each member who seeks its protection, not to exalt some and control others. Although each flock chooses its own pastor, the church is "universal; not ti'd to nation, dioces or parish, but consisting of many particular churches complete in themselves; gatherd, not by compulsion or the accident of dwelling nigh together, but by free consent, chusing both thir particular church and thir church-officers" (*Hirelings, CM* 6.64). In the image of a sheepfold of believers, Milton preserves the order and harmony that unites all men in the godly community, at the same time freeing each soul from rigid, external constraints.

Although its theology required each man to stand alone before God, Puritanism was a communal religion. Indeed, Austin Woolrych believes the single common denominator among the various forms of Puritanism was that "they all . . . pursued the ideal of a godly community on earth." The dualism of radical individualism and communality has produced conflicting social theories: some find in Puritanism the seeds of the ruthless individualism of industrial capitalism, and others see it as the last attempt in the West to create a Christian society.[2] Regardless of Puritanism's historical legacy, its dualism was essential to Milton's ideal community. Each man's individual center must first be free from external constraints; only then can he choose to join other circles of community in service that will lead finally to the divine circumference, which is indeed the true center of all things.

During the Smectymnuan controversy, Milton had hoped the Presbyterian model for community would serve man's spiritual needs. But, by the time he wrote "On the new forcers of Conscience under the Long Parliament" (1646), he realized that his former allies also advocated a pyramidal hierarchy, not a sheepfold of free believers.[3] When the Westminster Assembly convened in 1643 to consider the form of church government to replace episcopacy, a large majority favored the Presbyterian discipline. Aided by four Scottish commissioners, they proposed a compulsory national church organized by *classis* in an ascending order of jurisdiction. Within the Assembly, the Presbyterians were opposed by five prominent ministers who petitioned for toleration of Independent congregations. Outside the Assembly, a vocal minority supported the Dissenting Brethren, as did the predominantly Independent army whose political influence was growing daily. Ultimately, when Cromwell, a tolerationist, rose to power, the Presbyterian scheme was abandoned.

Meanwhile, between 1643 and 1646 as debate continued in the Westminster Assembly, pamphlet warfare raged in the presses. The five Independent ministers published their views in *An Apologetical Narration* (1644), which was answered by the Presbyterian Thomas Edwards ("shallow *Edwards*") in *Antapologia* (1644). Adam Stuart ("meer *A. S.*") wrote several anti-Independent pamphlets, and one of the Scottish commissioners, Samuel Rutherford (*"Rotherford"*), published formal defenses of Presbyterianism (1645–46). Besides arguing against the limitation of civil power in ecclesiastical matters, Presbyterians directly attacked the beliefs of sects their national church was designed to extirpate. Edwards's famous *Gangraena* (1646) catalogued and condemned numerous heresies, mentioning Milton disparagingly as a divorcer. Robert Baillie, a Scottish commissioner who Masson suggested might be "Scotch what d'ye call," wrote *A Dissuasive from the Errors of the Times* (1645) which also attacked Milton's views on divorce. And William Prynne opposed the Independents in *Twelve Questions* (1644), arguing that toleration results in "the sad effects . . . we have already experimentally felt by the late dangerous increase of many Anabaptistical, Antinomian, Heretical, Atheistical opinions, as of *The Soul's Mortality*, *Divorce at Pleasure*, &c., lately broached, preached, printed in this famous city; which I hope our Grand Council will speedily and carefully suppress."[4] Obviously, Milton had more than one reason to oppose the specific Presbyterians he ridicules in "The new forcers" sonnet. Not only would they "force . . . Consciences that Christ set free"; but, as a result of their insistence on conformity, they added their voices to the "barbarous noise" that railed at his unconventional views on divorce.

Whether the issue was domestic liberty or liberty of conscience, Milton's fundamental belief remained the same: because Christ freed man's soul from the external constraints of the Law, the function of the "Civill Sword" in a Christian community is only to preserve peace and order and to guarantee individual freedom. In both disputes and in the resulting sonnets (11, 12, and "On the new forcers"), Milton's enemies are the same: the Presbyterians and Scots, whose "rugged names" he derides in Sonnet 12 and deliberately forgets in "The new forcers" ("Scotch what d'ye call"). But we need not conclude, with Masson, that personal animus against the critics of the divorce treatises inspired the tailed sonnet.[5] Just as the condemnations of divorce by Edwards, Baillie, and Prynne stemmed from the same principles that made them "forcers of Conscience," so Milton attacks the same principle in both Sonnet 11 and "The new forcers" with the same satirical weapons. As Sonnet 11 labels his detractors "Owles and Cuckoes, Asses, Apes and Doggs," he intimates that the opponents of toleration are bestial. Repeating the joke of other pamphleteers, Milton suggests that "meer *A. S.*" is an ass, and spelling *Rutherford* "*Rotherford,*" he may hint that his opponent is an ox. Since *rother* means "ox," the name means "ox ford."[6] He strengthens the animal likeness by marveling at these two beasts of burden, who, having submitted themselves to the servile yoke of Presbyterianism, would teach others to "ride us." Like the zoo of Sonnets 11 and 12, the ox and ass have forfeited their humanity by denying liberty to the community.

These slurs about his opponents' bestiality are not mere name-calling; they reiterate the essential argument of Sonnet 11. Men who refuse to "quit their cloggs" and assume their God-given freedom have chosen to become beasts. As Latona rewarded the cruel "Hinds" with an outer form to match their inner beastliness, Milton calls the opponents of liberty what he believes they have already become. And as Sonnet 11 argues that those who refuse true liberty fall prey to "Licence," "On the new forcers" characterizes the antitolerationists as licentious indeed.

Although ridding themselves of prelacy, the Presbyterians failed to sustain the wisdom and goodness which alone make men free. From the beginning, they intended "to seise the widdow'd whore Pluralitie / From them whose sin [they] envi'd, not abhor'd." They are fornicators who seek out whores, not abhor (*ab-whore*) them. Because their sexual license has been clearly exposed in the opening lines, other terms applied to them acquire bawdy overtones. They are sexual "forcers," who have "thrown of" a Lord merely to "seise" his widow. Also, Milton may imply that they will sexually force and "ride" the citizenry unless it exposes their "tricks," "plots," and "packing." These last three words occur frequently in seventeenth-century dramas of sexual intrigue, against which Prynne raged so vehemently in *Histriomatrix*. For example, the *OED* cites Dekker's *Batchelors Banquet* (1603) for *packing:* "Then fals hee into a frantick vaine of Iealousie: watching his wives close packing." By associating Presbyterians with both whoredom and the intrigues of the Council of Trent, Milton further implies that these licentious clerics have defiled themselves with not only multiple lucrative church livings, but also the hierarchy and scheming of the Whore of Babylon, the Roman Catholic church.

Besides promoting ridicule and laughter, these veiled allusions to sexual misconduct advance Milton's argument in several ways. The Presbyterians' accusations, that his doctrine and *discipline* of divorce advocates sexual license, recoil upon themselves. Milton demonstrates again, as in Sonnets 11 and 12, that denying true liberty leads inevitably to license, really an enslavement to appetite. Finally, he exposes the opponents of liberty as hypocrites like the Pharisees who "make broad their phylacteries" (Matt. 23:5). They self-righteously abolish episcopacy, publicly criticizing its abuse of assigning one minister to several livings, when they really want to seize the benefices for themselves. Metaphorically, their own whoring surpasses the lewd "tricks" of the plays they condemn publicly. Indeed, because they lust after the "whore Pluralitie," want "to force" religious conformity, would "ride" England with a hierarchical system of church government, and are now more adept at "plots and packing" than the Council of Trent—*"New Presbyter"* has become *"Old Priest"* writ Large." He is a more licentious servant of the Whore of Babylon than not only the Anglican bishops whom he replaced, but even the Catholic priests whose offices the Reformation had promised to abolish.

The etymological word play (*priest* syncopates the Greek root *presbyter*), the puns on animal names (*A. S.* = "ass," *Rotherford* = "ox ford"), and the sexual jokes all serve the same purpose: to expose the truth behind the Presbyterians' self-righteousness. But the truth, as well as their longer name and worse vices, is also "writ Large" in this extended sonnet. The *sonetto caudato*, or tailed sonnet, is an Italian form used in the Renaissance for humorous or satirical verse. By appending any number of tails, each a half line and a couplet, to the sonnet proper, the sonneteer may lash his opponent with a satirical sting. Thus the form could be used as punishment. In seventeenth-century England, punishment was frequently meted out in public spectacles of flogging, branding, mutilation, and other brutalities to expose the villainy of the guilty, provide an object lesson on the wages of sin, and prevent repetition of the crime. A cutpurse whose hand was cut off had lost the tools of his trade.[7] In like manner, Milton's sonnet with a stinging tail is a public punishment that flogs, brands, and threatens to mutilate his opponents in order to expose the guilty, teach the reader, and put an end to the cycle of Catholic, then Anglican, then Presbyterian force.

At a notorious public spectacle, to which Milton alludes in line 17, S. L. (for "Seditious Libeller") was carved into William Prynne's cheek to brand him for railing against acting, a courtly amusement Queen Henrietta Maria much enjoyed. The Laudian party hoped to show all who saw the mutilated Prynne that his tirade was mere libel. They also cut off both his ears, later repeating the mutilation on the stumps for a different offense. The allusion to this public spectacle, which not only failed to silence the prolific Prynne, but in fact turned him into a revolutionary hero, suggests the cruelty and futility of physical force and highlights by contrast the humanity and effectiveness of Milton's method of punishment: the power of conviction inherent in the written word.

With a tailed sonnet, not a whip, he inflicts on the Presbyterians the common punishment for whores and whoremongers: flogging (see *King Lear* 4.6.162–65). Those who lust after the "whore Pluralitie" are lashed with stinging insults, since Milton's goal is to shock readers into an awareness of the Presbyters' hypocrisy, not to use physical force. With etymological wordplay, not an iron, Milton brands the new presbyter as "*Priest*," saying the Parliament "shall read this clearly in your charge," as if reading a judgment at a scene of public punishment. Again, the brand alerts readers to

Presbyterian hypocrisy without physical brutality. Finally, with a prophecy, not a knife, Milton threatens mutilation:

> That so the Parliament
> May with their wholsom and preventive Shears
> Clip your Phylacteries, though bauk your Ears.

Unlike the bloody severing of Prynne's ears, this punishment will do no physical harm; rather, it will surgically remove, with "wholsom . . . Shears," the Presbyters' guise of piety. Phylacteries were small boxes containing quotations from the Law, which Jews tied to their foreheads or wrists. These outward signs, seldom matched by inner piety, angered Jesus, who warned his disciples against such hypocrisy. By publicly clipping the Presbyters' phylacteries, Parliament will leave them naked before onlookers who will see their bestiality, licentiousness, and papistical scheming, which had been hidden beneath an outward show of righteousness.

This exposure will be more effective than physical punishment because Parliament's shears are "preventive" as well as "wholsom." The clipping, Milton believed, would cripple his opponents whose "plots" depended on the citizens' ignorance of the Presbyters' greed. In fact, Parliament will more than cripple them. In ancient times and more primitive societies, the punishment for rape, fornication, and adultery was castration, which left the culprit powerless to repeat his offense.[8] By clipping the Presbyterians' phylacteries (the disguise that allowed them "to seise the widdow'd whore Pluralitie"), Parliament will render these sexual "forcers" impotent. At long last, Milton believes, the cycles of force and corruption from Catholic to Anglican to Presbyterian will be broken.

In reference to this threatened mutilation, Donald C. Dorian has argued that the sonnet's tail contains a veiled threat to the Presbyters' official ministry by alluding to the Mosaic law which denies the priesthood to any man with a physical blemish. Dorian further notes that the ordination of priests emphasizes the importance of ears.[9] But Milton makes a point of not threatening the Presbyters' ears; instead, he proposes to clip the appendage, representing hypocrisy, which has allowed them to fornicate with "the widdow'd whore." This symbolic castration would not only prevent further abuses in the church, but, according to Mosaic law, end the Presbyters' ministry. In the list of forbidden blemishes, Leviticus does not mention ears, but denies the priesthood to any man that "hath his stones broken" (Lev. 21:20). Deuteronomy's strictures are even more severe: "He that is wounded in the stones, or hath his privy member cut off, shall not enter into the congregation of the Lord" (Deut. 23:1). Of course, Milton would not have denied the offending Presbyters freedom of worship (see also Isa. 56:3-5), but if, as Dorian believes, the poem alludes to Old Testament rules regarding the priesthood, the result suggests how the Law backfires upon those who would use external constraint "to force . . . Consciences that Christ set free."

In the public punishment that the sonnet initiates and expects in the future, true power resides in the word revealing the truth, not in physical force. Indeed, the sonnet demonstrates the power of the word not only by its stinging satire, but also by its physical appearance of potency. Since it is a *sonetto caudato* and *cauda* was often a synonym for *penis*,[10] the sonnet itself, with its two appended tails, becomes an emblem of potency that threatens the "forcers" with impotence.

This powerful sonnet also ridicules the desire of the "forcers" to exalt themselves. Although they have "thrown of" their "Prelate Lord" (with a possible pun on *Laud*),[11] they want to usurp his lofty seat by attempting to wield the "Civill Sword" against equals. Secretly, Milton jeers, such unremarkable men as "meer *A. S.*," "shallow *Edwards*," and "Scotch what d'ye call" aspire to become priests set high above underling congregations. For readers as familiar with the Bible as Milton's readers, the reference to phylacteries augments the exposé. In Matt. 23:6-12, after condemning the ostentatious display of phylacteries, Christ specifically warns his followers against exalting a priesthood above other believers. The Pharisees, he says,

> love the uppermost rooms at feasts, and the chief seats in the synagogues, and greetings in the markets, and to be called of men, Rabbi, Rabbi. But be not ye called Rabbi: for one is your Master, even Christ; and all ye are brethren. And call no man your father upon the earth: for one is your Father, which is in heaven. Neither be ye called

masters: for one is your Master, even Christ. But he that is greatest
among you shall be your servant. And whosoever shall exalt himself
shall be abased; and he that shall humble himself shall be exalted.

Not the brotherhood Christ outlines here, the "classic Hierarchy"
of Presbyterianism is pyramidal, like the "Prelaty" described in
The Reason of Church Government, and would raise its leaders to
a "bad eminence" (*PL* 2.6), like the tyrant Satan.

While punishing the aspiring priests, "On the new forcers"
publicly vindicates the good servants to their churches, who had
been falsely "nam'd and printed Hereticks." These "Men whose
Life, Learning, Faith, and pure intent / Would have been held in
high esteem with *Paul*" were probably the five Dissenting Brethren
of the Westminster Assembly. Milton associates these models for
church government by brotherhood rather than priesthood with
Paul because like him they advocated freedom of conscience: Paul
wrote to the Galatians, "Stand fast . . . in the liberty wherewith
Christ hath made us free, and be not entangled again with the yoke
of bondage" (Gal. 5:1). Also, they were ministers to gathered
churches much like the ones to which Paul addressed his letters.
Indeed, the Puritan ideal was to recreate the fellowship of
primitive Christian communities. Thus "On the new forcers"
publicly exposes and punishes the Presbyters for exalting themselves like Jewish Pharisees, Catholic priests, and Anglican
prelates, but it also publicly vindicates the ministers who strive
toward Milton's ideal of church government, a brotherhood
among believers.

Although in this sonnet of 1646 Milton still had faith that
Parliament would liberate individual conscience and eliminate
state-supported corruption, by 1648 that faith had been betrayed.
In May, the Presbyterian majority in Parliament passed a law
making persistence in heresy a capital offense.[12] What was worse,
instead of the scourge of corruption Milton had predicted,
Parliament had become a hotbed of financial abuses. To support
the war, it had borrowed, and never repaid, money from private
citizens, including John Milton, giving as surety only the "Public
Faith." Soon angry creditors, the scribblers of broadside ballads,
and Royalists whose property Parliament had confiscated made

the "Public Faith" a bitterly ironic synonym for extortion.[13] While many parliamentarians made fortunes in real estate and even bribery, the predominantly working-class army, every day becoming a greater threat to the predominantly bourgeois Parliament, were denied back pay unless they disbanded.[14] Because Parliament had failed to liberate truth and purge corruption, Milton turned, as he would again in *Paradise Lost*, to the "one just Man" (see 11.681, 818, 876, 890) who, he hoped, would restore "Truth, and Right" and "Public Faith." He addressed Sonnet 15 to General Thomas Fairfax.

From his youth, when at 17 he went to Holland to learn the art of warfare, Fairfax displayed admirable qualities of military leadership; and because of his success early in the Civil War, Parliament made him commander-in-chief of the New Model Army. His greatest fame accrued from his dashing courage during Charles's ignominious defeat at Naseby, where, without a helmet, he led several cavalry charges and seized the Royalist colors with his own hands. At the time of Milton's sonnet, he was besieging Colchester as part of his and Cromwell's successful efforts to quell widespread Royalist rebellions and counter an invasion on behalf of Charles by the Scots ("the fals North"). (The Scots had betrayed their former allies because they feared the King less than they feared the army occupying London.) Fairfax's virtues as a military leader were probably not the only traits that attracted Milton: the general valued learning and literature highly. The grandnephew of Edward Fairfax, who first translated Tasso's *Jerusalem Delivered* into English, Thomas later hired Andrew Marvell to tutor his daughter and spent his time after retiring from military service in literary pursuits—translating, writing history, paraphrasing Psalms, and composing original verse. Even before his retirement, Milton could have known how much Fairfax valued learning; he had performed an act remarkably similar to the one Milton recommends to the "Captain or Colonel, or Knight in Arms" who threatens the "Muses Bowre" in Sonnet 8. According to Aubrey, Fairfax's first order after capturing Oxford was to send a strong guard to protect the Bodleian Library from pillage.[15]

Understandably, Milton looked to him as the courageous and wise leader who could do what Parliament could not. Unfortunately, Fairfax did not possess political acumen to match his military prowess and respect for learning. He lost control of the General Council of the Army, refused either to participate in or forcefully oppose Charles's trial, and in 1650 retired to his country estate, taking little part in Commonwealth politics thereafter.[16]

Written before the decline of his influence, Sonnet 15 hails him in the style of Tasso's heroic sonnets as a conquering military hero and urges him to a still greater civic heroism. The opening quatrain introduces a larger-than-life figure who has taken not just England, Scotland, and Wales by storm, but all of Europe as well. The "rumors loud" of his victories have crossed the Channel, and his name "rings" throughout the continent, winning "praise" from Protestant allies and "envy" from Catholic enemies. Milton contrasts this one almost superhuman man, who remains "firm" and "unshak'n," to the multiple "jealous monarchs," who are amazed, and the "remotest kings," who are daunted by mere rumors.

The second quatrain ranks Fairfax among the fabulous heroes of the past. A modern Hercules, he must rid England of rebellion just as the ancient hero purged the Lernaean fens of the Hydra. This monster had one immortal head and nine others which, when crushed, regenerated themselves twofold. Like the heads of the fabled monster, numerous rebellions sprang up throughout England after Fairfax's victories in the first Civil War. As in Sonnets 11, 12, and "On the new forcers," Milton portrays the enemies of the community as bestial, but here they are monstrous as well. Moreover, Fairfax must subdue not only the Hydra of rebellion, but also a winged monster: "And the fals North displaies / Her brok'n league, to impe their serpent wings." Shawcross has argued from historical and manuscript evidence that lines 7–8 should be read, "And the fals North displaies / Her brok'n league, to impe her [not "their"] serpent wings," thus making the Scottish army a winged serpent, not the Hydra, which in literature has seldom been depicted with wings.[17] Even if Shawcross's speculation is incorrect, Milton establishes the bestial and monstrous nature of both enemies. If the Hydra of rebellion is the winged serpent, the "fals North" must also have feathers to be able to "impe [to graft new feathers onto damaged ones in order to improve flight] their serpent wings." Besides, a possible pun on *displaies*, meaning both "makes evident" and "spreads (as a peacock its tail)," more sharply focuses the portrait of Scotland as a monster that spreads its feathers, proudly displaying its treachery in breaking the Solemn League and Covenant.[18] The final lines of the sonnet may also convey overtones of monstrous ravening. After references to two monsters, a reader with literary acumen (as Fairfax was) might well associate the personifications "Avarice, and Rapine" which "share the land" with the traditional figure of a marauding dragon laying waste the kingdom. Milton asks the hero to slay these dragons too.

Like many of Milton's virtuous heroes and heroines (Abdiel, the lady of Sonnet 9, and himself facing the "barbarous noise" of detractors), Fairfax is surrounded on all sides by hostility—envy abroad and rebellion at home. Although he has so far proved more than a match for his enemies, for which the octave praises him lavishly, the sestet warns that his military heroism may have been "in vain." The sudden shift from praise to admonition at the volta is prompted by Milton's double attitude toward war.

He believed warfare justifiable and sometimes necessary to preserve the community. In *Of Education* he insists, "A compleate and generous Education" must prepare a man to perform "all the offices both private and publike of peace and war" (*YM* 2:378–79). In *A Second Defense* he asserts that soldiers are "organized and enrolled to be defenders of the laws, uniformed guardians of justice, champions of the church" and that "the true and proper end of their labors [is] not to sow and reap warfare, but to cultivate peace and safety for the human race" (*YM* 4[1]:649). And in *The History of Britain*, he even admits that the Roman legions "beate [the English] into some civilitie; likely else to have continu'd longer in a barbarous and savage manner of life" (*YM* 5[1]:61). Puritans in general were not pacifists, but depicted the Christian as a valiant warrior as often as a pilgrim journeying to the Celestial City. With equal force, the Christian knight, like Saint George, must challenge "this mighty sailewing'd monster [prelacy] that menaces to swallow up the Land" (*RCG*, *YM* 1:857) and the ever-present Satanic dragons within. Thus Sonnet 15 sincerely praises Fairfax as a warrior.

But Milton knew the limitations of war. In *Paradise Lost* God puts an end to the chaos of the fallen angels' war in heaven, announcing,

> I suspend thir doom;
> Whence in perpetual fight they needs must last
> Endless, and no solution will be found:
> War wearied hath perform'd what War can do,
> And to disorder'd rage let loose the reins,
> With Mountains as with Weapons arm'd, which makes
> Wild work in Heav'n.
>
> [6.692–98]

War itself can become a self-regenerating Hydra, and in Sonnet 15 Milton boldly confronts the commander-in-chief with the possible monstrousness of his own heroic efforts: "For what can Warr, but endless warr still breed?" The only purpose of external warfare, Milton insists, is to guarantee the freedom and safety of the community and the individual, who then must wage the hardest warfare of all: the war within. Just as each individual must make his heart upright and pure, a community must preserve virtue at the center of government. In *A Second Defense* Milton warns that defeating the Royalists was only a skirmish in a war against proliferating enemies at the center of the state and each man's soul:

> If, having done with war, you neglect the arts of peace, if warfare is your peace and liberty, war your only virtue, your supreme glory, you will find, believe me, that peace itself is your greatest enemy. Peace itself will be by far your hardest war, and what you thought liberty will prove to be your servitude. . . . Unless you expel avarice, ambition, and luxury from your minds, yes, and extravagance from your families as well, you will find at home and within that tyrant who, you believed, was to be sought abroad and in the field—now even more stubborn. In fact, many tyrants, impossible to endure, will from day to day hatch out from your very vitals. [*YM* 4(1):680–81]

In Sonnet 15 Royalist rebellions are the Hydra, and warfare itself can "still [ever] breed" like the Hydra. But internal vices, which "from day to day hatch out," also resemble the Hydra, and Fairfax is asked to confront all three manifestations of the monster. The only way to kill the Hydra is to burn the source from which new heads spring and bury the immortal head. So Sonnet 15 exhorts Fairfax to penetrate to the root of warfare's endless breeding, burn out its domestic origin at the center of the commonwealth, and bury the vices that physical force cannot expel.

To emphasize the progress from external to internal warfare, the sonnet presents the threats that surround Fairfax in descending order of geographical magnitude and distance from the center (from Europe to Britain to Parliament), but in ascending order of imminence and magnitude of danger (from the already-stunned European monarchies to the soon-to-be-quelled Royalist and Scottish rebellions to the present governmental corruption). And Milton is confident that Fairfax has the moral strength required to carry out the reform, just as he had the physical strength required to win the Civil War. Milton expresses this confidence by attributing Fairfax's victories to "firm unshak'n vertue." As Smart notes, *vertue* carries the Latin sense of "valour," and thus highlights Fairfax's renowned courage. But, citing Horatian parallels, Honigmann and Finley agree that the sonnet compliments Fairfax's moral virtue as well.[19] Both structure and diction strengthen the sonnet's plea: the Hercules who has demonstrated his *virtus* before national and international audiences must penetrate to the center of power and eradicate the source of the Hydra's regeneration by restoring moral *virtue* to the government.

Although Milton now depends on "one just Man" instead of Parliament's "wholsom and preventive Shears," the issues at stake in 1648 are the same that prompted him to castigate publicly "the new forcers": financial corruption and tyranny over conscience. In Sonnet 15 he condemns the "Public Fraud" of parliamentary corruption, and in "The new forcers" the Presbyterians' greed for multiple church livings. In Sonnet 15 he demands that "Truth, and Right" be freed "from Violence," in other words, that matters of conscience be exempt from force.[20] So too, in the tailed sonnet he insists that individual "Consciences that Christ set free" be exempt from "the Civill Sword." Sonnet 15 also echoes the motif of public vindication and punishment that concludes "The new forcers." Just as the tailed sonnet publicly defends the good names of the just and lashes, brands, and prophesies the mutilation of the guilty,

Sonnet 15 exhorts Fairfax to clear "Public Faith . . . from the shamefull brand / Of Public Fraud" and scourge the fraudulent.

Because Fairfax did not answer the call to cleanse the Lernaean swamp of governmental corruption, choosing instead a pastoral retreat at Nun Appleton House, Milton sought another "just Man" in 1652 to wield the "Civill Sword," Oliver Cromwell. Already successful at Preston (1648), Dunbar (1650), and Worcester (1651) in defeating the Scots, whose pact with Charles insisted upon the reestablishment of Presbyterianism in England, Cromwell seemed to many, as to Milton, "our cheif of men." Since he suppressed the Scots' armed attempt to "ride [England] with a classic Hierarchy" and openly supported religious toleration, claiming "he had rather that Mahometanism were permitted among us than that one of God's children should be persecuted,"[21] he was the man, Milton believed, to face a domestic form of the same evil he fought on the battlefield: the attempt to "bind . . . soules with secular chaines."

In 1652 a delegation, including four of the five Dissenting Brethren of the 1644 controversy over Presbyterianism, appealed to Parliament to reorganize the English church. They deplored the lack of any official manner of appointing preachers and the consequent spread of heresy. As proof of this spread, they produced the Racovian Catechism, a Socinian pamphlet licensed for printing by Milton himself. To remedy these ills, they proposed state commissions to oversee the selection, regulation, and maintenance of preachers, and drew up a list of the fundamentals of Christianity to which all approved preachers must subscribe. The Rump appointed a Committee for the Propagation of the Gospel to consider these proposals, and Cromwell was a member.

Milton probably experienced déjà vu during the Committee's deliberations, as he watched what seemed another Westminster Assembly; he was probably disillusioned when the Dissenting Brethren showed that their toleration of dissent extended only to themselves; and he was probably angered when the Committee summoned him to question his licensing of the Racovian Catechism. From his disillusionment, anger, and concern for freedom of conscience came an impassioned sonnet, "To the Lord Generall Cromwell May 1652 On the proposalls of certaine ministers at yᵉ Commtee for Propagation of the Gospell."[22]

The octave's portrait of Cromwell is as heroic as Sonnet 15's of Fairfax, the modern Hercules. The forceful verbs—"plough'd" (delayed and conspicuously placed to complete the opening quatrain's rhyme) and "reard"—emphasize the physical might of a general who not only subdues his enemies, but makes the streams of one battlefield run red with "blood of Scotts imbru'd," while a second "resounds [his] praises loud" and a third awards him the "laureat wreath" of victory. The sonnet marches from one victory to another, overriding the usual position of the volta, to invoke a sense of almost irresistible force. And the active verbs and striking visual and aural images depict a "glorious" conqueror who, cometlike, has pierced the surrounding clouds to blaze forth triumphant as he lifts a monument to God upon the neck of the personification, proud Fortune, now abased at his feet. With physical might, he has penetrated barriers against his own deeds and raised barriers against his enemies'.

In fact, the portrait of Cromwell is remarkably Herculean. Frequently, Renaissance painters and sculptors, notably Antonio del Pollaiuolo, represented Hercules Triumphant with a knee or foot on the neck or head of a defeated monster like the Nemean lion or Cacus. As an icon, this triumphant stance may be traced back to antiquity, and in early Christian art it represented the victory of virtue over vice.[23] Milton probably remembered this image, especially as represented in the portraits of Hercules, when describing Cromwell in such a heroic posture. He seems even more heroic than Fairfax, who still has a Herculean labor ahead of him, the Hydra of new rebellions. But Cromwell has already humbled not merely the treacherous Scots, but Fortune itself.

In subduing Fortune, he is revealed as an agent of divine providence to keep the tyranny of kingship and Scottish Presbyterianism from returning to England. What has enabled him to serve as God's scourge has been his "faith and matchless Fortitude." *Fortitudo*, as physical strength, was, of course, the distinguishing characteristic of Hercules. But during the Renaissance his physical attributes became a symbol of virtue in action. Often citing the story of Hercules at the Crossroads, where he chooses the road of Virtue over Pleasure, commentators like the Italian mythographer, Natale Conti, saw in the classical hero "honour, courage, and virtuous excellence of mind and body alike."[24] Sometimes allegorical interpretations transformed the monsters he defeated into vices; thus in cleansing the world of monstrous vice, he became a savior, a type of Christ. By the time Milton used the symbol to make his praise of Cromwell more vivid and significant, the portrait of Hercules Triumphant had become familiar, and his *virtus* was understood to include virtue as well. The sonnet emphasizes that both inner virtues, "faith" and "Fortitude" (as strength of will), and external "Fortitude" (as physical strength) have guided Cromwell to his victories.

Through faith animating strength, he has been able to serve as the agent of Providence to defeat Fortune. He has enacted the paradox of finding at the center, in the "upright heart and pure," the will of the circumference, God's providence. Milton insists, here as elsewhere, that seeking guidance within must precede and direct the exercise of physical might. In his famous exhortation to Cromwell in *A Second Defense*, he only touches "with brevity" on the victories at Preston, Dunbar, and Worcester, but dwells on "that piety, faith, justice, and moderation of soul which convince [him] that [Cromwell has] been raised by the power of God beyond all other men to this most exalted rank" (*YM* 4[1]:673–74). Indeed, Milton praises him as

> a soldier well-versed in self-knowledge . . . whatever enemy lay within—vain hopes, fears, desires—he had either previously destroyed within himself or had long since reduced to subjection. Commander first over himself, victor over himself, he had learned to achieve over himself the most effective triumph, and so, on the very first day that he took service against an external foe, he entered camp a veteran and past-master in all that concerned the soldier's life. [*YM* 4(1):667–68]

In Sonnet 16's striking image of a physical and spiritual hero, whose *virtus* / virtue has guided him to raise trophies "on the neck of crowned Fortune proud," several issues crucial to the sonnet are visualized. The hero who pierced barriers against his own actions has immobilized his enemy. With God's help he has humbled the mightiest monarch of the earth, Fortune. Finally, his physical heroism stems from his spiritual virtue. Because the picture carries this weight of symbolic meaning, it is likely that Milton was recalling the traditional emblems of Fortune so common and influential in the Middle Ages and Renaissance. The image, of course, echoes Josh. 10:24–25, in which Joshua calls his captains to place their feet on the necks of the defeated kings. But Fortune wears the crown in Sonnet 16, not an earthly king like Charles I. Ignoring this fact, editors have repeatedly glossed "crowned Fortune" as "Milton's exultant allusion . . . to the beheading of Charles and Cromwell's part therein."[25] This reading reduces an image rich in significance to a thin political allegory.

Pictures of the goddess Fortuna (sometimes called Occasion) had proliferated in England and Europe since the Middle Ages. A common medieval representation showed a crowned queen toppling kings with one turn of her wheel. In sixteenth- and seventeenth-century emblems, she is more often a lovely nude, draped with a thin stole blowing freely with the winds of change. Her hair, a forelock which flows to her front leaving the back of her head bald, signifies that fortune must be seized before it passes. Mounted on a wheel or ball, she stands triumphant above all men. More elaborate scenes depict kings either falling before her as she confiscates their crowns or following, chained to her wheel, in her triumph.

The subjugation of Fortune by divine providence or inner virtues also became a common emblem motif. Often the artist drew a hand with a rod or rope descending from heaven to topple Fortune from her proud height on the ball or wheel. In other emblems, more relevant to Milton's sonnet, an old man stands with his foot upon the neck of the goddess, who lies prostrate while he binds her with rope to her fallen wheel. This emblem was entitled *Sapiens Supra Fortunam*. (Similar emblems exalted the power of Poverty, Prudence, Constancy, and so forth.)[26] This image clearly resembles Milton's portrait of Cromwell, the Herculean hero who can rear God's trophies on Fortune's neck because of his "faith and matchless Fortitude."

Instead of copying any one painting or emblem to create the image he wanted, Milton seems to have coalesced several common iconographical motifs in his portrait of Cromwell. Paintings and statues of Hercules Triumphant, pictures detailing the abasement of kings before Fortune's higher sovereignty, and emblems of virtue's subjugation of Fortune herself have been fused to create a poetic image more resonant than the one-dimensional political allegory explained by previous editors. As a result, the image reminds the reader of Cromwell's military power, his virtues, his role as God's agent, and his superiority to Charles I. Both the defeat of King Charles by the goddess Fortuna and her defeat by Herculean Cromwell are suggested by the image. Probably, then, the point is not Milton's "malignity to Kings," as Bishop Richard Hurd claimed, and as Phillips feared when he omitted the allusion from the first printed version of the sonnet in Milton's *Letters of State* (1694).[27] Rather, it is that, while Charles surrendered his crown to a greater power (Fortune, not Cromwell), Cromwell, as the agent of Providence, has defeated "crowned Fortune" herself.

Despite this picture of the mighty warrior, Sonnet 16, like the sonnet to Fairfax, moves relentlessly inward. As we have already noted, virtue has animated Cromwell's physical strength. Also, like Fairfax, Abdiel, and Milton's many beleaguered heroes, Cromwell, although surrounded by external enemies, must penetrate to the center of virtue. By ploughing through a "cloud" of war, which had hemmed in the commonwealth, and detraction, which threatened to eclipse his own reputation, he has restored "peace" (not "warr") and "truth" (not "detractions") to the heart of government.[28] Because of his success in piercing these obstructions, Milton asks him to break even stronger bonds at the center of each citizen's soul. Instead of clouds, airy nothings which may be choking and deluding, but not binding, he must break the hard iron of the "secular chaines" threatening to "bind" free conscience. The paradox is characteristically Miltonic: the more palpable and dangerous threat is spiritual bondage at the center, while physical might faces only insubstantial and easily defeated enemies at the periphery.

Like the Hydra-headed rebellions plaguing Fairfax, the "new foes" facing Cromwell, intolerance and hire, have sprung up at home as soon as the Scots, also advocating intolerance and hire, were defeated in the field. As monstrous as the Hydra, these enemies are characterized as ravenous wolves with paws to enforce their will and maws to devour their prey. To the author of *Lycidas*, which condemns hirelings as "Blind mouths" who allow "the grim Wolf with privy paw" to devour the flock, and of *Means to Remove Hirelings*, which advocates a clergy supported by the free gifts of each congregation, the proposals for a state-supported clergy spelled financial abuses. Milton had already condemned the corruption resulting from hire graphically in the "New forcers." As it compares the Presbyterians' forcing and seizing to lust, Sonnet 16 describes the same actions as gluttony. To emphasize the voracity of the "hireling wolves," Milton isolates their salient features: a "paw," signifying state control over individual conscience, and a "maw," signifying greed for state-subsidized preaching positions. These harsh monosyllables, like those in Sonnets 11 and 12, form a concluding couplet, whereby Milton once again accentuates the bestiality of the enemies of human society. Like *Paradise Lost*, the sonnets dramatize a variety of heavenly, earthly, and hellish feasts, and Sonnet 16 concludes with a perversion of Milton's ideal communal feast. Not sharers, like Lawrence and Cyriack, in an earthly feast reflecting the heavenly one which the lady of Sonnet 9 awaits, these gluttons use their "paw" to stuff their "maw."

Although the enemies on the home front are more dangerous than those in the field, the sonnet offers hope that Cromwell, who stopped the Scottish advocates of force and hire, can restrain their English cousins. Since he "plough'd" through the "cloud" of war and detraction, he seems the natural choice to break the "chaines" of a state church. Since he "reard" trophies on the "neck" of a goddess who uncrowns kings, he can surely hobble the "paw" and muzzle the "maw" of a wolf. In other words, the physical actions praised in the octave exactly parallel those needed in the spiritual situations described in the sestet: breaking bonds and immobilizing the enemy. They are similar Herculean labors.

In Sonnet 16 Milton gauges the plea to suit the reader. Cromwell was primarily a warrior, and although in May, 1652, Milton had hopes of his governing abilities as well, he knew that Cromwell would respond most eagerly if the plea to end intolerance and hire were phrased as a rousing call to arms. But two months later Milton addressed a sonnet to a very different man, Henry Vane, the younger.

The son of a noted official in the administrations of James I and Charles I, Vane distinguished himself early in not only political successes, but also religious unorthodoxies. Disillusioned with the Church of England and elated by hopes for a holy commonwealth in the new world, he emigrated to America, becoming governor of the Massachusetts Bay Colony at only twenty-four. But soon his idealism confronted the two realities he would face for the rest of his life: war and intolerance. Located in the midst of a wilderness where Indian raids were a constant threat, the colony feared any sign of internal division. When Anne Hutchinson began to preach about the progressive revelation of the Holy Spirit and the young Governor Vane sympathized with her antinomian heresy, powerful John Winthrop and other conservative settlers were appalled. The godly discipline of a theocracy, they claimed, was the colony's only protection against chaos and license—whether from savage Indians without or visionary females within the community. Anne was tried, banished from the colony, and later massacred by Indians. Because of these conflicts, Vane was not reelected, and returned to England in 1637, having gained valuable experience: from his observations of Indian raids, he learned to avoid war whenever possible; during the persecution of Anne Hutchinson, he formulated his position on the separation of church and state; and in both war and internal disputes, he learned to value calm, but shrewd negotiation.[29]

Vane tried to use his experience to help build the holy commonwealth in England. As a lay member of the Westminster Assembly, he spoke for toleration. As a commissioner sent to Scotland in 1643, he helped negotiate the Solemn League and Covenant. Without yielding to demands for a Presbyterian settlement, he found a wording that satisfied both England, which wanted a purely civil treaty, and Scotland, which wanted a primarily religious covenant. As treasurer of the navy for eleven years and later a member of the Council of State, he negotiated to avoid war whenever possible, winning praise even from his enemies. "He was indeed a man," says Clarendon, "of . . . great understanding, which pierced into and discerned the purposes of other men with wonderful sagacity, whilst he had himself *vultum clausum*, that no man could make a guess of what he intended. He was of a temper not to be moved, and of rare dissimulation, and could comply when it was not seasonable to contradict, without losing ground by the condescension."[30] In the crises of 1652, Milton saw the talents of Vane, the tough negotiator and advocate of toleration, as precisely what England needed.

Despite Vane's and Cromwell's hopes for a European Protestant league, in 1652 a long-standing trade rivalry led to armed conflict between the English and Dutch, whose Protestantism might have made them natural allies. Vane played an important role in the crisis. As former treasurer of the navy and leading member of the navy committee, he ensured England's victory by maintaining a superior fleet. As a member of the Council of State and leader of the committee to negotiate a peace settlement, he penetrated the delaying tactics of the Dutch ambassadors. After one skirmish at sea, they denied that their government, all the while amassing a large fleet, had authorized the confrontation. Three days after the crafty but unsuccessful ambassadors left England, Milton sent Sonnet 17 to Vane, praising his ability "to unfold / The drift of hollow states, hard to be spelld" and his wisdom, as great as any senator's who ever "held / The helme of *Rome*."[31] In "drift," meaning both "plot" (*OED*, *sb*. 5) and "the fact or condition of being driven, as by a current" (*sb*. 2), and in "helme," Milton wittily alludes to Vane's service to the navy. So too in "hollow states," he puns on *Holland* and *hollow*, meaning "shallow" and perhaps even "low-lying" as Holland certainly is.[32]

But the Dutch War was not the only crisis of 1652: the Committee for the Propagation of the Gospel was still considering proposals for a state church. Thus Milton devotes the sestet to praising Vane's belief in the separation of church and state, perhaps hoping that two sonnets, one to England's foremost warrior, the other to its foremost statesman, would promote an alliance against the "forcers of Conscience." While Sonnet 16 figuratively calls Cromwell home from peripheral battlefields to war at the center of government, Sonnet 17 finds Vane already at work in the tough warfare of peace. Indeed, Richard Baxter, commenting on the years after Pym's death (1643), said that Vane "was that *within* the House, which *Cromwell* was *without*."[33]

In many ways the sonnet to Vane, the last of Milton's heroic sonnets, complements the other two. The Herculean heroes, Fairfax and Cromwell, must turn their conquering might, already proved on the battlefields, against the domestic enemies of the community: the "Avarice, and Rapine" of financial corruption and the "secular chaines" and "hireling wolves" of state-supported religion. In contrast, Vane depends on "gownes not armes" to repel the enemies of the community, handles supplies and finances efficiently during war, and knows the limits of the civil sword in spiritual matters. He is performing those labors the military heroes still must face. Sonnets 15 and 16 seek to persuade warriors to become statesmen, but Sonnet 17 describes a statesman directing a war only after efforts "to settle peace" by negotiation have failed. Fairfax and Cromwell are each summoned as the "one just Man" to purge the land, but Vane, a republican who later left government service when Cromwell disbanded the Rump, is compared to one of many virtuous senators in the Roman Republic prior to the Caesars. Like Fairfax and Cromwell, Vane is besieged on all sides—at sea, at the negotiating table, and in parliamentary committees. But, although distant enemies have yielded, the generals must still move inward to eradicate more central and tenacious enemies: greed and the abrogation of free conscience. Vane, however, moves in the opposite direction, and Sonnet 17 charts the ideal progress of Christian life as Milton conceived it: from the wise and virtuous center, through community service, to the circumference of God's will.

The opening line emphasizes Vane's wisdom, and the rest of the sonnet details how wisdom animates his actions. With his "sage counsell" (l. 1), he always seeks peace first (ll. 3–4), but cannot be deceived by trickery (ll. 5–6); he marshals force to win if war is necessary (ll. 7–9), but limits force in spiritual matters (ll. 9–12). Milton's arrangement of details suggests a cautious movement toward force and stresses the difference between its legitimate and illegitimate uses in order to convince the reader that Vane is indeed "old" (l. 1) in wisdom and should be considered religion's "eldest son" (l. 14). The sonnet's diction comes full circle, as does Vane's progress in service. Because his actions began at the center in wisdom (l. 1), which then guided him through the moral labyrinth of the fallen world (ll. 2–12), Vane arrives at the circumference as

God's chosen preserver of religion (ll. 13–14). But the sestet insists that true religion depends on freedom at the center. Once again the paradox of center and circumference is manifest: God's will is actuated only by the wise, virtuous, and free soul.

To signify the completeness of Vane's service, Milton avoids the strong volta he needed in Sonnets 15 ("O yet a nobler task . . .") and 16 ("yet much remaines . . .") to redirect the warriors from peripheral battles to new tasks on the home front. Sonnet 17 devotes one quatrain to Vane's wisdom and diplomatic avoidance of force, a second to his acumen as a negotiator and efficiency in administering the tools of force, a third to the limitation of force, and a two-line conclusion to his reward for service. To emphasize that all his service has depended on wisdom, Milton relates Vane's actions in a long series of infinitive phrases which complement the delayed subject and verb, "thou'hast learnt." Moreover, the other verbs Milton selects move from stasis to action to stasis, and the nouns frame two images of material power with scenes in which the dignity of age, not physical might, commands respect.

The first image pictures a "Senatour" (*senex* = "an elder") whose toga alone, as a symbol of office, repels armed force, and whose firm hand directs the state. The verbs, "held" and "settle," connote stability. The second image shows the statesman gradually arousing to action and wielding material power. We see him "unfold" treachery and "advise" how war may "Move"; we see how the as yet insubstantial treachery of "the drift of hollow states" is answered by the hardware of war, whose "nerves" are "Iron and Gold," "in all her equipage." In the third image Vane curbs action. He "severs" spiritual and civil power, and because he knows their "bounds," Milton hopes he will *bind* the civil "sword" in the 1652 controversy. The final image returns to stasis and the dignity of age. As a venerable lady, religion "leanes" on the same "firme hand" which could have "held / The helme of *Rome*."

Sonnet 17 envisions both war and religion as female ("warr . . . her two maine nerves . . . her equipage," "religion . . . her eldest son"), and both depend on Vane. One "leanes" on his "firme hand," while the other, after his attempts to secure peace, is "up*held*" by him, supported by his assent (*OED, v.* 4; emphasis mine). Because Vane knows when and when not to take the civil sword in hand, the "helme" of state (l. 3), the administration of "warr" (ll. 7–9), and "religion" (l. 13) all place themselves literally in his hands.

The circularity of Sonnet 17 is evident. It begins and ends emphasizing wisdom, focusing on pictures of venerated age, and praising Vane's statesmanship in the image of a "firme hand." In between, work must be done to fathom treachery, conduct a war, and limit civil force. But, as the sonnet begins in the hope to "settle peace," it ends with religion leaning "in peace" (peacefully or during a time of peace) upon Vane. Although England was virtually at war when the sonnet was written, Milton probably means that, because Vane knows the limits of civil power, religion, at least in 1652, is "in peace." In *A First Defense* Milton makes a similar point: "Men first came together to form a state in order to live in safety and freedom without violence or wrong; they founded a church to live in holiness and piety: The former has laws and the latter doctrine, which is quite different, and it is for this reason that war has followed war throughout our Christian world for so many years: namely, that magistrates and church are confused as to their jurisdictions" (*YM* 4(1):320–21). While Cromwell and Fairfax had to wage war in part because the Scots confused these jurisdictions, religion will be at peace when men like Vane keep civil and spiritual power distinct.

All four sonnets advocating policies that Milton deemed essential to the godly community in England dramatize the historical progress toward the Kingdom of God. Their heroes continue the work of past servants to religious and secular communities: Paul, Hercules, and virtuous Roman senators. And their villains are as bestial and monstrous as any that challenged Hercules: the ox and ass of submission to hierarchy, the Hydra of rebellion, and the wolf of greed. Still, the sonnets look forward to a future realization of the ideal community. The "New forcers" punishes the hypocrites with immediate exposure and predicts their future impotence. Sonnets 15 and 16 praise present victories over rebellion, while calling for a greater civic heroism. And Sonnet 17 previews the entire progress from center to circumference. Of course, Vane has not brought God's kingdom to earth, but he is thriving in his own pilgrimage of service, which is all anyone can do.

Amidst the disillusionments and frustrations of political controversy, the potential harmony of the Kingdom of God must have seemed at times unattainable. Referring to the five antiprelatical tracts, Joan Webber tells how Milton sustained his vision. As a Puritan activist, he was controversial, time-bound, and devoted to progress. But when speaking of his poetic vocation, he evoked a timeless world where contemplation and harmony are possible: "As soon as anything becomes poetic, it does transcend the chaos of the everyday world, and indicates an ability on the part of the author to transcend or transform it—to have his mind on consonance as well as party politics, and to hold action and contemplation in some kind of fusion where all is simultaneously ill and well."[34] In the sonnet which looks unflinchingly on one shocking defeat in the historical march to the New Jerusalem, Milton sustains this fusion. "Avenge O Lord" (Sonnet 18) clearly envisions the harmony and ultimate victory which transcend the carnage of the Waldensian massacre. The tension between present horror and future glory, earthly injustice and divine providence, stretches this lyric miniature to include a panoramic vision of the historical progress to the Kingdom of God.

The 1655 massacre of the Waldensians (Vaudois, Valdenses) was the climax of centuries of persecution for the sectaries living in a few Alpine valleys of northern Italy. Although claiming that their ancestors were primitive Christians converted by Paul on his journey to Spain, they were probably descended from the Poor Men of Lyons, a group of wandering ministers founded in the twelfth century by Peter Waldo (Pierre Valdes). A merchant of Lyons who sold his goods, gave his wealth to the poor, and preached literal obedience to the Gospel, Waldo did not intend to separate from Rome. But when he and his followers refused to obey orders against public preaching and teaching, they were excommunicated in 1215. Despite their wide following in southern France, northern Italy, Germany, and Bohemia, persecution soon forced them to retreat to strongholds in the Piedmont, which in the fifteenth century came under the control of the dukes of Savoy.

Because of the Waldensians' strategic location near Alpine passes and their close ties to Swiss, French, German, and Bohemian Protestants, Savoy renewed severe persecution in the 1540s. Fear that the valleys might become a base of operations for militant reformers led to outright war, but the Waldensians defended their homes so staunchly that in 1561 they won a treaty guaranteeing them toleration within defined limits. By 1655 their settlements had outgrown the limits, and in January the duke ordered their immediate retreat. The real power in Savoy was not the young duke, but his mother, Christine de Médici, the sister of Henrietta Maria (widow of Charles I) and a relative of Catherine de Médici (regent of France during the infamous Saint Bartholomew Day massacre). For reasons which historians have debated—the strategic location of the valleys, Counter Reformation zeal, even reprisal for the English Puritans' execution of her brother-in-law and Cromwell's massacre of Irish Catholics—Christine urged the April massacre.

Along with French troops and Irish soldiers, who were promised land in the Piedmont to replace their homes destroyed by Cromwell, the Savoy regiment was absolved by priests from the sins about to be committed, quartered in Waldensian homes within the limits of toleration, and ordered the next morning to purge the "heretics." Despite the soldiers' thoroughness and diabolical refinements of cruelty—dismemberment, sexual brutality, impalement of children on fences, the rolling of mothers and infants tied neck to heels over cliffs, even cannibalism—some survivors escaped and tried to reach friends in Switzerland and France through the Alpine passes. But many of these died of hunger and exposure.[35]

When news of the massacre reached England, Cromwell was appalled. Of course, he wanted an ally in the strategic valleys, but his speedy dispatch of generous personal funds to aid the survivors, his public campaign to raise more money, and his letters and envoy sent to urge restitution suggest that he was genuinely moved by the sufferings of fellow Protestants.[36] In letters, which Milton translated, to the duke of Savoy, the king of France, and the Protestant powers of Europe (Sweden, Denmark, the United Provinces, and Switzerland), Cromwell acted as the leader of European Protestantism, uniting his coreligionists and deploring the massacre. He wrote to the king of Sweden, "Even if Protestants differ among themselves on some trifling matters, yet ... their name and cause are common to them all and nearly the same" (*State Papers*, YM 5[2]:690). Similarly, Samuel Morland, the ambassador sent to protest to the duke of Savoy and distribute the proceeds of the collection to the survivors, later wrote in his history of the Waldensians, "The Interest of the chief Magistrate of England is, by all means to become Head of the Reformed Party throughout Europe."[37] Cromwell's hope to lead a European Protestant league did not produce only political rhetoric. At the time of the massacre, England and France were negotiating a treaty, which France wanted because of her rivalry with Spain, but Cromwell insisted that successful negotiations depended on French aid in guaranteeing the Waldensians' return to their homes and future toleration.

English Protestants shared Cromwell's horror and supported his collections and use of diplomatic pressure. The newsletters produced detailed accounts of the massacre, and, to boost contributions, Cromwell encouraged J. B. Stouppe, a Swiss minister, to publish *A Collection of the Several Papers Sent to His Highness the Lord Protector . . . Concerning The Bloody and Barbarous Massacres. . . .* Because Milton was Stouppe's friend, as well as the secretary selected, despite his blindness, to prepare state letters about the massacre, he probably had access to the papers prior to publication. Indeed, the accounts of the massacre, his involvement in England's official actions, and the Waldensians' history, which had sparked his interest before 1655, all influenced this celebrated sonnet.[38]

In particular, two aspects of his ideal of the Christian community prompted his impassioned response to the massacre: his views on church government and belief in an invisible church that transcends time and space. "On the new forcers" and Sonnets 15 and 16 plead that intolerance and hire be expunged so that churches may become true godly communities, and Milton's model for church government, based on free preaching from the scriptures and a ministry supported by the congregation, was the Waldensians. They practiced, he believed, the pure religion of the primitive church before it "fell off and turnd whore" (*Hirelings*, *CM* 6:81), accepting the temporal power and wealth bestowed by Constantine. Milton also praises their wandering preachers called *barba* ("guide" or "uncle" in Provençal) who were supported by alms. (See *Hirelings*, CM 6:80–81, 87.)

Their massacre not only horrified him, but proved the truth of his assertions in earlier sonnets: intolerance is the enemy of the ideal community and produces brutality and division, not unity. Stouppe's collection of narratives made clear that the soldiers were not merely reestablishing borders; their goal was genocide. In the accounts, Milton found his model for church unity, in which shepherd and flock freely minister to one another, shattered: "You might have seen here the legg of a Woman, there the head of a Child. Sometimes the privy Members of a man, the Intrails of another, and sometimes the pieces of another."[39] All that was left of their community were "bones / . . . scatter'd on the Alpine mountains cold."

But there was a larger community to succour the Waldensians. Because Milton believed in an invisible church, he advocated a godly community larger than the Christian commonwealth, a European Protestant league. In his first antiepiscopal tract, *Of Reformation* (1641), he advocated that England "cut away from the publick body the noysom, and diseased tumor of Prelacie, and come from Schisme to *unity* with our neighbour Reformed sister Churches" (*YM* 1:598). Even after Charles's execution, which stunned Europe, he asked, "Who knows not that there is a mutual bond of amity and brother-hood between man and man over all the World, neither is it the English Sea that can sever us from that duty and relation. . . . Nor is it distance of place that makes enmitie, but enmity that makes distance. He therfore that keeps peace with me, neer or remote, of whatsoever Nation, is to mee as farr as all civil and human offices an Englishman and a neighbour" (*TKM, YM* 3:214–15). Later, in *A Second Defense* (1654) he addressed all men of whatever nationality who agreed with his libertarian ideals: "the entire assembly and council of all the most influential men, cities, and nations everywhere" (*YM* 4[1]:554).

Moreover, he believed that reformed Christianity transcended time as well as space. Some communities had always rejected the worldliness of the Catholic church and preserved the simplicity of early Christians, and Milton considered the Waldensians among the first of these dissenters, praising them as "those ancientest

reformed churches of *Waldenses*, if they rather continu'd not pure
since the apostles" (*Hirelings, CM* 6:64). Since he idealized their
church government and considered them prime members of an
ancient and international community of reformed churches, he felt
their suffering as his own. A fellow in the fold of the purified faith,
he felt called to respond as not only Latin secretary to the Commonwealth of England, but also God's chosen poet and prophet.

His poetic response, "Avenge O Lord," has been universally
praised as his most powerful sonnet. Because of its headlong sweep,
rushing past line ends and through the volta, it has been compared
to a wave threatening to burst the constraints of sonnet form;
because of its predominance of long-*o* rhymes, it has been likened
to Lear's entrance carrying Cordelia's body: "Howl, howl, howl!
O, you are men of stones" (*King Lear* 5.3.258). But an early editor
of the sonnets, Mark Pattison, noted, "Of thought, or image, all
that there is is a borrowed thought, and one repeatedly borrowed."
Since this judgment, scholars have traced the extent of these
borrowings. Almost every phrase echoes the Bible. The paradox
that animates the sonnet's progress from bitter history to exultant
prophecy is Tertullian's well-worn dictum, "The blood of the
martyrs is the seed of the Church." The image of ashes turned to
seeds recalls the parable of the sower whose seeds "fell into good
ground, and brought forth fruit, some an *hundredfold*" (Matt.
13:3–9; emphasis mine), as well as the myths of Cadmus, who
sowed dragon's teeth which sprang up armed men, and Deucalion
and Pyrrha, who tossed stones over their shoulders to replenish the
earth after the flood. Commentators have found allusions to Virgil,
Petrarch, and Spenser in the sonnet's dense texture. So too,
Honigmann and Esther Menascé have discovered striking parallels
between Milton's diction and reports of the massacre in contemporary newsletters and Stouppe's collection. The authenticity
of these possible sources seems less relevant than the question, Why
is a medley of "hackneyed biblical phrases," clichés, literary
allusions, and borrowings from newsletters so moving?[40]

In Sonnet 18, as in *Lycidas*, Milton uses public, almost universal
language to express personal grief over a particular disaster.
Lycidas invokes the conventions of pastoral elegy, and Sonnet 18
uses words and images that had been voiced and heard by the

godly for centuries—by Jews crying for vengeance against the heathen, by an early Christian who recorded the cries of martyrs awaiting the final judgment (Rev. 6:9–10), by the Church Fathers, by a Renaissance humanist who deplored papal corruption, by an English Protestant who allegorized the defeat of Rome / Babylon, by the Waldensians themselves—in short, by many people of similar beliefs in many times and places. Such language provides a familiar, but ever-renewed public form in which personal emotions of rage and grief may be spent and transformed into peace and hope. It also encourages each mourner to feel, despite the separation occasioned by any death and the shattering of a community in the Waldensian massacre, that neither he nor the martyrs are alone. The echoes of past laments and consolations in Sonnet 18 assure the reader that the living and the dead form a community beyond death and time. Finally, although the massacre is recorded in ghastly particularity, the sonnet's allusive density places the single event in perspective. It becomes part of history and prophecy, not an isolated, meaningless atrocity. The reader imaginatively shares the fragmentation and slaughter of the Waldensians, but also their resurrection and reunification in language that links the reader, poet, and martyrs to a timeless and infinite community.

Indeed, the sonnet moves through time, locating this particular event in the historical progress to the Kingdom of God. As it opens, the massacre is past. The Waldensians have already been "slaughter'd"; now only their "scatter'd" bones remain as a memorial to their suffering. The scene seems even more desolate when Milton juxtaposes to the picture of fragmented bodies a brief history of the community, once "Sheep . . . in their antient Fold." While England still "worship't Stocks and Stones" (the idols of primitive religion, with perhaps a glance at the Catholic propensity for statues of saints), the Waldensians were practicing the pure Christianity of early converts. After a plea with God to "forget not" their faithful past, the poem seems to swell as if impelled by an irresistible force into a vivid account of the massacre. Milton recreates the immediate scene of horror both visually and aurally by recalling the newsletter reports of how soldiers rolled "Mother with Infant down the Rocks" and how "their moans / The Vales redoubl'd to the Hills." In Stouppe's *Collection* Milton read that during the massacre "did resound nothing else but the Cries, Lamentations and fearful scriechings, made yet more pitiful by the multitude of those Eccho's, which are in those Mountains and Rocks."[41]

After surveying the desolate scene of the massacre as it might have looked at the time of the sonnet's composition, recalling the proud history of the "Saints," and reliving the slaughter itself, Milton moves from present sorrow and defeat to future joy and victory. Here he pleads for what he promises in *Paradise Lost*: that Providence, working through natural fertility, will "bring forth / Infinite goodness, grace and mercy" (1.217–18) from such heinous cruelty, as it did from the Fall. He entreats God to transform the "blood and ashes" of the martyrs into seeds of new generations who will shun the Catholic Whore of Babylon ("the *Babylonian* wo") with her "triple Tyrant" pope, choose the purified faith, and increase God's fold "a hunderd-fold." Paradoxically, the massacre may not be a defeat, but the genesis of a glorious triumph in the historical progress to the Kingdom of God.

Sonnet 18 also unfolds a panorama of space, and many critics have noted the falling and rising imagery in the sonnet: from scenes of bones scattered "on the Alpine mountains," to mothers and children "roll'd . . . down the Rocks," to echoes "redoubl'd to the Hills, and . . . To Heav'n."[42] While Milton images Providence as working in history through natural fertility, he represents echo as lifting the martyrs' "moans" out of history into the timeless realm of "Heav'n." Tradition had made echo a manifestation of the divine harmony present in nature, as in George Herbert's poem, "Heaven," where echo relays God's answers to the eager questioner. And Sonnet 18 may also intimate a transcendence immanent in nature, even at the moment of the massacre.

The ambiguity of the lines,

> Their moans
> The Vales redoubl'd to the Hills, and they
> To Heav'n,

has often been ignored. By its case, *they* must be a second subject for *redoubl'd*, but its antecedent may be either *Hills* or *Saints*. The grammar of the sentence and the meaning of *redoubl'd* ("reechoed," [*OED, v.* 1, 4]) suggest the reading: the valleys reechoed the Waldensians' moans to the hills, and the hills reechoed the moans to heaven. But the position of *they*—between *their moans* and *their martyr'd blood*, and after *Saints . . . them . . . their groanes . . . their antient Fold*—suggests that *they* may be the Waldensians. If so, two readings seem possible: (1) the valleys re-echoed the Waldensians' moans to the hills, and the Waldensians repeated (*OED, v.* 1, 3) their moans to heaven and (2) through the valleys' echoes of their dying moans, the Waldensians themselves were translated to heaven. Although the second reading is ungrammatical (*they* cannot be the object of *redoubl'd*), the apparent parallelism of "their moans / . . . to the Hills, and they / To Heav'n" makes this reading credible.[43] In their total effect, the lines epitomize the central question of the sonnet: Does nature merely reecho the martyrs' repeated cries to an aloof heaven, or does it work through echo to enact God's providence, uniting the shattered Waldensian community to a far greater one?

This tension permeates the sonnet. Despite Milton's invocation of a communal response to familiar language and his dependence on the providential agency of history and nature, his faith was hard won. The sonnet may end in a vision of triumph wrested from defeat, but it begins as a cry for vengeance. The harsh consonants (*t, r, d*) and sibilants of the opening quatrain ("slaughter'd Saints, whose bones . . . scatter'd . . . mountains cold . . . Fathers worship't Stocks and Stones / Forget not") stress Milton's rage and strident demand for meaning. He almost seems to assault the "Lord," incredulous that He would allow such faithful servants, "who kept *thy* truth so pure" and were "*thy* Sheep" (emphasis mine), to be butchered. Commanding God to "avenge" their deaths, "forget not" their history, and "record their groanes," he seems to fear that the event has no providential significance. Even the final hope is based not on God's promise, but on his own imperative that God "sow" the blood and ashes of regeneration. Although the sonnet insists that the massacre have meaning, it ends with only an assertion of Milton's faith. God is silent.

Allen Grossman, criticizing what he calls the failure of Sonnet 18 to face the complexity of historical experience, believes that the Waldensian massacre was for Milton "the test as to whether the revolution effected an instauration of the value of existence or an irreparable devaluation leading to hopeless vulnerability in the extended body of the Protestant community." The massacre forced Milton to ask if the attempt to establish a new, nonhierarchical order of free Christians had not severed the individual from the harmonious feudal community of state, church, and cosmos. In other words, if the Revolution and Reformation, by destroying the intermediaries of king and priest, brought man into direct relation with God, why would Providence have abandoned a pure community like the Waldensians? Grossman concludes that, because Milton could not reconcile the event with a providential view of history, he wrote Sonnet 18 to "reconstitute the 'false surmise' of a sacramental universe."[44]

The violence and desolation recreated in Sonnet 18 suggest that Milton keenly felt the martyrs' terror when no Lamb of God appeared in power to save the sheep from slaughter. But the intense experience of abandonment renders the vision of nature and history reuniting the community all the more compelling. That vision was not a "false surmise" for Milton. Throughout the sonnets, nature is part of the cosmic community. As "the jolly hours lead on propitious *May*" in the dance of the seasons (Sonnet 1), as "the Suns bright circle warms" all climes (Sonnet 8), and as each year "*Favonius* re-inspire[s] / The frozen earth" (Sonnet 20), the souls of the martyrs may have been "redoubl'd" with the echoes of their groans from the isolated valleys of the Piedmont to the heavenly community. And from their martyrdom may "grow" a new earthly community. Nature, of course, participates in the circle which reunites all creation with the "one Almighty . . . from whom / All things proceed, and up to him return" (*PL* 5.469–70). Despite the vulnerability and apparent fragmentation of the godly community, Milton kept his faith that God gathers His sheep into the fold.

In Sonnet 18 he juxtaposes two symbols of good and evil community structure found throughout his canon: the sheepfold, representing a voluntary and unified religious community, and the mitre, representing the constraint and disunity inherent in a pyramidal hierarchy. The contrast between the Waldensians' "antient Fold" and the triple-peaked mitre of the pope ("The triple

Tyrant") defines the sonnet's final vision: the forced conformity imposed by the pope's tyranny will split when the new generation flees his jurisdiction to join the larger fold of which the Waldensians were one small part.

In these five sonnets—"On the new forcers," to Fairfax, to Cromwell, to Vane, and "On the late Massacher in *Piemont*"—Milton outlines the proper and improper uses of the "Civill Sword." As physical might, it must subdue enemies, like the Scots and Royalists, who try to limit individual freedom. As legal authority, it must expel corrupt parliamentarians and churchmen. But it must never force consciences; when it tries, unspeakable brutality is the result. Although Milton wrote pamphlets and sonnets about public policy, he was not primarily a statesman. He was a poet who believed the roles of private citizen and public servant were complementary, and in Sonnets 7, 19, and 22, he reflects upon the vocation of the poet in service to the godly community.

7.
The "better guide":
Center and Circumference

As a whole, Milton's sonnet sequence suggests an ideal progress of man in a community from perfection of the individual, to earthly love and service, to attainment of the Kingdom of God. A few sonnets—like Sonnet 14, which describes Catharine Thomason's ascent into heaven, and Sonnet 20, which invites Lawrence to share an earthly feast while awaiting the heavenly one—glimpse the complete progress from center to circumference. Many more show the perils and obstacles on the journey. Detractors rail against domestic liberty (11, 12), Scottish and Royalist armies threaten the godly community from without while corruption and greed undermine it from within (15, 16), and "forcers of Conscience" not only come between the individual and God, but can shatter an entire community ("On the new forcers," 18). To Milton, the failure to understand freedom has caused these blocks: man either wants tyranny over others' souls or has not learned that whoever loves liberty "must first be wise and good" (11). In several angry sonnets, he chastizes those who impede the progress to the ideal community.

In sonnets where other obstacles block the progress, he does not respond with anger. The exigencies of the fallen world, where we suffer for the sins of our first parents, sometimes delay the journey because the fall engendered death and discord. Although the young Milton of Sonnet 1 longs to serve poetry and love, he hears the discord of "the rude Bird of Hate" instead of the harmony of the nightingale. Although the older Milton of Sonnet 23 longs to embrace his wife, death has separated them. These sonnets are poignant, not angry, because they lament things as they are, harsh realities not to be improved by effort. The poet can only wait while earthly union is denied, trusting in future success or the promise of heavenly communion beyond measure.

Three sonnets in particular (7, 19, 22) dramatize Milton's struggle with obstacles to service in his own calling. Although in two he begins by chafing that his willing service is prevented by external forces beyond his control and in the third he praises his success almost to the end, all three finally reveal that pride, not time's flight or blindness, has impeded his progress. An anxious, rebellious, or self-congratulating heart cannot serve, because it is concentrating on the creature not the creator. In these sonnets, when Milton penetrates to the true center beneath his pride and restores his dependence on the divine circumference, his "better guide," he discovers that not only is service now possible, it is already perfected and accepted.

Puritan minds were obsessed by service, believing that each man had a particular calling, which William Perkins defined as "a certaine kind of life, ordained and imposed on man by God, for the common good."[1] Repudiating the Thomistic emphasis on the penal quality of labor, Puritans preached that fulfillment of one's earthly duties was the only way to live acceptably to God. Thus service to the community in one's calling became an essential form of Christian worship. Since divine providence ordained a man's calling according to his abilities and society's needs, one must not complain about his assignment. Cheerfulness and success in performing assigned tasks were evidence of election because only the elect have the power to feel a joyous sanctification enabling them to augment God's glory by service. Good works were signs of election already granted, not the means of purchasing salvation. Ever alert to these signs, Puritans frequently examined their souls and actions to measure their progress.

As a youth Milton felt singled out for arduous but glorious service, and later, in *The Reason of Church Government*, he acknowledged submission to the rigors of his calling as God's spokesman: "But when God commands to take the trumpet and blow a dolorous or a jarring blast, it lies not in mans will what he shall say, or what he shall conceal" (*YM* 1:803). He must bow to the will of "that eternall Spirit who can enrich with all utterance and knowledge, and sends out his Seraphim with the hallow'd fire of his Altar to touch and purify the lips of whom he pleases" (*YM* 1:820–21). Before he knew exactly what form his vocation would take, he devoted his youth and early manhood to tireless self-preparation. He studied under private tutors, in public schools, in the university; he retired to solitary scholarship at Hammersmith and Horton and toured Italy to augment his formal education; he practiced his poetic talents in Latin elegies, Italian sonnets, and a wide variety of genres from pastoral to satire to ode to masque. Yet frequently he was troubled by fears about a lack of productivity, on the one hand, and an unreadiness to produce, on the other. At twenty-three, he lamented that "no bud or blossom" had appeared to prove his "inward ripenes," and at twenty-nine, he still felt poetically unripe: to write *Lycidas* he had to shatter the laurel leaves of poetic excellence "before the mellowing year." He composed Sonnet 7 during one of these periods of doubt.

But questions still linger about exactly when this period was. Sonnet 7 was written in December–January of either 1631–32, Milton's last year at Cambridge, when he decided against a church career, or 1632–33, his first year of retired study, when he considered what career to pursue instead.[2] In either case, the sonnet indicates anxiety about his vocation at a turning point in his life. Some time after its composition, he included it in a letter to a friend, perhaps his former tutor Thomas Young, which considers the biblical admonition "that the day . . . is at hand wherin Christ comᵭands all to Labour while there is light" (*YM* 1:319). The friend probably disapproved of Milton's "studious retirement" and decision against a church career, but Milton ends the apology with a joke: "Having thus tired you singly, I should deale worse wᵗʰ a whole congregation, & spoyle all the patience of a Parish" (*YM* 1:320–21). Despite the jest, his anxiety about his calling was sufficient to prompt a written justification of his actions as concordant with God's will. The delay, he says, is not sloth, but "a sacred reverence & religious advisement how best to undergoe not taking thought of beeing late so it give advantage to be more fit" (*YM* 1:320). Never in the letter or sonnet does he mention any hope to be a poet. In both, his concern is less what his calling will be or what others may think of his delay, than that his waiting be in tune with God's will.

But as the sonnet opens, everything is out of tune. The speaker has lost track of his life and control of his destiny. Before he knew it, the "suttle theef," Time, insidiously stole his youth, and his days still "flie" away in a headlong rush before he can put them to use. Nor does Providence seem in control. The agents of divine concord, time and nature, produce only discord: one is a thief and brings the seasons "late," while the other is impotent to ripen "bud or blossom" when spring finally arrives. This discord is evident externally and internally in the speaker's life. Milton seemed younger than he was, and his external appearance at twenty-three "might deceive the truth" of his near manhood.[3] Internally, jealousy disrupts his belief in himself. In contrast to his slow start, others seem more in harmony with time and nature, which have brought their "inward ripenes" to bloom. Several poets and friends have been suggested as the originals for the "more timely-happy spirits," but who they were matters less than how the speaker perceives them.[4] They seem to enjoy time's steadier government of their lives (to be happy more on time) and to be more fortunate (*happy* = "having good hap") in the gifts of time than he. This thought has the potential to produce greater internal discord than jealousy. Time and nature, he hints in the pun on *happy*, may be subject to fortune, fickle and unjust, not divine providence, steady and just. Giving vent to his anxiety for eight lines, the frustrated youth has doubted, though almost imperceptibly, God's omnipotence.

Two forms of improper measurement have caused this discord. The speaker has counted his years ("my three and twentith yeer") and deeds ("no bud or blossom") exactly, finding them disproportionate. Also, he has measured himself, and the recipient of the letter has probably measured him, by the achievements of others. Although self-examination was fundamental to Milton's religion, such scorekeeping produces anxiety and jealousy because it assumes that, with sufficient effort, man can measure up. But finite and sinful, he always falls short of perfection, God's goal for all men. The speaker is in a quandary until he realizes that man cannot reckon God's will by counting and comparing. Neither the number of years and deeds nor one's relation to others' achievements measures a man's place in God's providence.

By not only describing but also reflecting the proper measurement of life in its cadences, the sestet restores the harmony lacking in the octave. To exorcise earthly measurement, the volta

checks the headlong rush of time with one-syllable words and
coordinate syntax, regularizes the halting rhythm of life's fitful
progress with an insistent beat, and mocks the petty account-
keeping of the octave with deliberate echoes: "Yet be it léss or
móre, or sóon or slów." Each heavily accented word recalls one of
the octave's anxious phrases: "ripenes doth much *less* appear,"
"*more* timely-happy spirits," "how *soon* hath Time," "my *late*
spring" (emphases mine). The remainder of the sestet contrasts
man's tally with God's promise: "It ["inward ripenes"] shall be
still in strictest measure eev'n." The perfect iambic pentameter of
the line mirrors the rhythm and harmony by which God justly
governs his universe (in even "measure"), ripening all things in
time with an infinity of beings in the stately dance of the cosmos
(another kind of even "measure"). Since no comma follows "eev'n"
in the manuscript, the line may also mean that the ripening will
proceed "in strictest measure eev'n / To" (in perfect degree equal
to) whatever place Milton is assigned in the beauteous pattern of
the whole dance. Where the discord of the octave resulted from
improper human measurement, the harmony of the sestet proceeds
from faith in God, the supreme artist who measures both action
and inaction in accordance with his plan.

Time once seemed a winged thief who steals precious years from
the youth; now it is a guide who "leads" him to assured fulfillment.
The speaker, who in the octave had lost track of his life and control
of his destiny, still does not know exactly where he is going in the
sestet, nor is he now master of his fate. The change the volta
initiates is so radical that the questions, Where? How much? and
When? become irrelevant. Mere surrender to "the will of Heav'n"
dispels the anxiety and jealousy rooted in pride, the speaker's
reliance on his achievements to justify his life.

Surrender of his will does not release man from the duty to serve,
but work can be a blessing, not a burden or a source of anxiety.
Because, to Milton, God created a universe where man is free to
follow or reject God's will, man can participate in the creation.
Joining with God as an artist of his own life, he can choose to
harmonize his deeds, not with earthly tallies or comparisons to his
peers, but with God's measure. In *An Apology for Smectymnuus*,
Milton asserts man's ability to make his life a work of art: "He who

would not be frustrate of his hope to write well hereafter in laudable things, ought him selfe to bee a true Poem, that is, a composition, and patterne of the best and honourablest things; not presuming to sing high praises of heroick men, or famous Cities, unlesse he have in himselfe the experience and the practice of all that which is praise-worthy" (*YM* 1:890). But how can sinful man create art acceptable to the divine artist? Only through Grace. And Milton ends Sonnet 7 with both an acknowledgment of his own responsibility and the hope of Grace: "All is, if I have grace to use it so, / As ever in my great task-Masters eye."

Most commentators agree that these lines refer to God's providence and man's responsibility, but many disagree about the precise meaning of the elliptical syntax. Suggested paraphrases include "All [that matters is]: whether I have grace to use it so, as ever [conscious of being] in my great Task master's [enjoining] eye" (Woodhouse): "All that matters is whether I have grace to use my ripeness in accordance with the will of God as one ever in His sight" (Svendsen); "All time is, if I have grace to use it so, as eternity in God's sight" (Dorian); "All my prospects, if I have grace to use my inward ripeness so, are still in favor with God" (my paraphrase of Fiske's view).[5] Unfortunately, these paraphrases fail Ockham's razor. Those by Woodhouse and Svendsen require the insertion after "is" of a colon, which does not appear in the Trinity Manuscript or either the 1645 or 1673 editions, and the substitution of a less common meaning for *if* ("whether") in an ordinary conditional phrase, "if I have grace." Dorian reads the adverb *ever* as an uncommon substantive, "eternity," when the phrase *as ever* ("still, as always") is common. And Fiske substitutes the biblical meaning, "in God's favor," for "in my great task-Masters eye"—a plausible but partial reading that slights the emphasis of the previous four lines on God's governance, not his favor.

In addition to elliptical syntax, two other problems obscure the meaning: the antecedent of *all* is unclear, and the *if* clause seems to make God's omniscience contingent on man's use of Grace. But if we read *all* as referring to the topic of the entire sestet—the eventual appearance of "inward ripenes" in deeds— then the *if* clause makes the speaker's deeds dependent on his use

of Grace, and the final lines become consistent with standard
Puritan theology. This reading suggests the paraphrase: "All that I
do, if I have grace to employ my inward ripeness thus, is done as
ever conscious of being in God's sight and having God's guidance."
This ending reasserts the central concern of sonnet and letter alike:
that Milton believes his action and inaction are in obedience to
God's will—as he says, "according to the praecept of my conscience, wch I firmly trust is not wthout god" (*YM* 1:319).

With Grace, man can harmonize his life with God's "measure,"
making his life a work of art. Still, he must "use" his "inward
ripenes," all the time knowing that he is watched by a "great task-
Masters eye." Sustaining this awareness, a difficult "task" in itself,
requires human grace, not the fretful anxiety and jealousy of the
octave. He must patiently await ripeness, trusting "the will of
Heav'n," despite the visible success of peers and the open disap-
proval of family and friends. Indeed, such a strenuous labor
performed with grace may itself be a sign of Grace. Milton devotes
a large part of his letter to proving that what appears to be "tardie
moving" has, in reality, required great effort. In choosing
"studious retirement," he has "held out . . . Long against so strong
opposition on the other side of every kind." Despite the temptations
of "Youth & Vanitie . . . Gaine, pride, & ambition"; "the desire of
house & family of his owne"; and "a desire of honour & repute, &
immortall fame" (*YM* 1:319-20)—he has awaited God's "advisement how best to undergoe." For him, as for the Son in
Paradise Regained who also resists worldly allurements, waiting is
the hardest "task" of all. At the end of Sonnet 7, the speaker hopes
Grace will enable him to perform whatever service his taskmaster
requires, but human grace will help him live as ever conscious of
being in the eyes of God, not peers or critical friends. By such
graceful living, man can participate in God's Graceful providence
to make his life part of the divine art.

Although the volta seems to shift the sonnet's mood abruptly
from anxiety to faith, and its subject from flight and theft to even
measurement, the change has been previewed. Despite worry over
time's headlong rush, the octave comprises regular, end-stopped,
iambic pentameter lines. A possible pun on *career* (a free and swift
course or a life's work) suggests that, although his "hasting dayes

flie on" without visible results, they are "full" of preparations for his "career." So too, the reference to his deceptive "semblance" anticipates the shift: just as he has nearly reached manhood even though his appearance is youthful, he may have already attained "inward ripenes" even if it has not yet appeared in deeds. These almost imperceptible hints in the octave become a complete transformation of attitude in the sestet.

A. S. P. Woodhouse finds in Sonnet 7 the first instance of this pattern which becomes characteristic of Milton's mature poetry: "the integral progression which carries the poet from one position or point of view at the beginning of the poem to another radically different at the end. The initial point of view is one that springs from Milton's extra-aesthetic experience, and it is transformed in the aesthetic experience which is the poem."[6] A conflict in his life is resolved "by the imposition of aesthetic pattern," producing in Sonnet 7 an experience that is "at once religious and aesthetic."[7] This striking insight may be extended to explain another way Milton conceived man's participation in God's art. In the process of writing Sonnet 7, he submitted his frustrations and fears to aesthetic discipline. As a result, the raw materials of life's muddle were transformed into a sonnet. The octave allows anxiety to spend its destructive energy, but because at the volta the form requires a shift, anxiety is contained. It cannot ultimately dominate the poem, and the new perspective of the sestet sees a pattern beneath the chaos—like the sonnet form that channels his emotions. Forming his life into art by submitting experience to its discipline, young Milton has rediscovered the place of his life in God's art. While trying to bring grace out of anxiety, he has restored his dependence on Grace.

At the end of Sonnet 7, his service is no longer blocked. In fact, by penetrating to the center to dispel fear and jealousy, he has found himself already at the circumference in God's presence. All his actions, even the seemingly inactive task of waiting, are service done before the eye of the taskmaster who commanded and approves them.

Long after the period of doubt which produced Sonnet 7, after Milton had acknowledged his vocation as poet and prophet to the new community, his "inward ripenes" had still produced no great poetic fruit, and the obstacles to performing the service to which he felt called seemed insurmountable because "that one Talent" he had spent his life nurturing was "lodg'd with [him] useless." The parable of the talent (Matt. 25:14–30) haunted Milton as it did many Puritans. In the letter containing Sonnet 7, he anticipates the friend's arguments by contrasting himself to the servant who was cast into outer darkness for hiding his one talent instead of investing it. By delaying, Milton is not hiding his talent, but prudently searching for the best investment. In *The Reason of Church Government*, he seems to feel more oppressed by the responsibilities accompanying God's gifts:

> Certain it is that he who hath obtain'd in more then the scantest measure to know any thing distinctly of God, and of his true worship, and what is infallibly good and happy in the state of mans life, what in it selfe evil and miserable, though vulgarly not so esteem'd, he that hath obtain'd to know this, the only high valuable wisdom indeed, remembring also that God even to a strictnesse requires the improvment of these his entrusted gifts, cannot but sustain a sorer burden of mind, and more pressing then any supportable toil, or waight, which the body can labour under; how and in what manner he shall dispose and employ those summes of knowledge and illumination, which God hath sent him into this world to trade with. [YM 1:801]

Then in Sonnet 19, when he thinks his talent hidden forever despite his eagerness to use it, he is plunged into such confusion and rebellion that he seems already cast into "outer darkness" with the slothful servant amidst "weeping and gnashing of teeth" (Matt. 25:30).

What has brought Milton to this impasse is blindness in the middle of life. After delays for "studious retirement" and preparation, then active duty on the front lines of pamphlet warfare, he now seems barred from answering the call to "leave something so written to aftertimes, as they should not willingly let it die" (RCG, YM 1:810). His "Talent"—in general, the entrusted gifts of God, and more specifically, his ability to speak for God,

particularly in poetry—seems "useless." Although the precise
dating of Sonnet 19 is controversial (late 1651–early 1652, when
Milton's blindness became complete, or 1655, the only possible
date if the sonnets were published in approximately chronological
order), most critics agree that Milton's anguish over his blindness
inspired it.[8] But, like the autobiographical sonnets on his twenty-
third year and his deceased wife, Sonnet 19 raises questions and
achieves a resolution which transcend biography.

One puzzling biographical problem has frequently sidetracked
criticism: the precise meaning of "my light is spent, / Ere half my
days, in this dark world and wide." Realizing that, at either forty-
four or forty-seven (depending on which date is preferred), Milton
would have exceeded thirty-five, half his biblical three score years
and ten, critics have offered several theories to explain "half my
days": half of his working life, his father's age at death (84), or the
life-span found in popular belief and mentioned in Plato and Isaiah
(100).[9] But for understanding the sonnet, Milton's exact age matters
less than his feeling of paralysis at the midpoint of life, the time
when his studious youth and active manhood should bear fruit. As
Dixon Fiske has shown, the middle of life, from twenty-five to
forty-five, was traditionally considered a turning point; and, like
Dante, "nel mezzo del cammin di nostra vita" (*Inferno* 1.1),
Milton, "ere half my days," has lost his way in the dark.[10] At first
the causes of the crisis seem different for the two poets. While
Dante has sinned, entangling himself in a dark wood of error,
Milton attributes his loss of light to blindness. But soon, despite
physical blindness, the speaker clearly sees that he has become no
less entangled than Dante in errors which have led him to the brink
of spiritual blindness. Indeed, the loss of eyesight is only the
prologue to a drama of man at the crossroads, turning away from
the darkness of pride toward the light of humble faith.

Although the speaker intends to depict his pitiable physical
condition in images of darkness ("light is spent . . . dark world and
wide . . . death to hide . . . light deny'd"), each word draws him
deeper into the darkness of confusion and error. Only his physical,
the least significant, light is spent; since the coming of "the true
Light, which lighteth every man that cometh into the world" (John

1:9), the world is no longer wholly dark; to consider his poetic abilities his sole "Talent," and one so valuable that God will punish its concealment with his most rigorous sentence, smacks of pride; and finally, his questioning the source of all light for denying him enough light to serve reveals how clouded his vision has become. As in Sonnet 7, his anxiety again makes him misconstrue godly measurement: he worries about counting ("half my days . . . one Talent") and thinks like a harried debtor ("spent . . . useless [with a pun on *use* = "usury"] . . . My true account"). In his fear and frustration, he sees the creator and savior of mankind as a chiding, account-demanding creditor.

Moreover, he is deluded about his own attitude, claiming to be not only blameless, but praiseworthy, with a "Soul more bent / To serve." The inescapable conclusion is that God is cruel and unjust. From the beginning of the meditation on his plight, "When I consider . . . ," the rehearsal of unjust suffering swells in subordinate clauses of internal considerations which only lead to greater frustration.[11] His self-pity runs away with his reason, plunging him so far into the darkness of error that he blurts out, not merely a complaint, but blasphemy: "Doth God exact day-labour, light deny'd?" Here at the center he finds the true source of his eagerness to serve and his anger at being frustrated: pride in exalting his hopes to perform glorious service above God's decree for his life. Finally confronted with the yawning abyss to which the pseudoreason and false self-knowledge caused by pride have led him, he retreats from the edge just in time with the qualification, "I fondly ask." As he falls to the darkest recess of the Inferno within his heart, patience brings the light of true reason to dispel his folly.

Although patience forestalls the prideful "murmur," the speaker has thought it and the reader has read it. Patience must now lead both through an almost purgatorial climb out of the Inferno of pride. By assuaging his anger and frustration, patience enables reason to correct the speaker's misconceptions about God. Where the octave ends by describing God as an Egyptian taskmaster who commands men to make bricks without straw, the sestet begins by stating that God has given man everything, including the ability to offer Him "man's work" which He does not need. Similarly, the misapplication of the parable of the talent is exposed. The over-valuation of self that interpreted the "one Talent which is death to hide" as his poetic talent alone is punctured by the reminder that submission to God's will is a sufficient investment of one's talent, whether it yields deeds or not: "Who best / Bear his milde yoak, they serve him best." Reason also corrects the speaker's misunderstanding of godly measurement. Not the chiding, account-demanding creditor described in the octave, the God of the sestet is a king who is beyond "need," favors man with "gifts," is served by countless "Thousands," and does not measure service by the number of deeds or the amount of energy expended.[12] Somewhat like Dante led by Virgil through Inferno and Purgatory, Milton has glimpsed "the Hell within him" (*PL* 4.20) and been led upward by patience and rectified reason. Reconsidering his calling, he has learned that to suffer and wait are acceptable service. The words he later wrote for the Son apply to his situation in Sonnet 19: "Who best / Can suffer, best can do" (*PR* 3.194–95).

But the sonnet does not end with the rather cold comfort of reason. After patience uses reason to dispel the danger of spiritual blindness, it leads the speaker, despite physical blindness, to a radiant vision of heaven. Trapped in the darkness of error and pride in the octave, he finds himself in the final tercet, like Dante, in Paradise viewing the heavenly throne from which legions of messenger angels "post o'er Land and Ocean" and before which still more angels "stand and waite" worshipping the divine light. H. F. Robins first suggested that the last line alludes to the two kinds of acceptable service performed by messenger and con-templative angels, but other critics have disagreed, claiming that it contrasts post angels to men on earth, not seraphim before God's throne.[13] The dispute is not inconsequential, because the speaker's final attitude (resignation, expectation, or exaltation) depends partly on its outcome. According to Robins, the comparison to seraphim exalts Milton from blindness to prophetic vision and the "Celestial Light" (*PL* 3.51–52) which eventually sparked his poetic "Talent" to create the promised masterwork.

But Milton did not adhere in *Paradise Lost* to the hierarchy of angelic orders established by the pseudo-Dionysius.[14] Blurring the distinctions between contemplative (seraphim, cherubim, thrones, and dominations) and messenger orders (virtues, powers, principalities, archangels, and angels), he described Uriel as both an "Arch-Angel" and

> one of the sev'n
> Who in God's presence, nearest to his Throne
> Stand ready at command, and are his Eyes
> That run through all the Heav'ns, or down to th' Earth
> Bear his swift errands over moist and dry,
> O'er Sea and Land.
>   [3.648–53]

Although Milton did not assign angelic duties exclusively by hierarchical degree, he differentiated two equally important types of service: to "bear his swift errands . . . / O'er Sea and Land" and to "stand ready at command." Thus Sonnet 19, which uses such similar language to distinguish angels who "post o'er Land and Ocean" from others who "only stand and waite," probably contrasts not two kinds of angels, but two kinds of angelic service. In this case the adverb *only* does not signify that the waiting angels do nothing else, but that they *merely* stand and wait. Although apparently inactive, their service of readiness is as acceptable as performance.

The purpose of the final allusion is to compare the blind, earth-bound speaker, who has learned to await patiently whatever God wills, to angels ranged before the divine effulgence, who serve God in the same manner. The comparison emphasizes not the immediate illumination of contemplation, as Robins claimed, but God's approval of the speaker's humble and apparently inactive service. Thus the sonnet ends in neither of two easy extremes: resignation because blindness has frustrated Milton's high hopes for service or exaltation because divine illumination will inspire a masterwork.[15] The speaker must "stand and waite" like the Son in *Paradise Regained*—seeming to do nothing now, but ready to do all when God commands. Such surrender of the will, which constitutes for Milton the most difficult service, produces an explosive tension of potential activity compressed into stillness.

The richness of the words *stand and waite* helps communicate the paradox of kinetic stasis that makes Sonnet 19 shimmer with tensile strength. Usually connoting passivity, these verbs can also signify active service. Paul exhorted the Ephesians "to stand against the wiles of the devil" (Eph. 6:11), and the psalmist advised, "Wait on the Lord" (Ps. 27:14). Such standing against evil requires strenuous effort, and awaiting the fullness of God's time is equivalent to waiting on God as a servant.[16] Like the young lover of Sonnet 1, the young poet of Sonnet 7, and the Son of *Paradise Regained*, Milton neither resigns himself to failure nor exults in future glory. The end of Sonnet 19 captures a dynamic poise between calm assurance that waiting is acceptable service and eager expectation of a call to more active work. At this point of balance, center meets circumference, and all obstacles to service—frustration, anxiety, anger, physical and the threat of spiritual blindness—are transcended.

In Sonnet 19, as in Sonnet 7, aesthetic pattern transforms the raw material of biography into the harmony of art. The opening line, "When I consider . . . ," initiates a mental journey. But unlike Henry Vane or Catharine Thomason, who ascend steadily to a heavenly reward for service, the speaker of Sonnet 19 descends until the volta checks his fall. No sooner do the considerations begin than pride takes over, muttering first person pronouns each of which drags the speaker deeper into the dark cave of self: "I consider . . . my light . . . my days . . . with me useless . . . my Soul . . . my Maker . . . My true account . . . I fondly ask." But the egotism is confined to seven and one-half lines. Not one first person pronoun trespasses the barrier between octave and sestet to taint the new theocentric vision with the old egocentric blindness: "God doth not need . . . his own gifts . . . his milde yoak . . . serve him . . . his State . . . his bidding."[17] In fact, because he gives full rein to pride, the speaker recognizes the blasphemous potential of his "murmur" early enough to "prevent" its reaching the traditional eight-line limit of an octave—just as prevenient Grace prevents the hardening of a rebel's heart. The early volta in the middle of line eight halts his fall, and the sestet lifts him beyond egotism, isolation, and blindness in a "dark world and wide" to place him among ministering angels in a vast, but cherished cosmos.

Just as in Sonnet 7, the radical transformation at the volta is previewed. As the rebellious speaker rushes over the words "my

Maker" and "my true account," he fails to recognize their import, which could stifle his muttering altogether. Man's "Maker" has given him everything, including the free will to choose obedience or rebellion. The only "true account" of service he can present (no matter that he has a "Soul more bent / To serve" with the "Talent" *he* thinks most important) is willing obedience to God's decrees. But this is exactly what the speaker is not doing at the moment he utters these words. In its torrent of error, the rebellious voice has exposed both the speaker's pride and the premises of his salvation. The patient voice merely amplifies and explains: because God is the "Maker," He "doth not need / Either man's work or his own gifts"; bearing "his milde yoak" is the best service and the only "true account." The rebellion permitted within the confines of the octave has activated reason, which returns faith to the sestet.

In Sonnet 7, Milton had only begun to realize the power of aesthetic form to calm passions and restore reason and faith. While the early sonnet vents anxiety and jealousy caused by self-doubt, Sonnet 19 doubts God himself. While the youth ends Sonnet 7 with an awareness of God's watchful eye on his deeds, the mature man ends Sonnet 19 with a dazzling vision of service in the divine presence. Perhaps, because Sonnet 19 journeys to the lowest ring of the hell within, it soars to the throne of God; because Milton trusted sonnet form to contain his anguish at the center, it brought him closer to the circumference. If so, Sonnet 19 illustrates Milton's meaning when he compares his chosen vocation, poetry, to his foresaken vocation, "the office of a pulpit," in their power "to allay the perturbations of the mind, and set the affections in right tune" (*RCG, YM* 1:816–17). As a poet, he used the grace of art to restore the inner harmony which reflects the Grace of God.

But the pressing needs of the new community had superseded the call to poetry, commanding Milton's services for almost twenty years. Still, he believed that God had called him to immediate service in prose treatises, and he postponed his poetic service indefinitely. Unlike Sonnets 7 and 19, which dramatize his struggles to overcome obstacles to service, Sonnet 22 seems to rejoice in the completed service of defending England before an international audience in memorable prose. As Latin secretary, Milton was commissioned by the Council of State in 1650 to answer

Salmasius's condemnation of the regicide, *Defensio Regia*. Despite doctors' warnings that, having nearly lost the sight of one eye, he would surely lose both if he undertook the task, he accepted the commission, publishing *Pro Populo Anglicano Defensio* in 1651. As predicted, he became completely blind, according to visitors' reports, in late 1651 or early 1652. Sonnet 22 surveys this period from the vantage of three years without the frustration or anger of his first blindness sonnet; indeed, he boasts of his service "in libertyes defence, my noble task."[18]

Almost universally, critics have contrasted this sonnet, as a statement of Milton's public attitude toward blindness, to Sonnet 19, the record of his private battle with despair. To support this view, they compare Sonnet 22 to his righteous rebuttal in *A Second Defense* of the gloating accusations that his blindness was God's swift judgment on the defender of regicide:

> Then let those who slander the judgments of God cease to speak evil and invent empty tales about me. Let them be sure that I feel neither regret nor shame for my lot, that I stand unmoved and steady in my resolution, that I neither discern nor endure the anger of God, that in fact I know and recognize in the most momentous affairs his fatherly mercy and kindness towards me, and especially in this fact, that with his consolation strengthening my spirit I bow to his divine will, dwelling more often on what he has bestowed on me than on what he has denied. Finally, let them rest assured that I would not exchange the consciousness of my achievement for any deed of theirs, be it ever so righteous, nor would I be deprived of the recollection of my deeds, ever a source of gratitude and repose.
>
> Finally, as to my blindness, I would rather have mine, if it be necessary, than either theirs, More, or yours. Your blindness, deeply implanted in the inmost faculties, obscures the mind, so that you may see nothing whole or real. Mine, which you make a reproach, merely deprives things of color and superficial appearance. What is true and essential in them is not lost to my intellectual vision. [*YM* 4(1):589]

The sonnet also repeats the following denial from *A Second Defense* of libels about his disfigurement: his eyes "have as much the appearance of being uninjured, and are as clear and bright, without a cloud, as the eyes of men who see most keenly" (*YM* 4[1]:583). In contrast to Sonnet 19, Milton refuses in Sonnet 22 to

"argue ... Against heavns hand or will" by asking such im-
pertinent questions as "Doth God exact day-labour, light deny'd?"
Nor has he lost, he claims, "heart [courage] or hope" that he can
continue to serve. This time when he considers his blindness, he sees
only a patriotic sacrifice, which has won him international fame.
While the considerations of Sonnet 19 led to frustration, anxiety,
and anger, "this thought" of sacrifice and fame leaves the speaker
of Sonnet 22 "Content" that he has fulfilled God's commands to
work while there is light and invest his talent.

I quarrel with this reading. Such boasting and self-vindication
may be justified, even necessary, when Milton is addressing an
international audience as the defender of England, his situation in
A Second Defense. Accusations about his disfigurement and God's
righteous punishment were really attacks on the justice of
England's cause and demanded forceful denial. But in Sonnet 22
Milton's audience is not "the entire assembly and council of all the
most influential men, cities, and nations everywhere" (*Def 2, YM*
4[1]:554). It is Cyriack Skinner, his personal "Friend" and former
student to whom he had recently addressed a jocular invitation to
mirth full of puns and academic jokes which laugh at men who
take themselves and their work too seriously.[19] In Sonnet 21 the
proper measurement of life requires accepting the ordinances of
"mild Heav'n" and not expecting "solid good" either from the law
(wrenched by lawyers), dedicated study (pursued to excess by
Archimedes), or international diplomacy (confused by the in-
scrutable intentions of Mazarin). Since Milton expected Cyriack to
learn this lesson, he probably intended his friend to question the
wisdom of his boast in Sonnet 22 to have lost his eyes

> overply'd
> In libertyes defence, my noble task,
> Of which all *Europe* talks from side to side.

Either the traditional reading of these lines is inadequate, or, in a
rare moral contradiction, Milton boasts in Sonnet 22 of what he
mocks in the immediately preceding sonnet: overwork, costly
study, and concern for the disposition of European powers.

Instead of proclaiming his contentment, as it seems to do, Sonnet
22 actually dramatizes his search for the meaning of his blindness.

In a futile attempt to understand it in terms of his self-image, he is tempted, as he was in Sonnet 19, by vanity, self-pity, self-deception, pride, and finally complete self-reliance—each temptation leading to the next until he is rescued from spiritual blindness at the last minute.

Before he finishes announcing the subject, his three years of blindness, he anxiously interrupts to assure himself alone, not Cyriack who can plainly see, that he is not disfigured. But this vain assurance provides little comfort, only reminding him of the discrepancy between appearance and reality. From the perspective of others' "outward view," his eyes may be "clear"; from his inward view, they are "bereft of light." Since the opening line, he has tried to distance himself from blindness by referring to his eyes in the third person ("these eys . . . thir seeing . . . thir idle orbs"), as separate beings who have merely "forgot" their wonted function.[20] Still, he seems all too aware of their darkness, describing it three times in succession: "[1] Bereft of light [2] thir seeing have forgot, / [3] Nor to thir idle orbs doth sight appear." A note of self-pity may intrude as he allows a list of what he can no longer see to spill over its expected conclusion at the end-stopped line: "Sun or Moon or Starre throughout the year, / Or man or woman." In fact, the redundant references to sightlessness and the catalogue of what he has lost extend the description of his pitiable plight one and a half lines beyond the limits of a quatrain.

Catching himself in midline with "yet," he refuses to let self-pity dominate the octave (and his thoughts). Although he cheers himself by rejecting rebellion and despair, Milton, as well as readers of Sonnet 19, knew that he was tempted by both. Murmuring about God's exacting "day-labour, light deny'd" constitutes arguing "against heavns hand or will," and fearing that his talent is "Lodg'd with [him] useless" is close to losing both "heart" and "hope." The mere mention that he neither argues with God nor abandons hope shows that these actions have crossed his mind, and such unsolicited denials inevitably sound defensive. To convince Cyriack (and perhaps himself) of his courage and hope, he claims to "bear vp and steer / Right onward" despite misfortune. But the entire second quatrain rings false. The commonplace phrase, *bate a jot*;[21] the alliterative cliché, *heart or hope*; and the trite nautical metaphor of putting up the helm and steering to the wind (*OED*: "bear up," *v.* 37) combine with the unsolicited denials to suggest that the speaker protests too much. In trying to counter self-pity, he may have fallen into another temptation: to self-deception. Retreating into a public role of unremitting patience, courage, and hope, he seems to deny that these virtues have been tempered in actual rebellion, fear, and despair.

In five lines of the sestet he finds the source of his strength in himself: the knowledge that he sacrificed his sight to write a defense of liberty which brought him worldly fame. Boasting about his "noble task" and implying that he can be justified by works alone, he confronts the temptation to pride, the error patience corrects first in Sonnet 19: "God doth not need / Either man's work or his own gifts." Indeed, self-deception and pride have fed one another. Both Milton and Cyriack knew that, although the confutation of Salmasius was widely read throughout Europe, the talking "from side to side" included as much criticism, indignation, and horror as praise.[22] Besides, if the world is merely a "vain mask" (a masquerade of vanity), as he claims immediately after his boast, what importance could worldly fame (more accurately, notoriety) possibly have? Self-deception and pride can breed falsifications, contradictions, and a self-reliance perilously close to Satan's when he proclaims himself "self-begot, self-rais'd" (*PL* 5.860).

The speaker's descent from temptations to vanity, self-pity, self-deception, pride, and absolute self-reliance has brought him once more to the brink of sin. Although in almost sanctimonious hauteur he believes himself contemptuous of "the worlds vain mask," the penultimate line is ambiguous. The prideful "thought" of his accomplishments might lead him through the "vain" (both conceited and futile) masquerade of the world—not immune to vanity and hypocrisy, as he believes, but one of the masked (both deceptive and blinded) participants. Because the mask of self-deception has masked (obstructed) his inner vision, pride threatens to harden his heart, making him "Content though [spiritually] blind" to the true source of his works. Like Sonnet 19, Sonnet 22 confronts the danger of spiritual, as well as the hardship of physical blindness.

At the last minute, with only five words instead of seven lines to spare, the speaker recoils from the brink. Realizing with what sin he proposes to rest "Content" and how "blind" it will make him, he appends a conditional phrase that negates his prideful "thought": "had I no better guide." As in Sonnet 6 where the final admission of love's power undercuts twelve lines of boasting, this masterful understatement rejects the vanity, self-pity, self-deception, and pride lurking in the previous thirteen and a half lines. Despite physical blindness, the speaker regains his inner vision by realizing that all works are guided by God's providence and all men are blind without God's guidance. "Of course, he has a better guide," is the reader response expected from the final conditional phrase. But Milton also expected the reader to know that God guides to salvation only those

> who renounce
> Thir own both righteous and unrighteous deeds,
> And live in [Christ] transplanted, and from [him]
> Receive new life.
> [*PL* 3.291–94]

Because God demands surrender of the total self, not merely a tribute of good works, Milton just slips under the wire of salvation at the end of Sonnet 22. In a grim paradox, self-reliance has tempted him toward a pit so dark that he could never have rescued himself. Yet, by acknowledging his dependence on the guide who permitted him to serve the community in the first place, he escapes the blindness and pride of justification by works alone.

As in Sonnet 19, the speaker of Sonnet 22 only sees light after he has glimpsed a dark inner hell—in the blasphemous accusation, "light deny'd," and the prideful boast, "Content though blind." But in each case the sin is only potential even as it is uttered: in Sonnet 19, he knows his question is "fondly" asked at the moment he asks it, and in Sonnet 22, his prideful thought "might" or might not become his guide. In both, Milton dramatizes how man must look inward and clearly see where his sinful thoughts are leading him before he can choose goodness. As an opponent of censorship and supporter of free conscience, he knew that

> Good and evil . . . in the field of this World grow up together almost inseparably; and the knowledge of good is so involv'd and interwoven with the knowledge of evill, and in so many cunning resemblances hardly to be discern'd, that those confused seeds which were impos'd on *Psyche* as an incessant labour to cull out, and sort asunder, were not more intermixt. It was from out the rinde of one apple tasted, that the knowledge of good and evil as two twins cleaving together leapt forth into the World. And perhaps this is that doom which *Adam* fell into of knowing good and evill, that is to say of knowing good by evill. [*Areop*, YM 2:514]

One of Adam's sons, the speaker of Sonnet 22 (also 19 and, to some degree, 7) comes to know good by first releasing his private thoughts in tentative syntax within the confines of sonnet form, then listening to what the thoughts reveal about his motives, and finally detecting the evil "involv'd and interwoven" in them. Within the safety of form, he can purge evil, restore good, and in the end bring an "upright heart and pure" before his "better guide."

The established critical view of Sonnet 22 as the expression of Milton's public attitude toward blindness reduces a poem to a static pronouncement. Whether in public or private, to convey the meaning of his blindness, he had to dramatize a progress from egocentricity to dependence on God (and other guides like Cyriack, who no doubt physically led him after his blindness). To deny anxiety, fear, frustration, rebellion, vanity, self-pity, self-deception, and pride would be, for Milton, to ignore the only way in a fallen world to know goodness: by knowing evil. In his second sonnet on his blindness, no less than his first, he proves dynamically that, although pride may stubbornly block the way, the journey from hellish center to divine circumference can be completed. But the whole journey, not just the point of embarkation or the final destination, is his attitude.

8.
The "well measur'd" Sonnet: Milton's Use of Sonnet Form

As Milton experimented with sequence content by celebrating an ideal community, he also experimented with sonnet form. Neither so ornate and mellifluous as the Elizabethan, so eccentric and rough as the metaphysical, nor so simple and clear as the neoclassical, Milton's style introduced several innovative techniques to English sonnet writing. His primary models were not the Petrarchists of either England or Italy; in fact, Parker can find no evidence that he had read any English sonnets before writing "O Nightingale."[1] Instead, as Prince has demonstrated in detail, he chose to imitate the poetic heirs of Pietro Bembo: Giovanni della Casa, whose sonnets are included in his earliest known book purchase, and Torquato Tasso, whose patron he visited in Italy.

From Bembo and his followers, Milton learned to combine "formality and intimacy" in his tone, to name ceremoniously the person to whom the sonnet is addressed in the opening line, to continue the apostrophe with relative clauses throughout the octave, and to strive for "a formal equivalent of spontaneous speech." From della Casa and Tasso, specifically, he learned *asprezza*, or a pleasing roughness, caused by complex and often surprising word order; rhythmic innovations; and *enjambment*, which ignores Petrarch's end-stopped lines and precise octave / sestet division.[2]

Although Milton's primary models were these sixteenth-century Italian poets and although he used the Italian rhyme scheme exclusively, some of his later sonnets incorporate elements of the Elizabethan form as well. Whereas in the Italian pattern, the asymmetrical, bipartite division into octave and sestet generally presents a problem and resolution, in the Elizabethan, the three quatrains and a couplet most often develop a theme in three stages and then clinch it in an epigrammatic conclusion—sometimes witty or paradoxical, sometimes grave or moral. Occasionally, Milton's sonnets evince a tripartite structure in content, if not in rhyme, and the surprising, poignant, witty, and aphoristic endings to several sonnets may owe some of their punch to their Elizabethan predecessors.

Whether Italian or Elizabethan in origin, various combinations of these and other techniques allowed Milton the freedom to create a sonnet form capable of sustaining the gravity of thought and intensity of emotion which his subject matter—no less than the ideal of a holy community—demanded. Because centuries of sonneteers had praised the rosy flush of a mistress's cheek or hoped to build "in sonnets pretty rooms" where love could flourish outside time and space, the form had become primarily an elegant, lyric miniature. Its strictures of rhyme, meter, and length seemed to limit its tonal range and fix its place in the hierarchy of poetic decorum. Nevertheless, Milton used the restraining form itself in ways that compelled this small instrument to resonate as it never had resonated before.

The traditional quatrain, octave, and tercet divisions provided him with signposts, where readers expected directions; and by observing, anticipating, overriding, or ignoring these limits, he enhanced the sonnet's semantic and syntactic meaning. To turn the reader's attention from the careering flight of man's time to the even measure of God's time (Sonnet 7), from physical battles against the treacherous Scots to the warfare of peace against governmental corruption (15), and from anxiety over law, studies, and diplomacy to relaxed good cheer (21), he used a strong, regularly placed volta. To imitate the prevenient grace that prevents the hardening of a rebel's heart, he anticipated the regular position of the volta (19). To evoke a sense of Cromwell's endless, irresistible sequence of victories, he delayed the volta until the middle of line 9 (16). And to depict the steady progress of earthly works to their heavenly reward, minimizing the interruption of death, he eliminated the volta altogether (14).

Some sonnets impose a modification of the Elizabethan structure over the Italian rhyme scheme to allow a three-stage development of thought. In Sonnet 17, the first quatrain compares Vane to a Roman senator, the second describes his diplomatic and ad-

ministrative skills, and the third praises his belief in the separation
of church and state. In Sonnet 20, the first irregular quatrain
laments the winter weather that prevents Milton's walks with
Lawrence, the second anticipates the spring, and the third
describes the feast that will entertain the friends despite the cold
and rain. And in Sonnet 23, each quatrain describes the vision of
Milton's wife in a simile: the first alludes to classical legend, the
second to Jewish tradition, and the third to Christian prophecy.

Just as he exploited the potential in the sonnet's structural
divisions, Milton knew the importance of poetic closure. In Sonnet
16, he ends with a couplet ("paw / . . . maw") which allows him to
emphasize the violence, greed, and bestiality of the opponents of
toleration, and in "The new forcers" the witty sting in the *sonetto
caudato*'s tail is the "charge" that new presbyters are simply old
priests "writ Large." Although he only used the couplet twice in his
English sonnets, the poignant conclusions to Sonnet 19 ("They also
serve who only stand and waite") and Sonnet 23 ("I wak'd, she
fled, and day brought back my night"), the aphorism that ends
Sonnet 20 ("He who of those delights can judge, and spare / To
interpose them oft, is not unwise"), and the final pun of Sonnet 10
("Honour'd *Margaret*") all have the effect of bringing these sonnets
to their inevitable ends. In other sonnets, however, the ending does
not round off the reader's experience; rather, it opens up a vista of
history or fable. Sonnets 8, 12, and 13 conclude with allusions to a
singer's preserving Athens from ruin, Sir John Cheke's teaching
Greek in an age of reformation and learning, and Casella's singing
to Dante in Purgatory. In each case, the final images broaden the
reader's understanding of the significance of the particular sonnet's
occasion and leave him with a panoramic vision not unlike that of
Cortez, "silent, upon a peak in Darien," in the final image of
Keats's sonnet, "On First Looking Into Chapman's Homer." Still
other endings surprise the reader by undercutting the proud
assertions that have dominated the sonnets: the speakers of Sonnets
6 and 22 finally admit to love's power over a seemingly
adamantine heart and God's guidance of a seemingly self-made
man.

The same freedom Milton enjoyed within the constraints of
sonnet structure characterizes his syntax, rhythmic variations, and
diction. He uses complex word order and periodic construction in

Sonnets 10 and 17 to turn the opening formal addresses to Lady Margaret Ley and Sir Henry Vane into stately compliments that suspend the sentence until the subject and verb complete the praise in line 11. Here, Milton extends the thought by periodicity to add dignity and weight to the compliment, but in Sonnet 19 he uses subordination, inversion, and the delayed subject and verb for very different effects: the complexity of the introductory adverbial clause ("When I consider . . . least he returning chide") intensifies tension to a climax in which the angry speaker murmurs the direct object ("Doth God exact . . .") before qualifying it with the main clause ("I fondly ask"). Although, in his sonnets, Milton preferred involved syntax, he could write simple subject-verb-object clauses when straightforward narration was required, as in the opening to Sonnet 11: "I did but prompt the age to quit their cloggs . . . When strait a barbarous noise environs me."

Only a few of the many possible examples will suffice to suggest the variety of effects Milton achieves with rhythm and diction. To ridicule the detractors of his divorce pamphlets in Sonnet 12, he employs harsh rhymes ("*Tetrachordon* . . . por'd on . . . word on . . . Gordon"; "Galasp . . . gasp . . . Asp"; "sleek . . . *Cheek* . . . Greek"), bizarrely broken lines ("Mile- / End Green"), and prominent caesuras, which make the lines limp along in a halting gait. The lament for the Waldensians (18), however, imitates the martyrs' moans with eleven long-*o* rhymes and rolls through line endings as the mothers and infants were rolled down the cliffs. Whereas the octave of Sonnet 19 avoids strong pauses in order to represent the swelling tide of the speaker's anger, the last line of Sonnet 23 intrudes them to retard reading and emphasize, by simplicity and understatement, the magnitude and finality of the dreamer's loss: "I wak'd, she fled, and day brought back my night." (Milton uses the same technique at the climax of *Paradise Lost:* "She pluck'd, she eat: / Earth felt the wound" [9.781–82]). He is also a master of circumlocutions which can either exalt the persons described—as with "that Old man eloquent" for Isocrates (10) and "the feirce *Epeirot* and the *African* bold" for Pyrrhus and Hannibal (17)—or degrade them to near oblivion—as with "meer A. S." and "Scotch what d'ye call" ("The new forcers").

Because Milton enjoyed so much freedom within fourteen lines of iambic pentameter rhyming *a b b a a b b a, c d e c d e* (with

variations in the sestet), Wordsworth's oft quoted praise of his
sonnets, "In his hands / The Thing became a trumpet," seems only
partially true.[3] Milton formed the sonnet into a flexible instrument,
tunable to the various requirements of celebrating an ideal
community: to a love song and a lament, a biting satire and an
invitation to dinner, a praise of heroism and of humble virtue.
Critics have often noted this freedom. Patrick Cruttwell attributes
"the peculiar flavour of Milton's sonnets . . . to the strange contrast
between the brief lyrical form and a language that seems made for
larger spaces. They are—almost—like fragments of epics." Paul
Fussell thinks the enjambment in his poetry produces "an effect of
strenuousness, of an energy that disdains containment, bursting
through the line endings as if they constituted impious bars to
liberty." And F. T. Prince has called Milton's selective adherence
to Italian metrical patterns "disciplined improvisation."[4] These
comments may suggest the answer to a puzzling question: Why did
Milton choose the sonnet sequence—a series of highly structured,
conventionalized lyrics with apparently little elbow room—to
present his ideal of a community?

Of course, he was busy and the sonnet came easily to hand if he
felt called to poetry when a friend died or during the Westminster
Assembly's deliberations or after the Waldensian massacre.
Perhaps for him as for Wordsworth, "in sundry moods 'twas
pastime to be bound / Within the Sonnet's scanty plot of ground."[5]
Besides, there was ample precedent for satirical, political, heroic,
and religious sonnets. Yet Milton had such a strong sense of poetic
decorum that he would not have chosen any form on the basis of
convenience, recreation, or authority alone. In fact, the sonnet
sequence is the perfect genre to convey his ideal because the
freedom he achieves within the limits of sonnet structure becomes
an aesthetic equivalent to the keystone of his ethics, politics, and
theology: disciplined liberty.

Neither license nor tyranny, this principle of freedom within
form—but a true, not a false, form—underlies many themes and
techniques of the sonnets. Men and women must be free to break
false marriages in order to be bound in true matrimonial harmony.
English music, if it would create a "well measur'd Song," must
learn "how to span / Words with just note and accent" lest the
license of Pan replace the ordered freedom of Apollo. Free con-

science must be subject to God and his word, but not the state, if the human center is to reach the divine circumference. Life must be measured in tune with divine harmony, not by earthly tallies or time's flight or politics or study, if man is to be free from anxiety so that he may both work and enjoy the cheerful hours God sends. And when the poet spends his fears, frustration, and pride freely, but safely within the restraining sonnet form, the grace of art helps restore true freedom and a sense of Grace in his life. By choosing a highly regulated pattern and exercising great liberty within its limits, Milton has mirrored in the form itself the unifying concern of his sequence: the ideal of a disciplined, but free community.

But Milton did not abandon the sonnet after his hopes for the ideal community were shattered; he used its disciplined liberty to enhance his major poetry. Wordsworth's friend, Henry Crabb Robinson, records in his diary on January 26, 1836, "By the bye, I wish I could here write down all Wordsworth has said about the sonnet lately—or record here the fine fourteen lines of Milton's *Paradise Lost* which he says are a perfect sonnet without rhyme. But I will hereafter find the passage."[6] Had Robinson pursued the matter, he would have found not one, but several sonnetlike lyrics in *Paradise Lost*.[7] The presence of these submerged sonnets seems to confirm traditional critical opinion that Milton's formal sonneteering, during his most politically active and least poetically productive years, served as an apprenticeship for the later masterpieces. But the interposition of sonnets also indicates his exploration of the lyric possibilities within epic form. As Rosalie Colie has noted, in the Renaissance experiments with *genera mista*, genres came to be seen as more then mere sets of conventions.[8] A smaller form encompassed within a larger form often became a metaphor for a kind of experience, and the submerged sonnets in *Paradise Lost* are this kind of metaphor. Their presence asserts Milton's heroic hope that one may still sing God's song in a fallen world.

Early in his poetic career, he had experimented with the submerged sonnet: in *Lycidas* (ll. 1-14, 50-63, 172-85), the third song of *Arcades*, and the Echo song of *Comus*, he practiced interposing fourteen-line verse paragraphs and rhymed stanzas within longer works. Although his later submerged sonnets do not always obey the fourteen-line limit, he had precedents for varying sonnet length.

The Italians had frequently extended the form in the *sonetto caudato*, and Shakespeare wrote one twelve-line sonnet (126) which divides syntactically and logically into octave and quatrain.[9] Nevertheless, the bipartite structure, imbalance of parts, and turn of thought so characteristic of the Italian sonnet are all present in each sonnet Milton interposed within his epic.

In this more ambitious mode he demonstrated his lifelong concern with "what the laws are of a true *Epic* poem, what of a *Dramatic*, what of a *Lyric*, what decorum is, which is the grand master peece to observe" (*Educ, YM* 2:405). To the champion of disciplined liberty, however, decorum did not demand inflexible obedience to generic "laws" of exclusion; it concerned the proper relations of the part to the whole. Miltonic decorum is an organic adjustment of character, speech, and action to both the needs of the individual scene and the poetic vision of the total work. The celestial, infernal, pre- and postlapsarian scenes of *Paradise Lost* include heavenly hallelujahs and the discourse of right reason, hellish oratory and sophistry, paradisaical love lyrics and prayers, and fallen man's lamentations. The poetic vision of *Paradise Lost* includes a panorama of all time and all space, a union between justice and mercy, a reconciliation of Providence and free will, and a promise of Grace despite sin. Thus there is room for lyric within the plenty of Milton's epic because his poetic vision can accommodate the lyric impulse in a fallen world.

Milton had precedents among critical theorists of Renaissance Italy for his interposition of lyric within epic. To Muzio the epic was encyclopedic: "The sovereign poem is a picture of the universe and therefore contains every style, every form, every image." Tasso agreed: "It is not unfitting for the heroic poet to leave the confines of his illustrious magnificence and incline his style . . . towards the enticements of the lyric mode . . . if he speaks in his own person or treats matters of ease."[10] Milton, perhaps more than any previous epic poet, was justified in yielding to "the enticements of the lyric mode." The universe pictured in *Paradise Lost* is not *Beowulf*'s lighted mead hall encompassed by darkness nor the hostile Mediterranean world through which Ulysses and Aeneas wander to find or found a home. It includes a paradise, a perfect place, which was irrevocably lost. In order to convey the tragic import of that loss, Milton had to find the proper mode to express man's blissful prelapsarian "ease." He found it in the lyric impulse.

The simplest and most spontaneous form of poetry, the pure lyric expresses the keenest possible realization of an emotion. The lyric speaker must surrender completely to his primary instinctual self; naked, stripped of sophistication, he commits himself, without reserve or circumspection, to the lyric impulse. Yet poets of a fallen world know all too well that what appears to be a cri de coeur demands all the calculation of art. Unlike narrative and dramatic poetry, which are curbed by the demands of story, the pure lyric has no built-in directions, nothing to sustain and guide it but the essential emotion it expresses. Thus poets have often felt the need to rein the lyric impulse by an imposed form, and the sonnet, the most rigid poetic structure, has provided a bridle for countless lyrics.

In Milton's paradise Adam and Eve, innocently unaware of "nice Art," can surrender unreservedly to the lyric impulse. Unsophisticated, literally naked, they sing of their love for each other and God, and their songs spontaneously become sonnetlike lyrics without the arduous labors of the fallen poet:

> for neither various style
> Nor holy rapture wanted they to praise
> Thir Maker, in fit strains pronounct or sung
> Unmeditated, such prompt eloquence
> Flow'd from thir lips, in Prose or numerous Verse,
> More tuneable than needed Lute or Harp
> To add more sweetness.
>
> [*PL* 5.146–52]

The "fit strains" of Eden mirror Adam and Eve's perfect recognition of divine immanence in the harmony of paradise, where

> The Birds thir choir apply; airs, vernal airs,
> Breathing the smell of field and grove, attune
> The trembling leaves, while Universal *Pan*
> Knit with the *Graces* and the *Hours* in dance
> Led on th' Eternal Spring.
>
> [4.264–68]

Although paradise is a "Wilderness of sweets . . . Wild above Rule or Art" (5.294, 297), it expresses God's art, the perfect union of spontaneity and rule, which makes the angelic dances before God's throne "regular / Then most, when most irregular they seem" (5.623–24). Because Adam and Eve are in tune with the harmonious art that governs God's universe, they may freely yield to the demands of the lyric impulse without the modifying parentheses or mental complications of a fallen world. Furthermore, the expressions of their particular epic *pietas*, their love for each other and God, become unpremeditated lyric verse.

In Book 4 of *Paradise Lost* Eve recites a sonnetlike lyric of total commitment to her husband:

> With thee conversing I forget all time,
> All seasons and thir change, all please alike.
> Sweet is the breath of morn, her rising sweet,
> With charm of earliest Birds; pleasant the Sun
> When first on this delightful Land he spreads
> His orient Beams, on herb, tree, fruit, and flow'r,
> Glist'ring with dew; fragrant the fertile earth
> After soft showers; and sweet the coming on
> Of grateful Ev'ning mild, then silent Night
> With this her solemn Bird and this fair Moon,
> And these the Gems of Heav'n, her starry train:
> But neither breath of Morn when she ascends
> With charm of earliest Birds, nor rising Sun
> On this delightful land, nor herb, fruit, flow'r,
> Glist'ring with dew, nor fragrance after showers,
> Nor grateful Ev'ning mild, nor silent Night
> With this her solemn Bird, nor walk by Moon,
> Or glittering Star-light without thee is sweet.
> [4.639–56]

Although the lyric has eighteen lines, it displays the characteristic bipartite structure, imbalance of parts, and volta of the Italian sonnet. In the first eleven lines, corresponding to the octave, Eve enumerates the glories she perceives everywhere when she is with her beloved. The near-sonnet turns at the opening of line 12 with a volta beginning, "But neither . . . ," and continues in seven lines, corresponding to the sestet, to reenumerate her bliss, none of which, she concludes, "without thee is sweet." Eve's emotional outburst, "With thee conversing I forget all time," is her spontaneous lyric response to Adam's gentle, domestic reminder that they must sleep in order to get up early for work. In her unfallen simplicity she only lists and relists the beauties of Eden, then surrenders to her love for Adam, Eden's most precious gift. Because her yielding to the lyric impulse, in spontaneity, total commitment, and simplicity, is in perfect harmony with God's ordered plan, her cri de coeur resembles a sonnet.

Before entering the virtuous Bower of Bliss to enjoy their pure sexual ecstasy, the innocent couple offer a lyric prayer to God. And again Milton gives their evensong a form very like the sonnet:

> Thou also mad'st the Night,
> Maker Omnipotent, and thou the Day,
> Which we in our appointed work imploy'd
> Have finisht happy in our mutual help
> And mutual love, the Crown of all our bliss
> Ordain'd by thee, and this delicious place
> For us too large, where thy abundance wants
> Partakers, and uncropt falls to the ground.
> But thou hast promis'd from us two a Race
> To fill the Earth, who shall with us extol
> Thy goodness infinite, both when we wake,
> And when we seek, as now, thy gift of sleep.
> [4.724–35]

The couple's devotions are simple; they observe no "other Rites / . . . but adoration pure / Which God likes best" (4.736–38). Their piety is a spontaneous response of thanksgiving to the universal Maker, for

> at thir shady Lodge arriv'd, both stood,
> Both turn'd, and under op'n Sky ador'd
> The God that made both Sky, Air, Earth and Heav'n
> Which they beheld.
> [4.720–23]

Although the prayer is only twelve lines long, its arrangement of thought resembles the Italian sonnet structure of two quatrains and a sestet separated by a volta. In the four full and two partial lines,

comparable to a sonnet's opening quatrain, Adam and Eve
acknowledge the omnipotence of God, who created day and night,
and rejoice in their ability to use God-given day to work in mutual
help and service to their Maker. In the following two and a half
lines, comparable to a second quatrain, they describe Eden's lush
fertility, which provides much more than two people need. The
miniature sonnet turns at the opening of line 9 and ends with a
brief request for offspring and an almost whispered good-night
prayer. The hushed reverence which closes the near-sonnet
resembles in its simplicity and emotional intensity the powerful
and poignant endings of Sonnets 19 and 23.

The sonnetlike lyrics in Eden thus express the lyric impulse in its
purest form with none of the reservations and complications
ushered in by the Fall. The love of "our first parents" is not marred
by the pressures of "Times winged Charriot hurrying near," for as
yet there is no time. Satan alone uses the language of carpe diem
when he sneers at the Edenic couple's joyous spontaneity:

> Live while ye may,
> Yet happy pair; enjoy, till I return,
> Short pleasures, for long woes are to succeed.
> [4.533–35]

Only in a fallen world must lyrics become "for short time an
endlesse moniment."

Of Milton's formal sonnets, only the Italian approach this pure
expression of the lyric impulse. His English sonnets confront
disappointment, devouring time, war, disillusionment, and death
in a fallen world. In the heroic sonnets he addressed to Fairfax and
Cromwell, he counsels each to turn his attention from victories in
the field to the more dangerous enemies at the commonwealth's
heart; "Avarice, and Rapine" in governmental corruption and
"hireling wolves" in the church must be defeated by "Truth, in
word mightier than [any force of untruth] in Arms" (*PL* 6.32). But
these are God's words of praise for Abdiel, the angel who refused to
be deceived by Satan's sophistry.

God's fifteen-line laud of the warrior angel in book 6 of *Paradise
Lost* is very similar to Milton's heroic sonnets to Fairfax and
Cromwell:

> Servant of God, well done, well hast thou fought
> The better fight, who single hast maintain'd
> Against revolted multitudes the Cause
> Of Truth, in word mightier than they in Arms;
> And for the testimony of Truth hast borne
> Universal reproach, far worse to bear
> Than violence: for this was all thy care
> To stand approv'd in sight of God, though Worlds
> Judg'd thee perverse: the easier conquest now
> Remains thee, aided by this host of friends,
> Back on thy foes more glorious to return
> Than scorn'd thou didst depart, and to subdue
> By force, who reason for thir Law refuse,
> Right reason for thir Law, and for thir King
> *Messiah*, who by right of merit Reigns.
>   [Ll. 29–43]

But the heavenly sonnet reverses the procedure of Milton's earthly
heroic sonnets. In the opening quatrain, which begins with the
characteristic vocative of the heroic sonnet (compare the openings
of Sonnets 15, 16, 17), God praises Abdiel's victory in the "better
fight" of truth over arms. In the following four and a half lines,
resembling a second quatrain, he commends Abdiel's courage in
choosing to stand alone rather than fall with his comrades in
Satan's troops, "though Worlds / Judg'd thee perverse." The turn
comes in midline with "the easier conquest now . . . ," and the final
six and a half lines exhort the angel to achieve the easier victory of
arms over the rebels. Milton's heavenly heroic sonnet displays the
proper order of warfare: the victory of truth and reason over inward vices before the triumph of arms over external threats. But
his earthly heroic sonnets must recall warriors from easy victories
over enemies in the field to the more arduous warfare of peace
against vices threatening the commonwealth from within. Still, the
heavenly decorum of Milton's epic demands a heroic sonnet, not
unlike those sonnets to Fairfax and Cromwell, in praise of the
warrior whose only care was "to stand approv'd in sight of God."

In contrast, the songs of hell mirror the confusion of the Satanic mind and the hellish "Universe of death" where "Nature
breeds, / Perverse, all monstrous, all prodigious things" (2.624–

25). As Lee M. Johnson and Roberts W. French have noted, Satan occasionally speaks in passages resembling sonnet structure.[11] But hell is a "partial" place, where devils try vainly to establish a rival empire of evil to oppose heaven's bliss, where Satan's family becomes a grotesque parody of the Holy Trinity, and where, playing the role of classical hero, Satan falls far short of Christ's and Abdiel's true heroism of "Patience and Heroic Martyrdom." Each time Satan tries to set himself apart as God's rival, the result is only a cheap imitation, a perversion, or a parody of God's all-encompassing divinity. In the inevitable comparison Satan is revealed clearly as no rival, but merely a distorted reflection in a carnival-fun-house mirror.

Even Satan's fourteen-line speeches are not sonnets, but merely sonnet-parodies. For example, in book 1 (ll. 242–255) Satan speaks fourteen lines which divide into octave and sestet separated by a volta. But his words of hatred for God invert the traditional function of the sonnet, to be a poem of love and praise. In these stirring lines addressed to Beëlzebub on the burning lake, there is no spontaneity, no surrender to naked emotion, no unsophistication. Satan's address is a calculated piece of rhetoric and sophistry in which he postures as an undaunted hero defying tyranny, in order to convince his former lieutenant to follow him again after their ignominious defeat in heaven. Despite their sonnet structure, the lines neither eventuate from the lyric impulse nor serve any lyric purpose. They are instead a parody both of the love sonnets Adam and Eve sing to each other and to God in Eden and of God's heroic sonnet praising a true hero, Abdiel, in heaven.

Whereas God sings heroic sonnets in heaven, and Adam and Eve sing spontaneous love sonnets in Eden, it is harder to sing of either love or heroism in "this dark world and wide." Nonetheless, it is possible, and Milton's entire poetic career testifies to both the possibility and the Herculean labors it requires. If fallen man would sing of love and heroism, he must sing in the dark,

> as the wakeful Bird
> Sings darkling, and in shadiest Covert hid
> Tunes her nocturnal Note.
>   [3.38–40]

And like the nightingale, the raped Philomela, he must make his song out of pain. In the invocation to book 3 of *Paradise Lost* Milton exhorts himself to follow the example of the nightingale and "feed on thoughts, that voluntary move / Harmonious numbers" (ll. 37–38), despite his blindness. The fifteen and a half lines, which follow his identification with the "wakeful Bird," form a sonnetlike prayer for the power to sing God's song in the darkness of a fallen world:

> Thus with the Year
> Seasons return, but not to me returns
> Day, or the sweet approach of Ev'n or Morn,
> Or sight of vernal bloom, or Summer's Rose,
> Or flocks, or herds, or human face divine;
> But cloud instead, and ever-during dark
> Surrounds me, from the cheerful ways of men
> Cut off, and for the Book of knowledge fair
> Presented with a Universal blanc
> Of Nature's works to me expung'd and ras'd,
> And wisdom at one entrance quite shut out.
> So much the rather thou Celestial Light
> Shine inward, and the mind through all her powers
> Irradiate, there plant eyes, all mist from thence
> Purge and disperse, that I may see and tell
> Of things invisible to mortal sight.
>
> [3.40–55]

The opening quatrain of four and a half lines lists earthly glories the poet will never again see, and the following six lines describe his enveloping darkness. At the volta, "So much the rather thou Celestial Light / Shine inward," Milton's lamentation becomes a humble prayer for the God-given power necessary to see and tell of heaven, to sing of love and heroism,

> though fall'n on evil days,
> On evil days though fall'n, and evil tongues;
> In darkness, and with dangers compast round,
> And solitude.
>
> [7.25–28]

The closing pages of Milton's epic demonstrate the lyric possibilities still present in an Edenless world. Michael does not sing heroic praises of the fallen couple, for they have yet to sally out and see their adversary, but his final words to them echo God's praise of Abdiel by asserting the primacy of inward virtues in the world of struggle they soon must face. Whereas God's sonnet praises a lonely heroism already achieved, Michael's thirteen-line sonnet encourages Adam and Eve to achieve a heroism of everyday virtue available to all men. After his tragic vision of future history, Adam testifies to his knowledge of true heroism; it signifies

> by small
> Accomplishing great things, by things deem'd weak
> Subverting worldly strong, and worldly wise
> By simply meek; that suffering for Truth's sake
> Is fortitude to highest victory.
>
> [12.566-70]

In the first six and a half lines, composing the octave of his sonnet, Michael assures Adam that this definition of true heroism is the height of knowledge, surpassing all earthly goals:

> This having learnt, thou hast attain'd the sum
> Of wisdom; hope no higher, though all the Stars
> Thou knew'st by name, and all th'ethereal Powers,
> All secrets of the deep, all Nature's works,
> Or works of God in Heav'n, Air, Earth, or Sea,
> And all the riches of this World enjoy'dst,
> And all the rule, one Empire.
>
> [12.575-81]

At the volta he turns Adam's attention from knowledge to action and the virtues from which it must spring:

> Only add
> Deeds to thy knowledge answerable, add Faith,
> Add Virtue, Patience, Temperance, add Love,
> By name to come call'd Charity, the soul
> Of all the rest: then wilt thou not be loath
> To leave this Paradise, but shalt possess
> A paradise within thee, happier far.
>
> [12.581-87]

The six-and-a-half-line sestet describes the way to regain paradise, if not in the perfect place irrevocably lost, at least within the soul. But the heroic charge is chastened by the bleak pageant of repeated human failure to build this paradise within, which the angel, Adam, and the reader have just witnessed. Nevertheless, Michael insists on the possibility of postlapsarian victory and future heroism. Here the lyric impulse expresses that hope which refuses to accept defeat or yield to despair despite all past or future failures, and this assertion of hope takes a lyric form, the sonnet. Although Michael cannot praise heroic victory, he can assert heroic hope.

Although fallen Eve must leave the garden with its flowers once tended so lovingly and its "nuptial Bower," she says, "by mee adorn'd" (11.280), she can echo both her unfallen love song to Adam and their evening prayer as she prepares to follow her mate into the unfamiliar world:

> Whence thou return'st, and whither went'st, I know;
> For God is also in sleep, and Dreams advise,
> Which he hath sent propitious, some great good
> Presaging, since with sorrow and heart's distress
> Wearied I fell asleep: but now lead on;
> In mee is no delay; with thee to go,
> Is to stay here; without thee here to stay,
> Is to go hence unwilling; thou to mee
> Art all things under Heav'n, all places thou,
> Who for my wilful crime art banisht hence.
> This further consolation yet secure
> I carry hence; though all by mee is lost,
> Such favor I unworthy am voutsaf't,
> By mee the Promis'd Seed shall all restore.
>
> [12.610–23]

Even in a fallen world she can recite a love sonnet of total commitment to Adam who will remain her Eden. In the first two quatrains, of four and a half and five and a half lines respectively, she describes her dream and reasserts that none of the joys of paradise "without thee is sweet." The volta comes at line 11, where Eve's sorrowful resolution to depart and guilt over her sin turn into hope of restoration and consolation in the "Promis'd Seed," her issue who will cancel all sin. Again, however, the lyric impulse is chastened; Adam, Eve, and the reader have witnessed all too recently the pain of domestic squabbling in which the former paradisaical lovers

> in mutual accusation spent
> The fruitless hours, but neither self-condemning,
> And of thir vain contést appear'd no end.
>   [9.1187–89]

Yet fallen Eve can still sing a lyric to the hope that refuses to let failure destroy love and looks toward the promise of each new child. Whereas the couple's prelapsarian sonnet-prayer celebrates their hope for offspring to share the garden's abundance and swell the prayers of thanksgiving, Eve's final sonnet only asserts her consoling hope for offspring to repair their parents' loss. The purpose is radically different, but the lyric hope and the lyric form remain.

How redeemed fallen, but penitent Eve really is at the end of book 12 may be measured when her final love sonnet is compared to another hellish sonnet-parody. Returning to hell after his successful corruption of Eden, Satan encounters the bridge which Sin and Death have built to link hell to earth. In malignant joy, Sin recites to her father and mate a fourteen-line parody of Eve's final love sonnet to Adam (10.354–67). Hellish creatures compose no true love sonnets. Eve willingly follows Adam in love and hope, for wherever he is, there is her Eden, and she knows that she will eventually bring "the Promis'd Seed" to earth. Sin, however, is drawn to Satan by the "secret harmony" of their mutual evil, for wherever Satan's corruption is, there she must come to extend the bounds of hell, and she immediately brings devouring Death to earth. Despite its sonnet structure, Sin's greeting is no lyric love song. It is an antilyric to an incestuous bond and the earth's destruction, a hideous inversion of Eve's song to love for her mate and hope for the earth's restoration.[12]

Milton ends his epic by narrating the beginning of life in the fallen world. The thirteen lines in sonnet structure, which conclude his epic, deny neither the tragedy of irrevocable loss nor the hope of future heroism and love:

> In either hand the hast'ning Angel caught
> Our ling'ring Parents, and to th' Eastern Gate
> Led them direct, and down the Cliff as fast
> To the subjected Plain; then disappear'd.
> They looking back, all th'Eastern side beheld
> Of Paradise, so late thir happy seat,
> Wav'd over by that flaming Brand, the Gate
> With dreadful Faces throng'd and fiery Arms:
> Some natural tears they dropp'd, but wip'd them soon;
> The World was all before them, where to choose
> Thir place of rest, and Providence thir guide:
> They hand in hand with wand'ring steps and slow,
> Through *Eden* took thir solitary way.
>
> [12.637–49]

In the opening quatrain Michael leads fallen man and woman through the gates of paradise then disappears, abandoning them to the world of their choice. In the second quatrain Adam and Eve look back upon the stern reminder of their sin, the flaming sword that forever prevents their return to the perfect place. At the volta the couple turn away from past ease toward future struggle, and in the five-line sestet they enter the fallen world "though sorrowing, yet in peace" (11.117).

Although these thirteen lines are narrative and no speaker comments, Milton here is not confined by the "laws" of genre. This conclusion is a remarkable mingling of generic expectations, which expresses the emotions appropriate to the single narrative scene of expulsion, the larger drama of the fall, and the epic vision of the total work. As the narrator refrains from comment, Adam, Eve, and the reader experience the tragedy of loss, the heroism of hope, and the ever-present possibility of lyric love simultaneously. Peter Hellings has said, "A sonnet will bear whatever a great writer can make it bear,"[13] and here Milton makes the sonnet-conclusion to his epic redefine "what the laws are of a true *Epic* poem, what of a *Dramatic*, what of a *Lyric*." The final lines of the subdued narrator take sonnet form, for, in Milton's total epic vision, the moment when life in the fallen world begins is at once a tragic, heroic, and lyric moment.

The couple weep for their tragic loss as they wander into a world of loneliness and sorrow. Yet, guided by Providence, they heroically confront a world of choice, "the race, where that immortall garland is to be run for, not without dust and heat." Though they face "trial . . . by what is contrary" (*Areop*, *YM* 2:515), their hope can wipe away tears, and, "hand in hand," they can find the mutual love which provides "apt and cheerfull conversation of man with woman, to comfort and refresh [them] against the evill of solitary life" (*DDD*, *YM* 2:235). By concluding his tragic epic with a lyric moment, Milton asserts that man can sing of love and heroism despite guilt over past sins, despite even the certainty of future failures.

The submerged sonnets in Milton's major epic graphically demonstrate the difference between man's pre- and postlapsarian states. The spontaneity and simplicity of one intense emotion expressed in the Edenic lyrics yield to the reservations, complications, and mixture of emotions and genres found in the final submerged sonnets. Man can reach the paradise within only if he achieves hard-won inner perfection. Eve must live with guilt until "blest *Mary*, second *Eve*" bears the "Redeemer ever blest" (*PL* 5.387, 12.573). The couple leave the garden both "solitary" and "hand in hand," both sorrowful and peaceful, both in fear and in hope. And even narrative may take lyric form in order to convey the complexity of emotions attending man's entrance into a fallen world. Thus in his final submerged sonnets Milton chastens the lyric impulse and form to match a world where life can seem "a long day's dying to augment our pain" (10.964); yet, like the nightingale, he sings even "in this dark world and wide" (Sonnet 19).[14]

These submerged sonnets demonstrate that Milton's sonneteering influenced his later poetry. But his sonnets also inspired future poets, like Wordsworth, who recorded this story:

> One afternoon in 1801, my sister read to me the sonnets of Milton. I had long been well acquainted with them, but I was particularly struck on that occasion with the dignified simplicity and majestic harmony that runs through most of them—in character so totally different from the Italian, and still more so from Shakespeare's fine sonnets. I took fire, if I may be allowed to say so, and produced three sonnets the same afternoon, the first I ever wrote, except an irregular one at school.[15]

Although the Romantics and Victorians praised Milton's sonnets, Dr. Samuel Johnson, the arbiter of eighteenth-century literary taste, was less complimentary. When asked why England's great epic poet wrote such poor sonnets, he replied, "Milton . . . was a genius that could cut a Colossus from a rock; but could not carve heads upon cherry-stones." In his *Lives of the English Poets*, Johnson summarily dismisses the sonnets: "They deserve not any particular criticism; for of the best it can only be said, that they are not bad. . . . The fabrick of a sonnet, however adapted to the Italian language, has never succeeded in ours, which, having greater variety of termination, requires the rhymes to be often changed."[16] Surely Johnson misrepresented the sonnet form in general and Milton's use of it in particular. Milton did not intend to create elegant, lyric miniatures like those of many Elizabethan and Italian sonneteers. He used the sonnet to capture moments of intense engagement between self and other during the period of his most active political involvement in creating a new English community. And the poet's duties to this community were many and important:

> to imbreed and cherish in a great people the seeds of vertu, and publick civility, to allay the perturbations of the mind, and set the affections in right tune, to celebrate in glorious and lofty Hymns the throne and equipage of Gods Almightinesse, and what he works, and what he suffers to be wrought with high providence in his Church, to sing the victorious agonies of Martyrs and Saints, the deeds and triumphs of just and pious Nations doing valiantly through faith against the enemies of Christ, to deplore the general relapses of Kingdoms and States from justice and Gods true worship. Lastly, whatsoever in religion is holy and sublime, in vertu amiable, or grave, whatsoever hath passion or admiration . . . all these things with a solid and treatable smoothnesse to paint out and describe. (*RCG, YM* 1:816–17)

Milton's sonnets fulfill all these lofty goals at a time when study and pamphleteering left him little leisure for more ambitious poetry.

Perhaps Dr. Johnson disliked the sonnets partly because they seemed neither fish nor fowl, neither the public poetry of an urbane Augustan satirist nor the private outpourings of a wounded Renaissance lover. Indeed, they participate in all three modes (private, social, and public) into which Earl Miner classifies seventeenth-century verse. One reason for their eclecticism is historical: they were written in response to the very events which shifted literary taste from Donne, who exalted the self and contracted the whole world into his bedroom, to Dryden, whose self is "premised on the historical existence and public validity of the world outside [his] own consciousness." If the poems in the private mode of the first half of the century seek "intense moments at which times seems to vanish" (see Sonnet 19), and poems in the public mode of the second half evoke "the sense of a *now* clearly related to a past and a future"[17] (see Sonnet 18), then Milton's sonnet sequence stands at the center of the poetic movements of the century, holding together, perhaps for the last time, both the lyric intensity of private and the historical consciousness of public poetry.

A more central reason for the mixture of public, social, and private modes in the sonnets is philosophical: they represent part of Milton's lifelong effort to define the relationship between the individual, his fellows, and God. An inclusive view of a holy community, from center to circumference, unites these diverse sonnets, creating a sequence like nothing Dr. Johnson had encountered before.

To compose a sonnet sequence, whether intentionally or not, which relates the individual to his fellows, history, the cosmos, and God, was to transform this minor lyric form. Considered as a sequence, Milton's sonnets present an ethical and cosmic vision second only to his later works in scope. Although they may have been exercises in his unceasing preparation for the promised masterpiece, or diversions, compliments, exhortations, and meditations written at odd moments snatched here and there from the pressing tasks of teaching, composing pamphlets, and translating government correspondence—nonetheless, the sequence stands beside *Lydicas* and *Comus* as a magnificent work in its own right.

Notes

Introduction

1. "At a Vacation Exercise in the College," in *John Milton: Complete Poems and Major Prose*, ed. Merritt Y. Hughes (New York: Odyssey Press, 1957), ll. 1, 30, 32–37. All quotations of Milton's poetry (except the sonnets) are from this edition and are cited by book and / or line numbers in the text.

2. Sonnet 7, *Milton's Sonnets*, ed. E. A. J. Honigmann (New York: St. Martin's Press, 1966). All sonnet quotations will be from this edition and will follow its numbering.

3. *RCG, YM* 1:810. All quotations of Milton's prose are from the Yale edition unless otherwise specified.

4. Michael Lloyd, *"Justa Edovardo King," N&Q* 203 (1958): 432–34 (see also Joseph Anthony Wittreich, Jr., " 'A Poet Amongst Poets': Milton and the Tradition of Prophecy," in *Milton and the Line of Vision*, ed. Joseph Anthony Wittreich, Jr. [Madison: University of Wisconsin Press, 1975], p. 115); Louis L. Martz, "The Rising Poet, 1645," in *The Lyric and Dramatic Milton*, ed. Joseph H. Summers (New York: Columbia University Press, 1965), p. 4; Arthur E. Barker, "Calm Regained Through Passion Spent: The Conclusions of the Miltonic Effort," in *The Prison and the Pinnacle*, ed. Balachandra Rajan (Toronto: University of Toronto Press, 1973), p. 16.

5. Honigmann, *Milton's Sonnets*, pp. 62–75; William McCarthy, "The Continuity of Milton's Sonnets," *PMLA* 92 (1977): 96, 104 (see also Laura Ann Bromley, "Continuity in Milton's Sonnets" [Ph.D. diss., Rutgers University, 1973]); Mary Ann Radzinowicz, *Toward Samson Agonistes: The Growth of Milton's Mind* (Princeton, N.J.: Princeton University Press, 1978), p. 131. Unfortunately, Radzinowicz's excellent study appeared too late to have assisted my work. Although she believes that the "sequential unity . . . presents the public and private evolution of the poet as a teacher of his nation" (p. 129), she agrees that the sonnets "are expressive of a sense of community which Milton never lost" (p. 138).

Chapter 1

1. J. W. Lever, *Sonnets of the English Renaissance* (London: Athlone Press, 1974), p. 3. See also S. K. Heninger, Jr., *Touches of Sweet Harmony: Pythagorean Cosmology and Renaissance Poetics* (San Marino, California: Huntington Library, 1974), p. 392.

2. Robert H. Deming, in "Love and Knowledge in the Renaissance Lyric," *TSLL* 16 (1974): 389–410, discusses how the Renaissance lyricist, in his quest to know the self, must separate from his true self a "created self" (which the reader sees) in order to overcome separation and achieve union with the self as "other."

3. These problems are examined exhaustively in the *Variorum* 1, 2(2).

4. J. W. Lever, *The Elizabethan Love Sonnet* (London: Methuen and Co., 1956), p. 169.

5. Maurice Kelley, in "Milton's Dante-Della Casa-Varchi Volume," *BNYPL* 66 (1962): 499–504, proves that Milton owned and read all three works. F. T. Prince, *The Italian Element in Milton's Verse* (Oxford: Oxford University Press, Clarendon Press, 1954), pp. 14–33 (see also Chap. 8 below). On Varchi, see Wilmon Brewer, *Sonnets and Sestinas* (Boston: Cornhill Publishing Co., 1937), p. 120.

6. In one sense, however, Milton's prose canon provides the explanations and details necessary for a full understanding of the sonnets and may be read as a kind of commentary similar to Dante's.

7. See Wyatt's "If waker care . . ." for allusions to his affair with Anne Boleyn, in *The Collected Poems of Sir Thomas Wyatt*, ed. Kenneth Muir and Patricia Thomson (Liverpool: Liverpool University Press, 1969), p. 78. See Surrey's "Th' Assyryans king . . . ," in *The Poems of Henry Howard, Earl of Surrey*, ed. F. M. Padelford (Seattle: University of Washington Press, 1920), pp. 77–78.

8. See Charles Bradford Mitchell, "The English Sonnet in the Seventeenth Century, Especially After Milton" (Ph.D. diss., Harvard University, 1939).

9. See Elkin Calhoun Wilson, *England's Eliza* (Cambridge, Mass.: Harvard University Press, 1939).

10. See Greville's "Under a throne I saw a virgin sit," Constable's Sonnet 2 of Decade 4 of *Diana*, and *The Faerie Queene* 6.10.5–16. Examining the symbolism of the "ermine" portrait of Elizabeth, Frances Yates writes, "We are intended to see in this picture Elizabeth as Petrarch's Laura, as a most chaste and beautiful lady, fit heroine of a sonnet sequence. Yet, as in Spenser's Gloriana-Belphoebe combination, the lady of the 'Ermine' portrait is not only a Petrarchan heroine in her private aspect; in her public aspect she is also a 'most royall queene or empresse' "

(*Astraea: The Imperial Theme in the Sixteenth Century* [Boston: Routledge and Kegan Paul, 1975], p. 114.)

11. The best example of such a sequence is Sir John Davies's *Hymnes to Astraea*, which consists of twenty-six sixteen-line acrostic poems using the letters *ELISA BETHA REGINA*. The collection may be called a sequence of Anacreontic sonnets for several reasons: each poem is divided into three sections resembling two quatrains and a sestet, the heroine is idealized in traditional sonnet language, and the Elizabethans often took the word *sonnet* to mean a "little song" of varying length and rhythm. (See Brewer, *Sonnets and Sestinas*, p. 145; and Wilson, *England's Eliza*, p. 239, n. 17.) Incidental allusions to Elizabeth appear in countless love sequences of the period, and, although the mistress of Greville's sequence *Caelica* may or may not be Elizabeth, at least three of his sonnets are definitely addressed to her.

12. H. R. Trevor-Roper, *Religion, the Reformation and Social Change* (London: Macmillan & Co., 1967). There are, of course, other theories about the events of this period: for example, the economic analysis of Puritanism proposed by Max Weber and R. H. Tawney, Michael Walzer's approach to radical politics through religion, and the Marxist perspective Christopher Hill focuses on England's revolution. Despite their differences, all these views agree on the important issue for this study: for whatever reason, seventeenth-century Europe experienced social upheaval and a proliferation of new definitions of community no longer based solely on the courtly ideal.

13. William Haller, *The Rise of Puritanism* (New York: Columbia University Press, 1938), p. 176; Michael Walzer, *The Revolution of the Saints: A Study in the Origins of Radical Politics* (New York: Atheneum, 1971), pp. 148–98.

14. Michael Fixler, *Milton and the Kingdoms of God* (London: Faber and Faber, 1964), pp. 77–78.

15. Christopher Hill, *The World Turned Upside Down: Radical Ideas During the English Revolution* (New York: Viking Press, 1972), pp. 292–93.

16. Christopher Hill, *Milton and the English Revolution* (New York: Viking Press, 1977), pp. 93–116.

17. James Holly Hanford, "The Chronology of Milton's Private Studies," and "The Youth of Milton," in *John Milton, Poet and Humanist: Essays by James Holly Hanford* (Cleveland, Ohio: Press of Western Reserve University, 1966), pp. 1–125.

18. This expansion of perspective was noted long ago by David Daiches, *Milton* (London: Hutchinson University Library, 1957). But few critics

have pursued the implications of such insights as the following two comments on Sonnets 8 and 13 represent: (1) "We begin, in 'Captain or Colonel, or Knight in Arms,' face to face with the anticipated Royalist officer; we end far away in time and place, listening to 'the repeated air of sad *Electra's* Poet.' That phrase itself . . . helps the withdrawal from seventeenth-century London to ancient Athens, and the withdrawal is part of the design and intention of the poem" (p. 132). (2) Sonnet 13 "ends, as so often with this type of Miltonic sonnet, with a comparison, a reference to the past, which brings the poem gently to rest in a distant land and time" (p. 136).

19. A similar process takes place in *Paradise Lost.* See M. M. Mahood, *Poetry and Humanism* (London: Jonathan Cape, 1950), pp. 180–81, and Louis L. Martz, *The Paradise Within: Studies in Vaughan, Traherne, and Milton* (New Haven, Conn.: Yale University Press, 1964), p. 110.

20. Gale H. Carithers, "Milton's Ludlow Mask: From Chaos to Community," *ELH* 33 (1966): 24.

21. Ibid., p. 35.

22. Edward S. Le Comte, *Yet Once More: Verbal and Psychological Pattern in Milton* (New York: Liberal Arts Press, 1953); *Milton's Unchanging Mind: Three Essays* (Port Washington, N.Y.: Kennikat Press, 1973).

23. For a representative sample of the discussion of Milton's allusiveness, see the following essays (listed in chronological order): James Whaler, "The Miltonic Simile," *PMLA* 46 (1931): 1034–74; William Empson, *Some Versions of Pastoral* (London: Chatto and Windus, 1935), pp. 170–91; Cleanth Brooks, "Milton and the New Criticism," *SR* 59 (1951): 1–22; L. D. Lerner, "The Miltonic Simile," *EIC* 4 (1954): 296–308; Geoffrey Hartman, "Milton's Counterplot," *ELH* 25 (1958): 1–12; Kingsley Widmer, "The Iconography of Renunciation: The Miltonic Simile," *ELH* 25 (1958): 258–69; Geoffrey Hartman, "Adam on the Grass with Balsamum," *ELH* 36 (1969): 168–92; Robert M. Adams, "Contra Hartman: Possible and Impossible Structures of Miltonic Imagery," in *Seventeenth-Century Imagery*, ed. Earl Miner (Berkeley: University of California Press, 1971), pp. 117–31; John C. Ulreich, Jr., "The Typological Structure of Milton's Imagery," *MiltonS* 5 (1973): 67–85.

Chapter 2

1. Honigmann, *Milton's Sonnets*, p. 87.

2. Honigmann's gloss, ibid., p. 89.

3. *The Complete Works of Geoffrey Chaucer*, ed. Walter W. Skeat, vol. 7, *Chaucerian and Other Pieces* (Oxford: Oxford University Press,

Clarendon Press, 1897), p. 355. See also Honigmann, *Milton's Sonnets*, pp. 85–86.

4. Sonnet 1 was almost certainly written while Milton was at Cambridge from 1625 to 1632.

5. John T. Shawcross, in "Milton's Italian Sonnets: An Interpretation," *UWR* 3 (1967): 27–33, has suggested that the woman addressed in the Italian sonnets is "probably not . . . a real person," but a "personification representing the inspiration through which man can raise earthly beauty and love to emulate heavenly beauty and love" (pp. 32–33). Because Milton describes the Lady's appearance and accomplishments in detail to Diodati in Sonnet 4, I cannot agree that she is purely a fiction, although she may be both real woman and symbol. She is a dark, foreign beauty, not, says Milton, the golden-haired, rosy-cheeked mistress of conventional sonneteers. She knows several languages, is both proud and modest, and sings beautifully. Furthermore, if she represents inspiration leading to heavenly love, why would Milton say, "Only grace from above may help" the man who hears her sing "ere amorous longing lingers in his heart" (Sonnet 2)? And why would he contrast the quick growth of the language of love on his tongue to the "slow heart and hard bosom" which has not yielded "as good a soil to Him who plants from Heaven" (Sonnet 3)? Shawcross's explanation that Milton "has not yet equated the two loves [for the lady and for God] fully" (p. 28) seems to be special pleading. See John S. Smart's convincing argument that Emilia might have been a member of the London colony of Italian musicians, "The Italian Singer in Milton's Sonnets," *The Musical Antiquary* 4 (1912): 91–97. See Hanford's denial that the Lady is a Dantesque embodiment of an ideal, "The Youth of Milton," pp. 33–34.

6. Denis de Rougement, *Love in the Western World*, trans. Montgomery Belgion (London: Faber and Faber, 1940), p. 267.

7. Prince, *The Italian Element in Milton's Verse*, p. 98; Sergio Baldi, "Poesie Italiane di Milton," *Studi Secenteschi* 7 (1966): p. 112.

8. John S. Smart, *The Sonnets of Milton* (1921; reprint ed., Oxford: Oxford University Press, Clarendon Press, 1966), p. 125. All translations of Italian sonnets are from this edition; Honigmann, *Milton's Sonnets*, uses Smart's translations.

9. In his essay asserting that Milton was tempted to engage in a homoerotic relationship with Diodati ("Milton and Diodati: An Essay in Psychodynamic Meaning," *MiltonS* 7 [1975]: 127–63), John T. Shawcross suggests that Emilia, perhaps a member of the Italian community in London associated with the Diodatis, may have served the tempted Milton as a surrogate for Diodati himself. Because he believes the warm friendship cooled in 1629–30, Shawcross concludes that the Italian sonnets "serve

Diodati fair warning that the kind of close relationship shared in the past is at an end" (p. 145). This speculation seems to conflict with Shawcross's earlier view (see n. 5 above) that Emilia is a personification allowing Milton to describe his quest for divine love in terms of human love.

10. A distinction must be made between Petrarch himself and his imitators. For example, Petrarch found in Laura the same mixture of pride and modesty Milton praises in Emilia. See John Carey's notes to Sonnet 4 in *The Poems of John Milton*, ed. John Carey and Alastair Fowler (London: Longmans, Green and Co., 1968), p. 94.

11. Prince, *The Italian Element in Milton's Verse*, p. 98.

12. In fact, sonneteering in Italian may have had a direct relation to his poetic aspirations. Perhaps some of those "trifles" which he says he "had in memory, compos'd at under twenty or therabout" and which "were receiv'd with written Encomiums, which the Italian is not forward to bestow on men of this side the *Alps*" (*RCG*, *YM* 1:809-10) were his Italian sonnets. Baldi thinks that the problem of reconciling Milton's youthful attitude with the linguistic maturity he shows in the sonnets can be solved by assuming that he wrote them first before he went to Italy and revised them during his trip ("Poesie Italiane di Milton," p. 105). If he did, then they were partly responsible for the encouragement he received from the Italian literati to attempt to "leave something so written to aftertimes, as they should not willingly let it die" (*RCG*, *YM* 1:810).

13. See Willie D. Reader, "Dramatic Structure and Prosodic Form in Milton's Sonnet 'On His Diseased Wife,'" *LangQ* 11(1972): 21-25, 28, for an analysis of the dramatic conflicts and structure of the poem. For a typological approach, see John C. Ulreich, Jr., "Typological Symbolism in Milton's Sonnet XXIII," *MiltonQ* 8 (1974): 7-10, and "The Typological Structure of Milton's Imagery." For a largely Neo-Platonic approach, see John J. Colaccio, " 'A Death Like Sleep': The Christology of Milton's Twenty-third Sonnet," *MiltonS* 6 (1974): 181-97. Although Colaccio asserts that the sonnet must be read from typological and Neo-Platonic perspectives, his conclusion (that the persona fails to realize "that the real or waking life is not the corporal life of man but life in God," p. 193) depends heavily on a Neo-Platonic reading. See also Dixon Fiske, "The Theme of Purification in Milton's Sonnet XXIII," *MiltonS* 8 (1975): 149-63, which, in the course of its Neo-Platonic reading, summarizes the thirty-year debate over which wife (Katherine or Mary) is the "Saint" or whether she is a specific woman at all.

14. Leo Spitzer, "Understanding Milton," *Hopkins Review* 4 (Summer, 1951): 16-27. Spitzer's original insight into the sonnet's tripartite structure has been refined by Ulreich, Fiske, and Colaccio (n. 13 above).

John Spenser Hill, in " 'Alcestis from the Grave': Image and Structure in Sonnet XXIII," *MiltonS* 10 (1977): 127–39, has noted how elements of the Alcestis story are echoed in the other two sections of the sonnet, suggesting that the classical comparison is not rejected, but assimilated to the Christian vision.

15. Charles and Katherine George point out the "total redefinition in the Anglican liturgy of the meaning of the ceremony of churching: from a rite of purification in the Judaistic pattern it became an expression simply of thanksgiving," in *The Protestant Mind of the English Reformation: 1570–1640* (Princeton, N.J.: Princeton University Press, 1961), p. 289. According to Keith V. Thomas, the Puritans denounced churching altogether and saw the belief that women were unclean as a primitive superstition, in "Women and the Civil War Sects," *Past and Present*, April 1958, p. 43. See Anthony Low's proof that Milton condemned the ceremony of churching, in "Milton's Last Sonnet," *MiltonQ* 9 (1975): 80–81.

16. Marilyn Williamson, "A Reading of Milton's Twenty-Third Sonnet," *MiltonS* 4 (1972): 141–49.

17. In terms of the "problem of the Ideal in our world," see Spitzer, "Understanding Milton," p. 22. For similar views see Thomas Wheeler, "Milton's Twenty-third Sonnet," in *Milton: Modern Essays in Criticism*, ed. Arthur E. Barker (New York: Oxford University Press, 1965), pp. 136–41; and John Huntley, "Milton's 23rd Sonnet," *ELH* 34 (1967): 468–81. In terms of lacking sufficient "Christian zeal," see Fiske, "The Theme of Purification," p. 157. In terms of "intellectual blindness," see Colaccio, " 'A Death Like Sleep,' " p. 181. Although not a specifically Neo-Platonic reading, Kurt Heinzelman's essay, " 'Cold Consolation': The Art of Milton's Last Sonnet," *MiltonS* 10 (1977): 111–25, agrees that the speaker's vision fails because of his narcissism. In his similes, says Heinzelman, the speaker has substituted a "graven image" of his own creation for his wife, and when his fiction fails in the last line, he learns the necessary limits of human thought. He is wrong to try to exalt his fiction above God's grace, the "full sight" promised in heaven.

18. Edward S. Le Comte, "The Veiled Face of Milton's Wife," *N&Q* n.s. 1 (1954): 245–46.

19. E. M. W. Tillyard, *The Metaphysicals and Milton* (London: Chatto and Windus, 1965), pp. 2–11.

20. An allusion to Heb. 12:26–29, the phrase *yet once more* has apocalyptic implications and "is associated by Milton, at various stages, with the entire redemptive mission of Christ, culminating in the Last Judgment and the enjoyment of heavenly bliss by those who are saved"

(Michael Lieb, " 'Yet Once More': The Formulaic Opening of *Lycidas*," *MiltonQ* 12 [1978]: 23–28). See also Wittreich, " 'A Poet Amongst Poets,' " pp. 117–18.

Chapter 3

1. There has been some critical argument over the exact dates of these seven sonnets. See the *Variorum* 2(2) for details, especially the argument for placing Sonnet 8 in 1642.

2. All six of the treatises published in this period (*The Doctrine and Discipline of Divorce*, 1643; *Of Education*, 1644; *The Judgement of Martin Bucer*, 1644; *Areopagitica*, 1644; *Tetrachordon*, 1645; *Colasterion*, 1645) were concerned with domestic liberty. *The Reason of Church Government* and *Apology for Smectymnuus* were published earlier than November, 1642.

3. In their return to biblical attitudes toward women, Puritans explicitly abjured Mariolatry and the courtly love exaltation of women. But woman's fall from her pedestal was a felix culpa because she acquired a more active role in the world, becoming man's loyal helpmeet. See William and Malleville Haller, "The Puritan Art of Love," *HLQ* 5 (1941–42): 235–72; William Haller, " 'Hail Wedded Love,' " *ELH* 13 (1946): 79–97; Roland Mushat Frye, "The Teachings of Classical Puritanism on Conjugal Love," *SRen* 2 (1955): 148–59; John L. Halkett, *Milton and the Idea of Matrimony: A Study of the Divorce Tracts and Paradise Lost* (New Haven, Conn.: Yale University Press, 1970).

4. For the clearest recent discussions of Milton's attitude toward women, see Barbara K. Lewalski, "Milton on Women—Yet Once More," *MiltonS* 6 (1974): 3–20; and Edward S. Le Comte, *Milton and Sex* (New York: Columbia University Press, 1978), pp. 118–20.

5. Cleanth Brooks and John E. Hardy noted some of these parallels in *Poems of Mr. John Milton: The 1645 Edition with Essays in Analysis* (New York: Harcourt, Brace and Co., 1951), p. 160.

6. Edward Phillips, *The Life of Milton*, in *The Early Lives of Milton*, ed. Helen Darbishire (London: Constable and Co., 1932), p. 64.

7. See Honigmann, *Milton's Sonnets*, p. 111, for evidence that Milton's and Lady Margaret's praise of the earl may not represent his character accurately.

8. C. V. Wedgwood, *Poetry and Politics Under the Stuarts* (Cambridge: Cambridge University Press, 1960), p. 84. See Milton's use of the catch phrase in Sonnet 15.

9. Smart, *The Sonnets of Milton*, p. 53.

10. Honigmann, *Milton's Sonnets*, pp. 49–50.

11. Sonnet 11: ibid., p. 117. It is perhaps coincidental, but in two sonnets of roughly the same period (1642–46) Milton uses the image of a pearl to represent what he values: Margaret's virtue and his own treatises on domestic liberty. Sonnet 13: Dante's last words to his musician friend in Purgatory begin, "Se nuova *legge* . . ." (*Purgatorio* 2.106; emphasis mine). See Nan Cooke Carpenter, "Milton and Music: Henry Lawes, Dante, and Casella," *ELR* 2 (1972): 237–42.

12. Smart first compared Sonnet 10 to three Italian sonnets with similar endings (*The Sonnets of Milton*, p. 55).

The Greek *Margarites* ("a pearl") was "taken from the Persian term for the jewel, Murvarid (child of light), in accordance with the beauteous notion that the oysters rising to the surface of the water at night and opening their shells in adoration, received into their mouths drops of dew congealed by the moon-beams into the pure and exquisite gem, resembling in its pure pale lustre nothing so much as the moon herself, '*la gran Margherita,*' as Dante calls her" (Charlotte M. Yonge, *History of Christian Names*, rev. ed. [1884; reprint ed., Detroit: Gale Research Company, 1966], p. 119). Although *margherita* may also mean "daisy," none of the sonnets to be discussed suggests this tertiary meaning.

In a typical complimentary sonnet written to celebrate the wedding of Margherita Farnese, Tasso compares the lady's radiant beauty to a starlike pearl:

> Né di feconda conca in ricco mare
> perla uscì mai sì luminosa e bella,
> né sì vago monil giamai fece ella
> a l'altre unita preziose e care,
> come costei ch'aver simil non pare
> di regio albergo esce in età novella,
> né gemma pur fra l'altre par, ma stella
> che risplenda nel ciel fra le men chiare.
> Quella ch'inanzi l'alba in oriente
> l'alme amorose a sospirar invita
> e riede poi con Imeneo la sera,
> somiglia appunto in giovenile schiera
> preziosa e mirabil *Margherita,*
> la fronte e gli occhi candida e lucente.

["Né di feconda conca . . . ," *Poesie*, ed. Francesco Flora (Milan: Riccardo Ricciardi Editore, 1952), pp. 855–56.]

("Never from a fertile shell in the rich sea arose a pearl so radiant and beautiful, nor did one ever make so lovely a necklace joined with others precious and dear, as this lady, who seems to have no equal among royalty, at her coming of age—not just a jewel among equals, but a star that blazes in the sky among lesser lights. This lady, who invites the amorous soul to sigh before the dawn in the east [as Venus, the Morning Star] and returns later with Hymen in the evening [as the Evening Star], resembles precisely among the youthful throng a precious and marvelous Margaret / pearl with her brow and eyes white and shining." [My translation])

Tasso uses the pun to highlight Margherita's beauty, which outshines other lovely, but lesser jewels in a necklace or stars in the sky.

So too, Tolomei addressed a sonnet, which ends like Sonnet 10, to Margherita Valesia, the Duchess of Savoy and sister to King Henry II of France, who became a learned collector of art and patroness of poets:

> Gratie, ch'a pochi il ciel largo destina;
> Nobilità chiara in humiltà di core,
> Giunto a sommo potere un sommo amore,
> Al disio di saper mente divina;
> Cortesia rara, altezza pellegrina,
> Vera, & salda virtute, eterno honore,
> Sapienza perfetta, alto valore,
> Che gli humili alza, & gli orgogliosi inchina;
> Castità pari a quella, ch'è nel cielo;
> Odio d'ogni viltà, vergogna honesta;
> Gloria, ch'altri a ben far infiamma, e invita;
> Angelica natura in human velo
> Fan, che 'l mondo riguarda, e adora questa
> Pretiosa, e celeste *Margherita.*

["Gratie, ch'a pochi . . . ," *De le rime di diversi nobili poeti Toscani,* ed. M. D. Atanagi (Venice: Lodovico Avanzo, 1565), p. 37.]

(Graces, to which generous heaven destines only a few; bright nobility in a humble heart, a superior love joined to superior power, a divine mind, to the desire to know; rare courtesy, a pilgrim loftiness, truth and steadfast virtue, eternal honor, perfect wisdom, high worth, which raises the humble and casts down the proud; chastity equal to that which is in heaven; hatred of all meanness, blushing modesty; glory, which inflames and invites others to do good; [these graces] make an angelic nature veiled in human form which the world gazes upon and adores, this precious and heavenly Margaret / pearl." [My translation])

Whereas Tasso uses the *Margherita / pearl* pun to set off the lady's physical radiance against lesser beauties, Tolomei puns in order to emphasize the purity and worth of his learned patroness's virtue. In other sonnets dedicated to the duchess, Tolomei continues the motif of a pearllike virtue that is both precious and radiant in a base and darkened world. In one he plays on her name's association with pearls without actually punning to demonstrate how the virtue and beauty symbolized by her name compensate for his inability to honor her as she deserves:

> Non potendo con arte formar belle
> Le belle membra di colei, che spinse
> Argo, et Troia a furor, mentre le pinse
> Quell'accorto discepolo d'Apelle;
> Egli adornando queste parti, & quelle
> D'ostro, d'oro, & di gemme intorno cinse,
> E così riccamente ornolle, e finse,
> Che risplendean quasi notturne stelle:
> Così non potend'io con basse rime
> Degnamente scolpir l'alta bellezza
> E la chiara virtù, che Francia mostra;
> M'ingegno almen di farle parer prime,
> Con fine, & ricche perle, e con vaghezza
> Celeste, impressa in lor da la man vostra.
> ["Non potendo con arte . . . ," *De le rime*, p. 39]

("Unable to match with the beauty of art the beautiful limbs of the lady who, while he painted them, drove Argos and Troy to fury—that shrewd disciple of Apelles, adorning these parts and those with purple [*ostro*—a purple matter extracted from oysters] and gold, girded them around with jewels; and so richly he ornamented and represented them that they shone almost like the stars at night: likewise, I, unable with my base verses to sculpture adequately the lofty beauty and the shining virtue which France shows, strive at least to make them seem foremost with fine and rich pearls and with heavenly grace impressed upon them by your hand." [My translation])

The poet claims that not his poetic skill, but the pearls in Margherita's name are sufficient to adorn his verses, making his lady, as Apelles made Helen, shine like stars in the night. In several other sonnets Tolomei contrasts her unique brilliance to earthly darkness: her virtue gleams as a "fida stella del cielo" ("faithful star of heaven") in the midst of "il cieco mondo" ("the blind world").

Although secular Italian Renaissance poets, comparing women to pearls, emphasized primarily their similarity in radiance and value, a vast Catholic literature had for centuries used the comparison to symbolize innocence, virtue, and the Kingdom of God as well. Hymns to Saint Margaret frequently included the *Margherita* pun. See D. W. Robertson, Jr., "The Pearl as a Symbol," *MLN* 65 (1950): 155–61, and P. M. Kean, *The Pearl: An Interpretation* (New York: Barnes and Noble, Inc., 1967), pp. 138–61. Puritans, on the other hand, exalted a good woman's active service above the beauty, purity, and value of pearls. Perhaps because the

Geneva Bible translates Prov. 31:10 as "Who shal finde a vertuous woman? for her price is farre above the pearles," it became a common-place in seventeenth-century domestic conduct books to compare a good woman to a pearl. In *A Plaine and Familiar Exposition of the Ten Commandments*, John Dod expands the analogy, asserting that a good wife's service makes her worth all her husband's wealth:

> And shee may be well valued above the pearles. For no Iewels can doe that good that a good wife can and doth. For if he have griefe within, or businesse or troubles in his outward estate, other things be dumbe, & cannot helpe him: but she can refresh his soule with good counsel, oversee his businesse in wisedome, helpe his body in and against sicknesse and infirmitie, & incourage him in his calling, and be a stay and succour to him in all things. Therefore also those be most miserable and base minded men, that set their desire so much upon the outward things of this world, that if their wife and their wealth were laide in the balance together, they would sooner part with ten wives one after another, then loose their filthie lucre and worldly commoditie. [London: H. Lownes for T. Man, 1606, Pollard and Redgrave no. 6969, p. 368]

Since Dod could presume that his readers knew their Bible, chapter and verse, and since the comparison had become a commonplace in older Catholic literature, he may intend here to compliment the ideal wife as the pearl of great price that Jesus says, in Matt. 13:45–46, the kingdom of heaven resembles. Like the kingdom of heaven, to which domestic bliss was often compared in Puritan conduct books, the worth of a good wife is far beyond worldly riches, even beyond earthly pearls: she is a heavenly pearl of great earthly price.

Thus literary and religious traditions influential in Milton's poetic development provide ample precedents for comparing the outstanding virtues and worth of a lady to a shining and precious pearl, especially if her name is Margaret.

13. I am indebted to Robert B. Hinman for first suggesting to me that Sonnet 10 may end in a pun.

14. Smart, *The Sonnets of Milton*, pp. 68–71; Honigmann, *Milton's Sonnets*, pp. 134–35; Lois Spencer, "The Professional and Literary Connections of George Thomason," *Library* 13 (1958): 102–18.

15. James Holly Hanford, "Milton in Italy," *AnM* 5 (1964): 59–60. Milton would probably have known Catharine for as long as he knew George, because the Thomasons were married not much later than 1631. Smart, *The Sonnets of Milton*, p. 69.

16. Robert L. Ramsay, "Morality Themes in Milton's Poetry," *SP* 15 (1918): 142; Honigmann, *Milton's Sonnets*, p. 46. On condemnation of the

sonnet, see George Saintsbury, "Milton," *The Cambridge History of English Literature*, ed. A. W. Ward and A. R. Waller (New York: Macmillan Co., 1933), 7:131; William Riley Parker, *Milton: A Biography* (Oxford: Oxford University Press, Clarendon Press, 1968), 1: 304–5.

17. See William Kerrigan's discussion of the interest in "assumption" that Milton displays in his early poetry and of how this interest led to his later mortalism, in "The Heretical Milton: From Assumption to Mortalism," *ELR* 5 (1975): 125–66.

18. H. J. C. Grierson has shown that *Theams* is used here in a musical sense. The term refers to a plainsong or *canto fermo* of a contrapuntal piece ("The Text of Milton," *TLS*, 15 Jan. 1925, p. 40).

19. Smart, *The Sonnets of Milton*, pp. 69–70.

20. Spencer, "The Professional and Literary Connections," pp. 114–15.

21. Lois Spencer, "The Politics of George Thomason," *Library* 14 (1959): 11–27; John J. McAleer, "The King's Pamphlets," *LC* 27 (1961): 163–75.

Chapter 4

1. Dod, *A Plaine and Familiar Exposition*, p. 366.

2. William Perkins, *Christian Oeconomie: or, A Short Survey of the Right Manner of Erecting and Ordering a Familie, according to the Scriptures* (London, 1609), Pollard and Redgrave no. 19677, epistle of dedication by Thomas Pickering, and p. 670.

3. See Smart, *The Sonnets of Milton*, pp. 47–49. Honigmann, *Milton's Sonnets*, disagrees with this dating (pp. 101–3). The *Variorum* replies to his objections, 2(2): 374–75.

4. *The Anonymous Life* which Darbishire (*Early Lives*, p. 32) attributes to John Phillips.

5. Honigmann has also noted the humor in comparing the soldier to Alexander, *Milton's Sonnets*, p. 104.

6. Smart, *The Sonnets of Milton*, pp. 49–50.

7. This sonnet, in which a fictional reader is deliberately addressed, lends itself well to the kind of "affective stylistics" Stanley Fish analyzes in *Surprised by Sin* (London: Macmillan and Co., 1967). The officer is tripped up, then taught a lesson in a manner similar to the surprising of the sinful reader of *Paradise Lost*. E. R. Gregory, in " 'Lift not thy speare against the Muses bowre,' " *MiltonQ* 11 (1977):112–13, believes the sonnet's irony is directed against the poet, not the soldier. Because Mary Powell's desertion closely preceded the sonnet, Gregory argues that a

depressed Milton now saw his home as no "Muses Bowre" and poetry as not insuring immortality, but as transient as the now destroyed home of Pindar and the Athenian walls. This reading seems to contradict Milton's numerous tributes in poetry and prose to the quasi-divine power of poetry. The poem itself, unlike Sonnet 22, contains no hint to alert the reader to the supposed irony.

8. Parker, *Biography*, 1:232.

9. Elijah Fenton, in his *Life of Milton* which accompanied Bishop Thomas Newton's eighteenth-century edition, noted that Deborah Milton could recite whole sections of Homer, Ovid, and Euripides because she had read these authors so often to her father. See also P. W. Timberlake, "Milton and Euripides," *Essays in Dramatic Literature: The Parrott Presentation Volume: By Pupils . . .* , ed. Hardin Craig (Princeton, N.J.: Princeton University Press, 1935), pp. 317–18.

10. "Stesichorus, or his alleged predecessor Xanthus of Lydia . . . made a bad pun on ['Αλέκτρα] in defiance of quantity, interpreting the Doric form as meaning 'unwedded,' as from α privative + λέκτρον" (*The Oxford Classical Dictionary*, ed. N. G. L. Hammond and H. H. Scullard (Oxford: Oxford University Press, Clarendon Press, 1970), p. 378).

11. Quoted in Chilton Latham Powell, *English Domestic Relations 1487–1653* (New York: Columbia University Press, 1917), p. 91.

12. Halkett, *Milton and the Idea of Matrimony*, pp. 98–99.

13. A similar view of creation is expressed in *Paradise Lost* (7.168–72). Kester Svendsen's analysis of *The Doctrine and Discipline of Divorce* points out that Milton uses images of health and order to describe his ideas on divorce and images of disease and chaos to describe opponents' objections, in "Science and Structure in Milton's *Doctrine of Divorce*," *PMLA* 67 (1952): 435–45.

14. J. H., *The Censure of the Rota* (1660), quoted in Honigmann, *Milton's Sonnets*, p. 123.

15. See Heninger, *Touches of Sweet Harmony*, pp. 154–55, for a seventeenth-century table of tetrads.

16. Leo Spitzer, *Classical and Christian Ideas of World Harmony*, ed. Anna Granville Hatcher (Baltimore, Md.: Johns Hopkins Press, 1963), pp. 46–47.

17. See the *Variorum* 2(2): 389, for a list of Milton's detractors.

18. See Marjorie Hope Nicolson, *John Milton: A Reader's Guide to His Poetry* (1963; reprint ed., New York: Octagon Books, 1971), p. 165.

19. Among them Cicero; see Smart, *The Sonnets of Milton*, pp. 59–60.

20. William Riley Parker, "Milton's Sonnet: 'I did but prompt,' 6," *Explicator* 8 (1949–1950): Item 3.

21. Alexander Ross, British mythographer and Milton's contemporary, wrote in *Mystogogus Poeticus* (1653),

> Our savior Christ is the true *Apollo* . . . he is the Son of God, and the God of Wisdom, the great Prophet, the Son of *Latona*, that is, of an obscure maid: the true God of Physick who cureth all our infirmities; and the God of Musick too for that harmony of affections and Communion of Saints in the Church is from him. . . . Gods Church is the true *Diana*, the daughter of God, the sister of the son of righteousnesse, who is a virgin in purity, and yet a fruitfull mother of spiritual children. [Quoted from Thomas E. Maresca, "The Latona Myth in Milton's Sonnet XII," *MLN* 76 (1961): 493]

22. Ovid, *Metamorphoses* 6. 331ff.

23. Honigmann, *Milton's Sonnets*, p. 117.

24. Nathaniel H. Henry, "Who Meant Licence When They Cried Liberty?" *MLN* 66 (1951): 509–13.

25. My reading of lines 13–14 agrees with the *Variorum*: "*They* (those who fail to understand these principles of true liberty) *roave*, shoot away from the *mark* (*OED*: rove, *v.* 2); and this despite all the *wast of wealth* (expenditure that has proved useless by not attaining the end, true liberty) and *loss* of lives" (2(2):398). Lee Sheridan Cox, in "Milton's 'I Did but Prompt,' ll. 13–14," *ELN* 3 (1965–1966): 102–4, reads the lines thus: "For [all] the waste we see, we see how [far] men rove from the mark." This reading suggests that the carnage of the war is a direct result of the detractors' misunderstanding of true liberty. Such a view slightly distorts Milton's conception of war as presented in the sonnets addressed to warriors and statesmen and in the heavenly war of *Paradise Lost*. Warfare, with all its carnage, is justified when it is waged by men and angels (like Vane and Abdiel) who have first tried to be "wise and good" and then gone to war. Certainly, the war in heaven results in futile carnage; but looking at the chaos, we do not see how far from the mark of true liberty the good angels have shot (the kind of reading Cox suggests). We may perhaps see how far Satan has already fallen by looking at the chaos he has caused. But in Sonnet 11, Milton addresses men who are on his own side in the Civil War. He does not suggest that they cease the carnage of the war, but rather that they fight like Abdiel. Then all the property damage and loss of lives would not be a complete "wast" and "loss." But, since they have not first sought wisdom and goodness within, as did Abdiel, their war against external tyranny means nothing. They will merely be slaves to internal tyranny.

26. Although in the 1673 edition of his poems, Milton placed "A Book was writ . . ." before "I did but prompt . . . ," the order is reversed in the Trinity manuscript. Smart (*The Sonnets of Milton*), Honigmann (*Milton's*

Sonnets), and the *Variorum* all consider "I did but prompt . . ." the earlier of the two sonnets.

27. See also *Prol* 7: "Learning brings more Blessings to Men than Ignorance" (*YM* 1:299) for an extended discussion of the civilizing power of learning.

28. W. F. Smith, in "Milton's Sonnet on 'Tetrachordon': 'Like,' " *N&Q*, ser. 12, 2 (1916): 7, relates the Crassus anecdote and cites the resulting Latin proverb, which Milton may also have had in mind: "Similem habent lactucam labra" ("Like lips, like lettuce").

29. Smart (*The Sonnets of Milton*, p. 63) and others have read lines 12–13 to mean that Milton's age hated learning not worse than, but as much as toad or asp. Leaving aside for the moment the problem of whether or not Cheke's age hated learning (see n. 33 below), let us assume that Milton means his own age, at least, did hate learning. It seems to me that by using the comparative *wors*, he suggests a relationship of better or worse, not equivalency. Thus if his age hated learning *worse* than toad or asp, they liked toad or asp *better* than learning.

30. See also Irene Samuel, "Milton on Comedy and Satire," *HLQ* 35 (1972): 107–30.

31. Honigmann, *Milton's Sonnets*, pp. 124–25.

32. See *Tetrachordon* (*YM* 2:716). Milton includes Cheke's praise of Bucer in testimonies he includes in the preface to *The Judgement of Martin Bucer*.

33. Debate over the meaning of lines 12–14 has been vigorous. Many commentators, citing criticism from Cheke and his contemporaries that their own age hated learning, read the lines ironically to mean that both Cheke's and Milton's ages hated learning as much as they hated loathsome animals. See the *Variorum* for a summary of the debate, 2(2):391–92.

34. *Colasterion* opens by revealing Milton's hopes for "som peece of diligence, or lerned discretion" from his critics and lamenting his frustration at the name-calling and slander they produced instead (*YM* 2: 722).

Chapter 5

1. See Chapter 4, n. 26. Sonnets 12, 13, and 14 did not appear in this order in the 1673 edition.

2. Letter to Buonmattei, *YM* 1:329–30; see Chapter 4 above.

3. Dixon Davis Fiske, "Milton's Sonnets" (Ph.D. diss., Princeton University, 1969), p. 231.

4. Hughes, *John Milton*, p. 86.

5. For details of Lawes's biography, see Willa M. Evans, *Henry Lawes: Musician and Friend of Poets* (London: Oxford University Press, 1941).

6. Although written in 1645, the sonnet was not published until 1648, when it was included in Lawes's *Choice Psalms.* The sonnet may, however, have been intended to accompany Lawes's *Ayres and Dialogues* (1653) because in one manuscript version the sonnet is entitled, "To M.ʳ Hen: Laws on the publishing of his Aires." See the *Variorum* 2(2):399.

7. Cicero, *De senectute, De amicitia, De divinatione,* trans. William Armstead Falconer (Cambridge, Mass.: Harvard University Press, 1964), p. 135; Michel de Montaigne, "On Vanity," *The Essays of Michel de Montaigne,* trans. Jacob Zeitlin (New York: Alfred A. Knopf, 1934), 3:179.

8. Dante Alighieri, *The Divine Comedy of Dante Alighieri,* vol. 2, *Purgatorio,* trans. John D. Sinclair (New York: Oxford University Press, 1939), 2.76–78. All quotations and translations are from this edition and will be cited in the text by canto and line.

9. Parker, *Biography,* 1:286.

10. In identifying the unstated pun on Lawes's name, which results from an awareness of these lines from the *Purgatorio,* Nan Cooke Carpenter ("Milton and Music," p. 242) has shown that Milton expected his reader to remember not only the episode, but also all the implications of the comparison: "As Dante requests a love song so Milton suggests that if a new law—a new composer, musical canon or rule, even governmental law—does not interfere, Henry will continue to produce the songs so much admired by Milton and others."

11. These days were doubly dark for Lawes as well. Not only was his patron, the king, about to be executed, but his brother and fellow musician William was killed in the battle at Chester. This news may have been one reason for Henry's delay in publishing his *Ayres,* the book for which Milton's sonnet may have been intended (Smart, *The Sonnets of Milton,* p. 65; Honigmann, *Milton's Sonnets,* p. 129).

12. Although there is some disagreement about the sonnet's date, editors who believe that the sonnets are, for the most part, numbered chronologically suggest the winter of 1655–56. See the *Variorum* 2(2): 470.

13. Smart, having collected the biographical details of the Lawrences, argues convincingly that the sonnet is addressed to Edward, not his younger brother Henry (*The Sonnets of Milton,* pp. 98–101).

14. Richard Lovelace, "The Grasse-hopper." See Earl Miner, *The Cavalier Mode from Jonson to Cotton* (Princeton, N.J.: Princeton University Press, 1971), pp. 282–305, for a discussion of the significance of winter in Cavalier verse.

15. See Ralph W. Condee, "Milton's Gawdy-Day with Lawrence," *Directions in Literary Criticism: Contemporary Approaches to Literature*, ed. Stanley Weintraub and Philip Young (University Park: Pennsylvania State University Press, 1973), pp. 86–92, for a similar view of the sonnet.

16. In its meaning, Sonnet 20 follows a tripartite structure, resembling the Shakespearean pattern of three quatrains and an epigrammatic conclusion of two lines. The rhyme, however, is strictly Italian. By the third quatrain, I mean lines 9–12, all of which describe the proposed feast.

17. Many commentators have noted the Horatian elements in Sonnets 20 and 21. John H. Finley, Jr., however, has made the most extensive study of the Horatian overtones in many other sonnets. See "Milton and Horace: A Study of Milton's Sonnets," *Harvard Studies in Classical Philology* 48 (1937): 29–73.

18. Darbishire, *Early Lives*, p. 59.

19. Milton makes it clear in the discussion of angelic eating and sexuality that unfallen man and angels are near equals and can thus be friends. Raphael himself states that a fellowship exists between angels and man: "Nor less think wee in Heav'n of thee on Earth / Than of our fellow servant" (*PL* 8.224–25).

20. See the *Variorum* 2(2):474–76, for a summary of the debate. Even the editors, Woodhouse and Bush, disagree.

21. Stanley Fish, in "Interpreting the *Variorum*," *Critical Inquiry* 2 (1976):466–68, has suggested that Milton intended *spare* to be deliberately ambiguous so that the burden of the poem's meaning would be thrown back upon the reader, who must interpret the proper use of "those delights" for himself.

22. For the known facts of Skinner's ancestry and biography, see Smart, *The Sonnets of Milton*, pp. 102–5. For proof of his friendship with Oldenburg, see *Familiar Letters*, 18, *CM* 12:79.

23. Milton quotes Coke in *Hirelings* (*CM* 6:74). John Aubrey in his life of James Harrington described Skinner as "scholar to John Milton" (*Brief Lives*, ed. Andrew Clark [Oxford: Oxford University Press, Clarendon Press, 1898], 1:290. Phillips's *Life* indicates that Milton taught his students arithmetic, geometry, and trigonometry (Darbishire, *Early Lives*, p. 61). Much earlier, during his own days of study at Hammersmith and Horton, he made special trips into London, as he said, "to become acquainted with some new discovery in mathematics or music, in which I then took the keenest pleasure" (*Def 2*, *YM* 4[1]:614).

24. This comparison was first made by Honigmann, *Milton's Sonnets*, p. 185.

25. Ibid.

26. Proclus, *A Commentary on the First Book of Euclid's Elements*, trans. Glenn R. Morrow (Princeton, N.J.: Princeton University Press, 1970), pp. 56–57. It is likely that Milton knew this famous quip for several reasons. First, according to Anthony Wood, Simon Grynaeus found in England manuscripts of Proclus's commentary, the locus classicus of the story, which he later published as part of his 1533 Greek edition of Euclid's *Elements* (see William Smith, *Dictionary of Greek and Roman Biography and Mythology* [London: Taylor and Walton, 1846], 2:71). Grynaeus's edition, including Proclus's commentary, served as the basis for all other Greek texts until the nineteenth century (see Morrow, in Proclus, *Commentary*, pp. xxiii, xliv). Second, Proclus's works were widely known in seventeenth-century England: there are references to him in John Dee's preface to Henry Billingsley's 1570 English translation of *The Elements*, in Isaac Barrow's 1660 translation, and in the works of Bacon, Burton, Browne, Jonson, and Hobbes. Third, the "royal road" story was also available in a Latin edition of Proclus, translated in 1560 by Francesco Barozzi. Fourth, and most conclusive, in 1621 Sir Henry Savile, an advocate of the study of mathematics at Oxford, published his open lectures on Euclid's *Elements*, which include the story of King Ptolemy's asking Euclid, "an via esset aliqua ad Geometriam magis compendiara sua" ("whether any other road to geometry is a *shorter way* for him") (Sir Henry Savile, *Praelectiones Tresdecim in Principium Elementorum Euclidis* [Oxford: John Lichfield and James Short, 1621], p. 9). Finally the story had already become proverbial by the seventeenth century: we find variants of the answer, "There is no royal / easy way . . ." in Seneca, Propertius, Cicero, La Fontaine, and Browne. In fact, Milton may have intended to reverse the proverb in claiming that there was a *Ready and Easy Way to Establish a Free Commonwealth*.

27. The echo of the Euclidian definition was first noted by Honigmann, *Milton's Sonnets*, p. 185.

28. Sir Thomas Browne, *Pseudodoxia Epidemica*, in *The Works of Sir Thomas Browne*, ed. Geoffrey Keynes (Chicago: University of Chicago Press, 1964), 2:156, 541, 542; Robert Burton, *Anatomy of Melancholy*, ed. Floyd Dell and Paul Jordan-Smith (New York: Tudor Publishing Co., 1948), pp. 96, 262, 455, 461.

29. Plutarch, *The Lives of the Noble Grecians and Romaines*, trans. Sir Thomas North (London: Richard Field for Thomas Wight, 1603), Pollard and Redgrave no. 20068, pp. 313–16. Most of the existing legends about Archimedes are related in this section. Milton had, of course, read Plutarch, and there are numerous references in his prose to the *Lives*.

30. Vitruvius, *On Architecture*, trans. Frank Granger, Loeb Classical

Library (Cambridge, Mass.: Harvard University Press, 1956), 2:203–7. We know Milton knew Vitruvius's work well because he recommends study of it in *Of Education* (*YM* 2:390).

31. Fiske, "Milton's Sonnets," pp. 310–11.

32. Honigmann, *Milton's Sonnets*, p. 185.

33. Aubrey, *Brief Lives*, 1:289. On Milton's wit, see Anthony Wood, *Oxford Annals*, in Darbishire, *Early Lives*, p. 39.

Chapter 6

1. See, for example, *RCG* (*YM* 1:837), *TKM* (*YM* 3:240–41), *Hirelings* (*CM* 6:76), *Lycidas* (ll. 113–31), *PL* (4.178–93).

2. Austin Woolrych, "Puritanism, Politics, and Society," in *The English Revolution: 1600–1660*, ed. E. W. Ives (New York: Barnes and Noble, Inc., 1968), pp. 87–88. On the conflicting social theories: for the former view, see Max Weber, *The Protestant Ethic and the Spirit of Capitalism*, trans. Talcott Parsons (London: George Allen and Unwin, Ltd., 1930); and R. H. Tawney, *Religion and the Rise of Capitalism* (New York: Harcourt, Brace and Co., 1926). For opposing views, see Trevor-Roper, *Religion, the Reformation and Social Change*; Walzer, *The Revolution of the Saints*; and Chapter 1, nn. 12, 13. See also Christopher Hill, "Individuals and Communities," in *Society and Puritanism in Pre-Revolutionary England*, 2d ed. (New York: Schocken Books, 1967), pp. 482–500.

3. There is some argument about the exact date. See the *Variorum* 2(2): 508–9.

4. Quoted in David Masson, *The Life of John Milton Narrated in Connexion with the Political, Ecclesiastical, and Literary History of His Time*, vol. 3 (London: Macmillan and Co., 1873), p. 299.

5. Ibid., 3:466–71.

6. The name puns were first noted by Honigmann, *Milton's Sonnets*, p. 200.

7. Harry Elmer Barnes, *The Story of Punishment: A Record of Man's Inhumanity to Man* (Boston: Stratford Co., 1930), pp. 56–62.

8. Ibid., pp. 60–61.

9. Donald C. Dorian, " 'On the new forcers of Conscience,' line 17," *MLN* 56 (1941): 62–64.

10. Le Comte, *Milton and Sex*, p. 65. Le Comte's detailed analysis of the riot of sexual puns and allusions in the three prose defenses proves that Milton believed the kind of bawdry found in "The new forcers" to be an appropriate satirical strategy (pp. 60–67).

11. Honigmann, *Milton's Sonnets*, p. 197.

12. Masson, *Life of Milton*, 3:600–601.

13. Wedgwood, *Poetry and Politics*, p. 84; Honigmann, *Milton's Sonnets*, pp. 142–43.

14. For a concise summary of parliamentary abuses, see Smart, *The Sonnets of Milton*, p. 75, and Honigmann, *Milton's Sonnets*, pp. 143–44. For Milton's own view of the Long Parliament, see the digression following his *History of Britain*, which was suppressed in the 1670 edition (*YM* 5(1):440–51).

15. Aubrey, *Brief Lives*, 1:250–51.

16. For a detailed account of Fairfax's life, see *The Dictionary of National Biography*, s.v. "Fairfax, Thomas, Third Lord Fairfax."

17. The Hydra is described as "winged" in a controverted passage in Euripides' *Ion* (l. 195), but Fiske lists several Renaissance paintings which depict a winged Hydra ("Milton's Sonnets," pp. 82–83); John T. Shawcross, "Milton's 'Fairfax' Sonnet," *N&Q* 200 (1955): 195–96.

18. The pun was first noted by Denis H. Burden in his edition, *The Shorter Poems of John Milton* (New York: Barnes and Noble, 1970), p. 138. Don Cameron Allen argues that for Milton *winged serpent* was synonymous with *dragon*, in "Milton's Winged Serpents," *MLN* 59 (1944): 537–38.

19. Smart, *The Sonnets of Milton*, p. 74; Honigmann, *Milton's Sonnets*, p. 141; Finley, "Milton and Horace," pp. 41, 59. Fairfax was a man of principle. Although Scotland had previously broken the Solemn League, in 1650 Fairfax chose to resign rather than break the Covenant by leading an army into Scotland.

20. Honigmann, *Milton's Sonnets*, pp. 141–42.

21. Quoted in Smart, *The Sonnets of Milton*, p. 77.

22. Smart, *The Sonnets of Milton*, pp. 76–77; Honigmann, *Milton's Sonnets*, pp. 145–46; *Variorum* 2(2):416–19.

23. See Sergio Ortolani, *Il Pollaiuolo* (Milan: Ulrico Hoepli, 1948), pls. 21, 83, 104–5, 114. For an examination of the icon, see Adolf Katzenellenbogen, *Allegories of the Virtues and Vices in Mediaeval Art*, trans. Alan J. P. Crick (1939; reprint ed., New York: W. W. Norton and Co., 1964), pp. vii, 14–17. For a discussion of Milton's use of the icon in describing the war in heaven, see Roland Mushat Frye, *Milton's Imagery and the Visual Arts: Iconographic Tradition in the Epic Poems* (Princeton, N.J.: Princeton University Press, 1978), pp. 51–52.

24. Quoted in G. Karl Galinsky, *The Herakles Theme* (Totowa, N.J.: Rowman and Littlefield, 1972), pp. 197–202. For discussions of Milton's

conception of "fortitude," see John M. Steadman, *Milton and the Renaissance Hero* (Oxford: Oxford University Press, Clarendon Press, 1967), pp. 23–42; and A. B. Chambers, "Wisdom and Fortitude in *Samson Agonistes*," *PMLA* 78 (1963): 315–20.

25. *Variorum* 2(2):424.

26. Geffrey Whitney, *A Choice of Emblemes*, ed. Henry Green (1586; facsimile ed., New York: Benjamin Blom, 1967), p. 181. Howard R. Patch, *The Goddess Fortuna in Medieval Literature* (Cambridge, Mass.: Harvard University Press, 1927), frontispiece, pls. 3, 5, 10, 12. Gottfried Kirchner, *Fortuna in Dichtung und Emblematik des Barock* (Stuttgart: J. B. Metzlersche, 1970), illustrations 3, 13, 21–24, 26, 30, 33, 35. Arthur Henkel and Albrecht Schöne, *Emblemata: Handbuch zur Sinnbildkunst des XVI. und XVII. Jahrhunderts* (Stuttgart: J. B. Metzlersche, 1967), Figs. 1802–3, 1808.

27. *Variorum* 2(2):424. See *John Milton's Complete Poetical Works Reproduced in Photographic Facsimile*, ed. Harris Francis Fletcher (Urbana: University of Illinois Press, 1943), 1:372, for a facsimile of Sonnet 16 as printed by Phillips.

28. Honigmann (*Milton's Sonnets*, pp. 146–47) glosses "peace and truth" as a common catch phrase of the 1640s and 1650s, which echoed the concluding promise of the Solemn League and Covenant (1643) to establish truth (true religion) and peace. Milton's use of the phrase would then contrast the perfidious Scots, whose belief in forcing consciences was not "true religion" and had thus led to the bloody warfare so vividly described in the sonnet, to the faithful Cromwell, who supported toleration, Milton's ideal of "true religion," and who had ended the war.

29. See J. H. Adamson and H. F. Folland, *Sir Henry Vane: His Life and Times: 1613–62* (Boston: Gambit, 1973), pp. 53–120.

30. Edward Hyde, Earl of Clarendon, *The History of the Rebellion and Civil Wars in England* (Oxford: Oxford University Press, Clarendon Press, 1816), 2:480.

31. See George Sikes, *The Life and Death of Sir Henry Vane* (n.p., 1662), pp. 93–102.

32. Honigmann, *Milton's Sonnets*, pp. 159–60. *Variorum* 2(2):428.

33. Richard Baxter, *Reliquiae Baxterianae* (London, 1696), Wing no. B 1370, Pt. 1, p. 75.

34. Joan Webber, *The Eloquent "I": Style and Self in Seventeenth-Century Prose* (Madison: University of Wisconsin Press, 1968), p. 202.

35. Walter F. Adeney, "Waldenses," *Encyclopedia of Religion and Ethics*, ed. James Hastings, vol. 12 (New York: Charles Scribner's Sons, 1922), pp. 663–73.

36. See W. Arthur Turner, "Cromwell and the Piedmont Massacres," *N&Q* 193 (1948): 135–36, for a suggestion that Cromwell's motives were strategic as well as humane.

37. Samuel Morland, *The History of the Evangelical Churches of the Valleys of the Piemont* (London: Henry Hills, 1658), dedicatory epistle.

38. On Milton's access to the papers, see Esther Menascé, "Milton e i Valdesi: Segnalazione di una fonte del sonetto sul 'massacro,' " *Bollettino della Società di Studi Valdesi* 88 (June, 1967): 23. Milton's reference to the Waldensians in his Commonplace Book (*YM* 1:379) indicates that he had read Pierre Gilles's history of their church, which was published in 1644 in Geneva. See also *FKM* (*YM* 3:227), *Eikon* (*YM* 3:513–14), and *Def 2* (*YM* 4[1]:658), all published before 1655.

39. J. B. Stouppe, *A Collection of the Several Papers Sent to His Highness the Lord Protector . . . Concerning the Bloody and Barbarous Massacres . . .* (London, 1655), p. 36.

40. Sonnet compared to wave: Parker, *Biography*, 1:460–61. Compared to *Lear:* Patrick Cruttwell, *The English Sonnet* (London: Longmans Green and Co., Ltd., 1966), p. 32. Mark Pattison, *The Sonnets of John Milton* (London: Kegan Paul, Trench, Trübner and Co., Ltd., 1892), pp. 58–59. On echoes of the Bible, see the *Variorum* 2(2):439–41, and Charles E. Goldstein, "The Hebrew Element in Milton's Sonnet XVIII," *MiltonQ* 9 (1975): 111–14. Tertullian, *Apologeticus* 50:535, in *Patrologiae . . . latina*, ed. J. P. Migne, 1:603. On ashes turned to seeds, see Kester Svendsen, "Milton's Sonnet on the Massacre in Piedmont," *Shakespeare Association Bulletin* 20 (1945): 155; and Sheila Blanchard, "Milton's Foothill: Pattern in the Piedmont Sonnet," *Genre* 4 (1971): 39–44.

On literary allusions: Thomas B. Stroup, in "Dido, the Phoenix, and Milton's Sonnet XVIII," *MiltonQ* 4 (1970): 57–60, finds an echo of Dido's dying prophecy of eternal enmity between Rome and Carthage in Sonnet 18. Smart (*The Sonnets of Milton*, p. 93) finds in "*Babylonian* wo" an allusion to Petrarch's sonnet condemning the papal court which begins, "Fontana di dolore. . . ." Milton had quoted the sonnet in *Of Reformation*. Roberts W. French, in "Spenser and Sonnet XVIII," *MiltonQ*, 5 (1971): 51–52, finds in Sonnet 18 an allusion to Arthur's storming Orgoglio's castle in *The Faerie Queene* (1.8.36–37). Arthur captures Duessa, the Whore of Babylon, who wears a triple crown; then he hears the martyrs underneath a bloody altar calling for vengeance. On newsletter reports, see Honigmann, *Milton's Sonnets*, pp. 164–66; Menascé, "Milton e i Valdesi," pp. 24–29. On "hackneyed biblical phrases," see Pattison, *The Sonnets*, p. 59.

41. Stouppe, *Collection*, pp. 33–34.

42. See, for example, Taylor Stoehr, "Syntax and Poetic Form in Milton's Sonnets," *ES* 45 (1964): 300; and Lawrence Hyman, "Milton's 'On the Late Massacre in Piedmont,' " *ELN* 3 (1965–1966): 26–29.

43. Milton's mortalism does not preclude this ambiguity. From the point of view of an omniscient God and the Waldensians themselves, their assumption into heaven is immediate. Referring to the dead who await the resurrection, Milton says in *De Doctrina*, "It will seem that they die and are with Christ at the same moment" (*YM* 6:410).

44. Allen Grossman, "Milton's Sonnet 'On the late massacre in Piemont': A Note on the Vulnerability of Persons in a Revolutionary Situation," *Tri-Quarterly* 23–24 (Winter / Spring, 1972): 292, 300. Nicholas R. Jones, however, in "The Education of the Faithful in Milton's Piedmontese Sonnet," *MiltonS* 10 (1977): 167–76, describes the sonnet not as a personal outcry, but as a lesson in which a fictive speaker dramatizes for the reader the growth of wisdom from faith.

Chapter 7

1. Quoted in George and George, *The Protestant Mind*, p. 128.

2. The date of the sonnet was assumed to be close to Milton's twenty-third birthday, December 9, 1631, until William Riley Parker, in "Some Problems in the Chronology of Milton's Early Poems," *RES* 11 (1935): 276–83, proposed that, because of the way Milton often used the Latin phrase *anno aetatis*, he meant the year between his twenty-third and twenty-fourth birthdays when he wrote "my three and twentith yeer." If Parker's assumption is correct, the poem was written in 1632–1633, much closer to the composition of the letter to which it was appended. Although this redating is approved by Diekhoff, Hanford, Hughes, and Woodhouse, Dixon Fiske reexamines Parker's evidence and disagrees ("Milton's Sonnets," pp. 111–18); and William B. Hunter, Jr., in "The Date of Milton's Sonnet 7," *ELN* 13 (1975): 10–14, presents new evidence to refute Parker. He believes that, because "the age of twenty-three had been appointed by the Canons of 1604 as the earliest date for one's ordination as a deacon" (p. 11) and fifteen of Milton's twenty classmates had already been ordained by the time he was twenty-three, Sonnet 7 reveals his deep concern over his decision against ordination and was written in 1631–1632.

3. Aubrey attributes Milton's nickname, "the Lady of Christ's College," to his fair complexion (Darbishire, *Early Lives*, p. 3). In *A Second Defense*, Milton himself refers to his youthful appearance (*YM* 4[1]:583).

4. The most likely candidates are Spenser, who had composed a verse letter resembling Sonnet 7; Charles Diodati, who, although younger than Milton, was years ahead in school; Thomas Randolph, who had already produced some popular poetic dramas at Cambridge; Abraham Cowley, who published *Poetical Blossoms* (1633) at fifteen, long antedating any "bud or blossom" from Milton; and his already ordained classmates. See Roland M. Smith, "Spenser and Milton: An Early Analogue," *MLN* 60 (1945): 394-98; Donald C. Dorian, *The English Diodatis* (New Brunswick, N.J.: Rutgers University Press, 1950), pp. 122-23, 142-44; Smart, *The Sonnets of Milton*, p. 46; Arthur H. Nethercot, "Milton, Jonson, and the Young Cowley," *MLN* 49 (1934): 158-62; Hunter, "The Date of Milton's Sonnet 7," pp. 10-14.

5. A. S. P. Woodhouse, "Notes on Milton's Early Development," *UTQ* 13 (1943): 96; Kester Svendsen, "Milton's 'On his having arrived at the age of twenty-three,' " *Explicator* 7 (1949), item 53; Donald C. Dorian, "Milton's 'On his having arrived at the age of Twenty-Three,' " *Explicator* 8 (1949), item 10; Fiske, "Milton's Sonnets," pp. 201-3.

6. A. S. P. Woodhouse, *Milton the Poet* (Toronto: J. M. Dent & Sons, 1955), pp. 5-6.

7. Woodhouse, "Notes on Milton's Early Development," p. 97.

8. On dates, see the *Variorum* 2(2):442-52, for a summary of the debate. Two less likely dates, 1642 and 1644, have been proposed by Lysander Kemp, in "On a Sonnet by Milton," *Hopkins Review* 6, no. 2 (Fall 1952): 80-83, who believes that loss of poetic inspiration is the subject of the sonnet, and Honigmann (*Milton's Sonnets*, pp. 172-74) who suggests that the sonnet resulted from Milton's first realization that his eyes were growing weak. However, Earl Daniels (*The Art of Reading Poetry* [New York: Farrar and Rinehart, 1941], pp. 34-36), Lysander Kemp ("On a Sonnet by Milton," pp. 80-83), Parker (*Biography*, 1:468-72, 2:1042-43), and Evelyn J. Hinz ("New Light 'On His Blindness,' " *MSE* 2, no. 1 (1969): 1-10) deny that blindness is the major subject of the sonnet.

9. Donald C. Dorian, "Milton's 'On His Blindness,' " *Explicator* 10 (1951-1952), item 16; and Gary A. Stringer, "Milton's 'Thorn in the Flesh': Pauline Didacticism in Sonnet XIX," *MiltonS* 10 (1977): 151; William Riley Parker, "The Dates of Milton's Sonnets on Blindness," *PMLA* 73 (1958): 199; John T. Shawcross, "Milton's Sonnet 19: Its Date of Authorship and its Interpretation," *N&Q* 202 (1957): 442-46; and Emile Saillens, "The Dating of Milton's Sonnet XIX," *TLS*, 6 October 1961, p. 672.

10. Dixon Davis Fiske, "Milton in the Middle of Life: Sonnet XIX," *ELH* 41 (1974): 37–49. See also C. J. Morse, "The Dating of Milton's Sonnet XIX," *TLS*, 15 September 1961, p. 620.

11. Thomas B. Stroup, " 'When I Consider': Milton's Sonnet XIX," *SP* 69 (1972): 245, has found in Sonnet 19 the tripartite structure of the Ignatian meditation.

12. See Joseph Pequigney, "Milton's Sonnet XIX Reconsidered," *TSLL* 8 (1967): 485–98, for a similar interpretation.

13. Harry F. Robins, "Milton's First Sonnet on his Blindness," *RES*, n.s. 7 (1956) 360–66.

14. Fitzroy Pyle, "Milton's First Sonnet on his Blindness," *RES*, n.s. 9 (1958): 376–87. See also C. A. Patrides, "Renaissance Thought on the Celestial Hierarchy: The Decline of a Tradition," *JHI* 20 (1959): 155–66; and "Renaissance Views on the 'Unconfused Orders Angellick,' " *JHI* 23 (1962): 265–67.

15. For a representative statement of the view that emphasizes resignation, see Smart, *The Sonnets of Milton*, p. 95.

16. See James L. Jackson and Walter E. Weese, " '. . . Who Only Stand and Wait': Milton's Sonnet 'On His Blindness,' " *MLN* 72 (1957): 91–93, for an explication of Milton's use of *stand* in Sonnet 19. See also Boyd M. Berry, "Puritan Soldiers in Paradise Lost," *MLQ* 35 (1974): 396: "Standing is the perfect verb to represent this Puritan mode of heroism. From the sonnet on his blindness on, it became a crucial verb in Milton's poetry. Standing is an act, a gesture; . . . it requires effort."

17. See Paul Goodman, *The Structure of Literature* (Chicago: University of Chicago Press, 1954), pp. 204–15.

18. The clue to Sonnet 22's date is *this three years day*, which may mean "three years ago today" or merely "for three years" (Smart, *The Sonnets of Milton*, p. 106; B. Nicholson, "Milton, Sonnet XXII," *N&Q* ser. 4, 11 [1873]: 349). If the term is thought to refer to an anniversary and if Milton's memory of the onset of complete blindness agrees with the reports of visitors, Sonnet 22 was probably written in February, 1655, prior to the composition of Sonnet 18 (no earlier than May–June, 1655). Thus the assumption that the sonnets are numbered chronologically in the 1673 edition is false. But the term *three years day* may be taken more loosely, and Milton may have remembered the onset of complete blindness to have occurred as late as September, 1652. Thus the sonnet may have been written in late 1655, making room for 19, 20 (a late autumn or winter poem), and 21 (possibly written for the same occasion as 20) between 18 and 22. See the *Variorum* 2(2):481–83; and Fiske, "Milton's Sonnets," pp. 151–54.

19. Hugh M. Richmond, in *The Christian Revolutionary: John Milton* (Berkeley: University of California Press, 1974), p. 93, has also noted a slight irony in Sonnet 22's apparent praise of overwork after Sonnet 21's reproaches.

20. For a similar view, see Fiske, "Milton's Sonnets," p. 315.

21. Variations of *one jot, any jot, no jot, not a jot* appear twenty-five times in Shakespeare's plays, including "bate one jot of ceremony" in *Coriolanus* 2.2.138–39. Variations of the phrase appear at least four times in Milton's prose. See also *OED*, "bate," v^2, 5b; and "jot," sb^1.

22. William Riley Parker, *Milton's Contemporary Reputation* (Columbus: Ohio State University Press, 1940), pp. 34–39. Christopher Hill, *Milton and the English Revolution*, pp. 227–28.

Chapter 8

1. Parker, *Biography*, 1:58.

2. Prince, *The Italian Element in Milton's Verse*, pp. 17, 21–33.

3. William Wordsworth, "Scorn not the Sonnet . . . ," *The Poetical Works of William Wordsworth*, ed. Ernest de Selincourt and Helen Darbishire (Oxford: Oxford University Press, Clarendon Press, 1946), 3:20–21.

4. Cruttwell, *The English Sonnet*, p. 31; Paul Fussell, *Poetic Meter and Poetic Form* (New York: Random House, 1965), p. 117; Prince, *The Italian Element in Milton's Verse*, p. 89.

5. Wordsworth, "Nuns fret not . . . ," *Works*, de Selincourt, 3:1.

6. Henry Crabb Robinson, *The Diary of Henry Crabb Robinson: An Abridgement*, ed. Derek Hudson (London: Oxford University Press, 1967), p. 153.

7. For a different perspective on the sonnets in all three of Milton's major poems, see Lee M. Johnson, "Milton's Blank Verse Sonnets," *MiltonS* 5 (1973): 129–53. Johnson examines many more sonnets than are noted here, but confines his discussion to passages of exactly fourteen lines. He argues that Milton uses these sonnets "to Christianize classical heroism," and he does not consider the implications of Milton's placing lyrics within the epic structure.

8. Rosalie Colie, *The Resources of Kind: Genre-Theory in the Renaissance*, ed. Barbara K. Lewalski (Berkeley: University of California Press, 1973), pp. 19–31.

9. The Elizabethans often used the term *sonnet* loosely to refer to short lyrics of varying lengths. See Chapter 1, n. 11.

10. Girolamo Muzio, *Rime diverse del Mutio Iustinopolitano* (Venice,

1551), fol. 80; Torquato Tasso, *Le prose diverse di Torquato Tasso*, ed. Cesare Guasti (Florence, 1875), 1:51–52; both quoted in John M. Steadman, "Demetrius, Tasso, and Stylistic Variation in *Paradise Lost*," *ES* 47 (1966): 330, p. 336, n. 28.

11. Lee M. Johnson, "Milton's Blank Verse Sonnets," pp. 135–38. Roberts W. French has discussed a Satanic "mock sonnet" in "Satan's Sonnet," *MiltonQ* 11 (1977): 113–14.

12. See Lee M. Johnson, "Milton's Blank Verse Sonnets," p. 145.

13. Peter Hellings, "A Note on the Sonnets of Milton," *Life and Letters* 64 (1950): 167.

14. Much as at the end of *Paradise Lost* Adam and Eve leave the garden "though sorrowing, yet in peace," at the end of *Samson Agonistes* the Danites leave the tragic scene "with peace and consolation . . . / And calm of mind, all passion spent." Their departure is also a lyric moment, and the final chorus of Milton's tragedy is a submerged sonnet of fourteen lines rhyming *a b a b c d c d e f e f e f*. Lee M. Johnson refers to several fourteen-line passages in *Paradise Regained* as public sonnets ("Milton's Blank Verse Sonnets," pp. 147–48). There are, however, neither lyric nor heroic submerged sonnets in Milton's brief epic, which is a masterpiece of dialectic and rhetoric. Lyric interludes are not often appropriate in this stylistically restrained work, and where songs or praises of heroism suit the needs of decorum, Milton employs angelic hymns instead of sonnets.

15. Note prefixed to "I grieved for Buonaparté . . . ," in William Wordsworth, *The Poetical Works of William Wordsworth*, ed. William Knight (London: Macmillan and Company, 1896), 2:323.

16. On the Romantics and Victorians, see *Milton's Sonnets*, ed. A. W. Verity (Cambridge: Cambridge University Press, 1916), pp. xxx–xxxi; George Sanderlin, "The Influence of Milton and Wordsworth on the Early Victorian Sonnet," *ELH* 5 (1938): 225–51; and Raymond D. Havens, *The Influence of Milton on English Poetry* (Cambridge, Mass.: Harvard University Press, 1922), pp. 478–548. On Johnson, see James Boswell, *Boswell's Life of Johnson*, ed. George Birkbeck Hill, rev. and enl. L. F. Powell (Oxford: Oxford University Press, Clarendon Press, 1934), 4:305; Samuel Johnson, "Milton," *The Lives of the English Poets*, in *Samuel Johnson's Literary Criticism*, ed. R. D. Stock (Lincoln: University of Nebraska Press, 1974), p. 214.

17. Earl Miner, *The Restoration Mode from Milton to Dryden* (Princeton, N.J.: Princeton University Press, 1974), pp. 7, 46.

Index

Titles of Milton's works are entered separately under their English titles. Pages of the most extended discussions of Milton's sonnets are given in boldface type.